30

Arms Control Verification and the *New* Role of On-Site Inspection

Arms Control Verification and the *New* Role of On-Site Inspection

Edited by

Lewis A. Dunn

with

Amy E. Gordon

Science Applications International
Corporation

Lexington Books

D.C. Heath and Company/Lexington, Massachusetts/Toronto

Library of Congress Cataloging-in-Publication Data

Arms control verification and the *new* role of on-site inspection / edited by Lewis A. Dunn, with Amy E. Gordon
  p. cm.
Includes index.
ISBN 0–669–21411–6 (alk. paper)
1. Arms control—Verification. I. Dunn, Lewis A.
UA12.5053 1989
327.1′74—dc20   89–12597
                                               CIP

Published simultaneously in Canada
Printed in the United States of America
Casebound International Standard Book Number: 0–669–21411–6
Paperbound International Standard Book Number: 0–669–21534–1
Library of Congress Catalog Card Number: 89–12597

The paper used in this publication meets the minimum requirements of American National Standard for Information Sciences—Permanence of Paper for Printed Library Materials, ANSI Z39.48–1984. ∞™

Year and number of this printing:

89 90 91 92 10 9 8 7 6 5 4 3 2 1

Contents

Preface

On-site inspection is essential to verifying compliance with the Intermediate-Range and Shorter-Range Nuclear Forces (INF) Treaty, which eliminates U.S. and Soviet ground based intermediate-range and shorter-range missiles. Breaking new ground, U.S. and Soviet inspectors have carried out over three hundred on-site inspections at INF missile bases and related facilities in the United States, Eastern and Western Europe, and the Soviet Union. U.S. and Soviet inspectors also will be stationed on a continuous basis for thirteen years at one missile production plant in each other's country.

Soviet and U.S. acceptance of intrusive on-site inspection in the INF Treaty has set a precedent for future arms control verification. Verification of proposed 50 percent reductions of U.S.-Soviet strategic nuclear forces and of a future complete and total ban on chemical weapons also will depend heavily on on-site inspection techniques. On-site inspection is all but certain to figure prominently in future conventional arms control in Europe, both for monitoring reductions of forces and for enhancing confidence and stability.

Some U.S. defense experts, legislators, and officials have begun, however, to voice reservations about on-site inspection. Its benefits have been questioned, whether to monitor compliance and treaty implementation, to build political confidence, or to help open up the Soviet Union and Eastern Europe. Concerns also have been raised about the financial costs of preparing for and carrying out on-site inspections, and there is fear of possible losses of information about sensitive U.S. national security, nuclear weapons-related, intelligence, and commercial activities. There also may be legal complications with constitutional implications.

These new concerns have been greatest for mandatory short-notice inspection of sites at which activities in violation of an agreement are suspected. Such suspect site inspections (or, as they are sometimes known, anytime, anywhere challenge inspections) have been proposed for both future START (Strategic Arms Reductions Talks) and chemical weapons treaties. But routine on-site inspections also have come under close scrutiny (for example, from baseline inspections establishing a data base for treaty implementation to close-out inspections for confirming cessation of activities), as have short-notice inspections of previously agreed sites.

Against the background of this growing debate, specific chapters of this book assess the role of the different types of on-site inspection in future nuclear, chemical, and conventional weapons negotiations. Other chapters draw lessons from past experience with on-site inspection, set out an approach to manage the legal issues it can raise, examine changing congressional and Soviet attitudes toward it, and propose an overall strategy for on-site inspection.

Taken together, this book's discussions should help policymakers and congressional staffs, academics and policy researchers wrestling with the question of how to balance the benefits, costs, and risks of on-site inspection for future arms control verification. Its examination of past experiences and legal issues should be of particular interest to defense industry officials likely to be subject to future on-site inspections as well as to on-site inspection planners. Concerned citizens will find insights into the verification issues likely to be a prominent part of ratification debates of future arms control agreements.

Expanding prospects for arms control agreements in the years ahead will place new demands on means of treaty verification. But new-found skepticism threatens to replace long-standing enthusiasm for on-site inspection. This would be a mistake. Routine and short-notice on-site inspections of agreed sites can enhance arms control verification, while building political confidence and contributing to the broader goal of a more open Soviet Union. A balanced and realistic approach to on-site inspection, therefore, is needed. Reflected in the chapters that follow, such an approach would seek to contain the potential costs and risks of on-site inspection, while still taking advantage of its promise for future arms control agreements.

Acknowledgments

T his book grows out of a series of meetings on "On-Site Inspection in Arms Control Verification Regimes," which were held from April, 1988 through March, 1989. The meetings were organized by the Center for National Security Negotiations, with support from the Ford Foundation and from Science Applications International Corporation.

The editors would like to thank the many participants, whose generous contributions of time and thought made the workshop meetings extremely productive. They also thank the authors who presented papers at the meetings as well as those who revised informal contributions into more formal papers.

Financial support from the Ford Foundation, and from Science Applications International Corporation, was essential to the success of this project. In particular, Enid Schoettle, on behalf of the Foundation, encouraged and supported our efforts at all stages. The Foundation's support is deeply appreciated.

Many thanks also are due to Frank Jenkins, Director of the Center for National Security Negotiations, for his steady counsel and encouragement throughout the course of the project. Mrs. Donna Fenton provided first class support for administration of the meetings and preparations for this book.

Introduction

Since entry into force of the Intermediate-Range and Shorter-Range Nuclear Forces (INF) Treaty in June 1988, nearly 300 on-site inspections have been conducted by the United States at Soviet missile facilities in Eastern Europe and in the Soviet Union.[1] Soviet inspectors have checked U.S. INF missile bases and related facilities in Western Europe and the United States. On-site inspection figures prominently in U.S.-Soviet negotiations for strategic arms reductions and in multilateral talks on conventional forces in Europe and a global chemical weapons ban. A long-standing proponent of on-site inspection, the United States is experiencing widespread acceptance of its proposals for the first time.

The prospect of on-site inspection across the arms control spectrum has paradoxically raised a series of new issues and concerns. Some American experts and observers are voicing doubts about its payoffs. Others, including government officials and defense and chemical industry executives, are concerned about its risks and costs. This debate may further polarize the positions of proponents and opponents rather than help to clarify the issues it has raised. New-found skepticism threatens to replace traditional enthusiasm for on-site inspection.

With heightened controversy about on-site inspection's future arms control role, the Center for National Security Negotiations (CNSN), with the support of the Ford Foundation, sponsored a series of meetings in 1988–1989 on "On-Site Inspection in Arms Control Verification Regimes." Three main questions were addressed: What can be learned from past experience with on-site inspection? What are the payoffs, risks, and costs associated with it? What role should on-site inspection play in future arms control agreements?

Based on material from these CNSN meetings, the chapters of this book interweave historical, operational, technical, and political assessments of on-site inspection in arms control. The contributing authors bring to bear a broad spectrum of backgrounds, ranging from experience as negotiators and inspectors, through expertise in particular verification technologies, to knowledge of domestic U.S. and Soviet policy environments. Their analyses make possible a more balanced evaluation of what on-site inspection can and cannot contribute to the realization of U.S. arms control and national security goals in the decade ahead.

In part I, which examines experience with on-site inspection, the authors share insights and operational lessons from their direct involvement in organizing inspections under the INF agreement, on-site inspections in Europe under the 1986 Stockholm Accord, monitoring International Atomic Energy Agency (IAEA) safeguards, and confronting the technical problems of on-site inspection procedures for a nuclear test ban. An overview of the postwar ups and downs of on-site inspection helps to draw out the many, and often conflicting, purposes served by past proposals for such inspections in U.S. arms control and disarmament diplomacy.

Edward J. Lacey, Principal Deputy Director of the U.S. On-Site Inspection Agency, reflects on the INF inspections in Europe, the United States, and the Soviet Union. Despite the short start-up time and steep learning curve, this historic experience with on-site inspection has been a success. Concerns that fulfillment of the verification protocol of the INF Treaty would require a large and unmanageable organization have proved unfounded. As Lacey notes, the process of inspections has been neither unwieldy nor unworkable. It has provided useful precedents for procedures, organizational structure, and working relationships with the Soviets that may help to facilitate future inspections. Not least, greater confidence in treaty implementation and an increase in predictability in the U.S.-Soviet relationship have been, in Lacey's view, important results of the use of on-site inspection to verify compliance with the INF Treaty.

In a precedent-setting step, the 1986 Stockholm Accord of the Conference on Disarmament in Europe established the U.S. right to inspect military exercises on Soviet and Eastern bloc territory. Don O. Stovall argues in chapter 2 that on-site inspection under the Stockholm Accord has helped to open up the East, a U.S. goal for more than four decades. As former head of the Stockholm inspections for the United States, Stovall observed increased levels of cooperation between East and West and improvements in both sides' understanding of operational practices on the other side. He suggests that the increase in transparency afforded by these inspections is a major benefit, which can build confidence that treaty terms are being met.

Nearly three decades of International Atomic Energy Agency (IAEA) safeguards on peaceful nuclear facilities represents the most extended experience to date with on-site inspection. A variety of useful practical lessons, especially for multilateral verification regimes in chemical weapons and conventional arms control, are drawn from this experience by Archelaus R. Turrentine in chapter 3. IAEA experience, he suggests, demonstrates the value of information collected continuously over a long period of time. In addition, many of the technologies developed for safeguards, such as cameras, seals, sampling techniques, and procedures for shipment of samples, could usefully be transferred to other arms control areas. But Turrentine also warns against direct extrapolation from the safeguards model without taking into account the unique characteristics of peaceful nuclear activities and the different nature of other treaty-limited items or activities.

The earliest work on on-site inspection techniques was prompted by U.S. proposals for on-site inspection to verify compliance with a comprehensive ban on nuclear testing. Work began in the Geneva Group of Experts, formed at the urging of the United States in 1958, and has continued since the 1960s as part of overall U.S. research on monitoring problems and methods. Carl Romney describes research and the evolution of scientific thinking on the technical problems of monitoring a comprehensive ban on nuclear weapons testing in chapter 4. As Romney notes, on-site inspection of suspicious events has been seen as a way to help discriminate between earthquakes, conventional explosions, and underground nuclear tests. Over the years, however, it has remained difficult to establish agreed technical criteria for initiation of on-site inspections. Additionally, the effectiveness of on-site inspections depends in good measure on the ability of seismic means to locate accurately a suspect site for inspection. Seismic capabilities, however, have lacked sufficient accuracy to narrow the search area to manageable proportions.

Concluding part I, Timothy J. Pounds in chapter 5 surveys the record of on-site inspection proposals from the 1946 Baruch Plan for international control of atomic energy to the Reagan initiatives that led to the INF and Stockholm inspections. Such proposals have served many purposes in U.S. arms control and nuclear diplomacy, at different times, for different people. Calls for on-site inspection have variously been a verification means to monitor Soviet compliance, a measure to increase transparency and build confidence, an instrument of political confrontation designed to seize the high ground and put the Soviets on the arms control defensive, a political quid pro quo to build alliance consensus, and a bureaucratic ploy to block arms control agreements while appearing to support them. That said, by the end of the Reagan years, on-site inspection had become an integral part of arms control verification, less a means of political one-upmanship than of political confidence building.

Beginning part II's discussion of on-site inspection in possible future nuclear, conventional, and chemical weapons arms control agreements, in chapter 6, James R. Blackwell examines on-site inspection for verification of nuclear arms reductions. Blackwell, drawing on his extensive experience in crafting verification provisions for the INF treaty, argues that there are significant differences between the benefits, risks, and costs of different types of on-site inspections. He is skeptical of the verification value of most types of short-notice inspections, calling in particular for a shift away from pursuit of unqualified short-notice (or challenge) inspections of suspect sites. To Blackwell, the risks to sensitive U.S. facilities, as well as the costs of preparations for matching suspect-site inspections by the Soviets, more than outweigh any modest deterrent effect of such inspections on Soviet noncompliance. By contrast, he holds that the broad access to the Soviet infrastructure for strategic and intermediate-range systems provided by routine inspections under INF and a future START (Strategic Arms Reductions Talks) agreement would strengthen U.S. confidence in Soviet compliance. It also would add to the costs of cheating.

Turning to conventional arms control negotiations, in (chapter 7) Christopher J. Makins stresses the importance of distinguishing on-site inspection from what he terms on-site observation. On-site inspection concerns the verification of specific limits or reductions of conventional forces (for example, counting tanks to determine that they do not exceed an agreed number). By contrast, on-site observation covers a variety of measures designed to promote security by identifying normal patterns of Eastern bloc activity and any deviations from them. Makins questions the utility of on-site inspection to monitor the extremely numerous, small, and mobile items at issue in conventional arms reductions in Europe. Instead he views increasing the transparency of the Soviet and Warsaw Pact military posture by on-site observation as a more appropriate goal. This could provide more usable information, deter or complicate illegal activities, and might help provide warning of surprise attack.

The burden on on-site inspection is especially high in the area of chemical weapons arms control, as John Barrett notes in chapter 8. Extensive systematic on-site inspections and continuous monitoring with instruments (such as of storage sites for declared chemical weapons) already are a key part of verification in the draft Chemical Weapons Convention. Discussion also is well along on possible short-notice, suspect-site inspections aimed at detecting cheating at hidden sites or misuse of known facilities (so-called anytime, anywhere inspections). Routine and systematic inspections, Barrett believes, can be especially useful, particularly in offering Third World countries without extensive national intelligence capabilities a much better window on their neighbors' chemical programs. The benefits of suspect-site inspections without a right of refusal, by contrast, appear considerably more limited. Besides, for many developing countries (particularly those in the Middle East), a decision to adhere to a convention would depend most on assurances of assistance in the face of threatened or actual chemical weapons use by a treaty holdout or violator. A well-thought-out strategy for enforcing compliance, Barrett concludes, will likely be equally critical to the success of a complete and total chemical weapons ban.

The prospect of wide-ranging on-site inspection has raised a number of cross-cutting political and legal issues that are examined in part III. Janne

E. Nolan in chapter 9 stresses that the INF ratification hearings have focused congressional and public attention on on-site inspection not as an abstract symbol of tough, high-confidence verification but as a practical monitoring means with its own benefits, costs, and risks. In an atmosphere of fiscal constraint, moreover, Congress will scrutinize on-site inspection in START (and other treaties) to determine what it would add to overall U.S. verification capabilities. Congress also is likely, Nolan proposes, to become increasingly uneasy about the intrusiveness of such inspections, responding to concerns of the U.S. defense industry. Most important, provisions for on-site inspection may not suffice to answer all questions about verifying Soviet compliance with a future START agreement. This will all but ensure a contentious debate over START ratification. Greater efforts are needed to win congressional acceptance of realistic demands on verification, which weigh the military significance of possible undetected illegal activities against the overall benefits of an agreement. This will require, she argues, bringing Congress into the treaty-making process well in advance of treaty ratification.

Soviet acceptance of on-site inspection in the INF Treaty and the Stockholm Accord, as well as in the draft Chemical Weapons Convention, START, and conventional arms negotiations, reversed traditional Soviet efforts to limit the scope and variety of verification measures, especially on-site inspection. William C. Potter argues in chapter 10 that this important shift must be seen in the broader context of new trends in Soviet foreign policy, known as the "new thinking." Acceptance of intrusive on-site inspection measures is intended, in Soviet eyes, to reduce suspicions and concerns, build confidence, and provide a less error-prone view of each side's military activities. This new acceptance of on-site inspection is seen by the Soviets to be particularly appropriate for a world in which strategic parity exists and in which the superpowers must recognize the other's legitimate security requirements. Soviet calculations of the risks and benefits of intrusiveness, Potter stresses, also have changed. Despite their long-standing tradition of secrecy and control in politics and society, they appear prepared to live with intrusive on-site inspection as the price of arms control progress which will, in turn, support Gorbachev's policy of perestroika.

The potential infringement of on-site inspection measures on the rights of privacy and property guaranteed to American citizens by the U.S. Constitution is examined by David A. Koplow in chapter 11. Koplow demonstrates that, for the most part, on-site inspections will not cause serious legal or constitutional problems. This is partly so because most inspections will take place at government sites or because advance consent and provisions for compensation can be negotiated with private defense contractor facilities. But suspect-site, challenge inspections without a right of refusal, as proposed for verification of the START agreement and the Convention on Chemical Weapons, could clash with constitutional protection under the Fourth

Amendment against unreasonable search and seizure. Even here, however, Koplow argues that proper attention in the negotiating process to the design of inspection requirements could mitigate these potential problems.

By way of conclusion, we set out the elements of a long-term strategy for using on-site inspection to serve U.S. arms control and national security goals. This strategy emphasizes what on-site inspection does best while suggesting steps to contain its risks and costs.

Routine and short-notice inspections of agreed, declared locations can increase the difficulties, expense, and risk of detection by other monitoring means of illegal activities. Such inspections can help, as well, to strengthen public assurance that treaty provisions are being faithfully carried out, to build confidence, and to increase transparency of the Eastern bloc and Soviet Union. By contrast, it is highly unlikely, barring a mistake by the evader, that a suspect-site inspection would be permitted to find a violation. The United States should revise its support for unqualified suspect-site inspection by adding a right to refuse requests for such inspections, subject to certain conditions. This also would reduce significantly the potential risks and costs of on-site inspection. "Red teaming" (role-playing as the adversary) and mock inspections also need to be continued to reduce risks to sensitive national security related information.

Finally, for some arms control limits, high-confidence verification of some treaty provisions may not be attainable, regardless of the mix of verification means. Nevertheless, an agreement might still serve U.S. interests. Conversely, not even the best verification can make up for a poor agreement. These considerations also need to be reflected in a long-term strategy for use of on-site inspection in arms control verification.

Note

1. The INF Treaty calls for a variety of on-site inspections, including baseline, elimination and closeout inspections, short-notice inspections (with a quota) of missile bases and support facilities, and continuous perimeter portal monitoring but does not include any provision for suspect-site inspections.

I
Past Experience

1

On-Site Inspection: The INF Experience

Edward J. Lacey

O n December 8, 1987, President Ronald Reagan and Soviet leader Mikhail Gorbachev signed the Treaty Between the United States of America and the Union of Soviet Socialist Republics on the Elimination of Their Intermediate-Range and Shorter-Range Nuclear Missiles, more commonly known as the INF Treaty. This historic event marked the culmination of seven years of on-again, off-again negotiations and resulted in the first superpower arms control agreement to eliminate offensive nuclear weapons—nearly 2,700 U.S. and Soviet missiles with ranges between 500 and 5,500 kilometers. It also ushered in a new era in arms control verification: the age of on-site inspection.

For over forty years, beginning with the Baruch Plan in 1946, the United States had sought to establish on-site inspection as a means of verifying compliance with arms control agreements. With the signing of the INF Treaty, this goal became a reality.

The Soviet Union had previously shown some willingness to accept limited on-site inspection in a multilateral context and, bilaterally, in the unratified 1976 Peaceful Nuclear Explosions Treaty. The INF Treaty represented a major new departure, however, in both the scope and intrusiveness of its on-site inspection regime. For the first time in history, U.S. and Soviet personnel would be allowed to inspect operational nuclear missile bases and support facilities of the other side, with attendant direct hands-on access to the missiles themselves. They also would be permitted to maintain a continuous presence on the other's national territory to monitor the portal of a missile production facility.

The On-Site Inspection Agency

The task of implementing this unprecedented on-site inspection regime for the United States has been assigned to the On-Site Inspection Agency (OSIA). Even as the ink was drying on the INF Treaty, a Pentagon task force with support from other government agencies was laying the groundwork for the new agency. OSIA was established on January 15, 1988. Its twofold mission was to carry out the required inspections of Soviet INF facilities and elimination activities and to ensure that the Soviet Union was able to exercise its treaty-mandated inspection rights.

The short time between the signing of the INF Treaty and its entry into force on June 1, 1988, dictated that OSIA be given immediate access to substantial personnel, financial, and logistical resources. Accordingly, it was established as an independent operating agency of the Department of Defense, much like the Defense Nuclear Agency and the Defense Communications Agency. The director of the agency is appointed by the secretary of defense and reports to a Department of Defense executive committee consisting of the under secretaries of defense for acquisition and policy and the vice-chairman of the Joint Chiefs of Staff. Over 100 uniformed personnel from every service of the armed forces was assigned to OSIA headquarters, and the agency received almost $90 million in reprogrammed funds.

The importance of interagency cooperation and support to the OSIA mission was recognized at the outset. As a consequence, a small number of civilians from various government agencies were assigned to OSIA headquarters, and a much larger number were selected to serve as inspectors of Soviet facilities and as escorts for Soviet inspection personnel. The principal deputy director of the agency is appointed by the director of the Arms Control and Disarmament Agency, while a deputy director for international negotiations is assigned from the Department of State and a deputy director for counterintelligence from the Federal Bureau of Investigation.

The organization of OSIA directly parallels its mission (figure 1–1). The largest component is the Operations Directorate consisting of two divisions. The Inspection Division performs the INF Treaty–specified inspections of Soviet facilities in the Soviet Union, Czechoslovakia, and the German Democratic Republic. The Escort Division is responsible for facilitating and supervising Soviet access to U.S. INF facilities in the United States and five West European basing countries: Belgium, the Federal Republic of Germany, Italy, the Netherlands, and the United Kingdom. The Portal Monitoring Directorate is responsible for directing an OSIA detachment at the Votkinsk Missile Assembly Plant in the Soviet Union and for overseeing a similar Soviet detachment in Utah. The Support Directorate, responsible for everything from budget and personnel management to the procurement of cold weather clothing and the provision of airlift for inspection and escort operations, rounds out the principal organizational structure.

The Inspections

The INF treaty and its integral Protocol on Inspections provides for five types of on-site inspection: baseline, closeout, quota, elimination, and portal

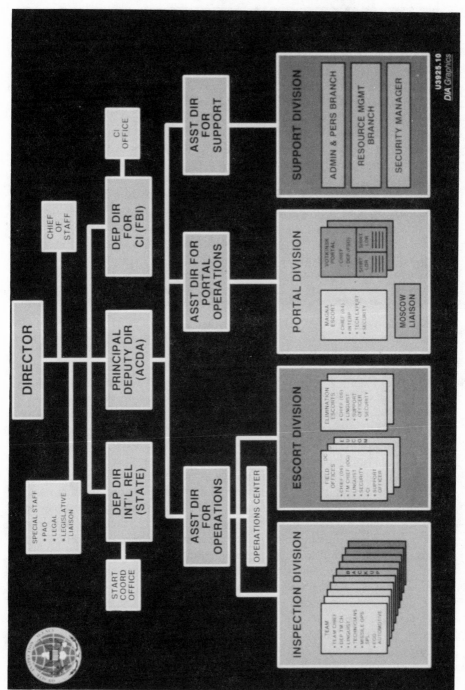

Figure 1–1.

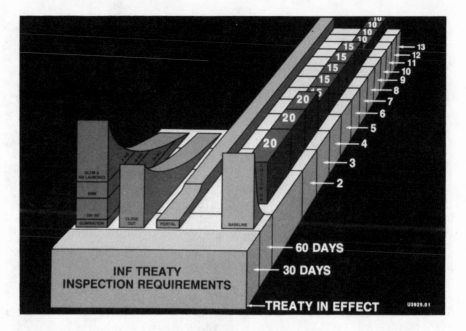

Figure 1–2.

monitoring. (figure 1–2). The baseline inspections were intended to assist in verifying the exchange of data between the two sides contained in the treaty's Memorandum of Understanding (MOU). These inspections had to be carried out between thirty and ninety days after the treaty entered into force.

After all treaty-limited items are removed from an INF base or facility and all INF-related activity has ceased, a closeout inspection of the site may be carried out to confirm that it no longer is engaged in INF operations. Follow-up inspections of facilities contained in the MOU are permitted after the baseline period for thirteen years. These inspections, known as quota inspections, are intended to confirm that the terms of the treaty are being adhered to. The stringent time lines specified in the inspection protocol permit a quota inspection to be underway within as little as thirty hours.

Elimination inspections are designed to confirm the elimination of treaty-limited missiles, launchers, and associated equipment in accordance with the procedures set forth in the treaty's Protocol on Eliminations. The conduct of elimination inspections is not merely a right guaranteed by the INF Treaty; it is an obligation. Both sides are required by the treaty to monitor the elimination of these items. Finally, portal monitoring inspections consist of reciprocal, continuous, on-site inspection activities at two former INF missile production facilities, one each in the United States and the Soviet Union.

Concept of Operations

OSIA inspection teams are comprised of up to ten to twenty inspectors, depending on the type of inspection. The portal monitoring detachments are limited to thirty members. Escort teams are not limited in size but tend to parallel the Soviet inspection teams in numbers and organization.

Each OSIA inspection team is led by a senior team leader and a deputy. As required by the INF Treaty, two dedicated Russian linguists are assigned to the teams as interpreters. Other team members include missile operations specialists and technical experts.

Outgoing inspection teams are forward deployed to gateway activities established by OSIA in Frankfurt, Germany, and Yokota, Japan. The gateways shorten the transportation legs required, reducing the fatigue inspectors endure on their continent-spanning inspection trips. At the gateways, the teams are briefed on the facilities they are to inspect and are issued their equipment—typically consisting of tape measures, meter sticks, cameras, compasses, and occasionally portable scales. The required notifications are issued through the Nuclear Risk Reduction Center in the State Department. At the appropriate time, the teams depart the gateway for the treaty-specified point of entry—Moscow or Ulan Ude in the Soviet Union. After completing their inspections, the OSIA teams return to the gateways, report on their inspection activities, store their equipment, and resume their normal, non-inspection duties.

Baseline Inspections

On July 1, 1988, U.S. and Soviet inspectors began the baseline inspection inventory process that would account for all of the INF treaty–limited equipment specified in the then recently updated (June 1) MOU. Some sites in both the Soviet Union and the United States contained multiple inspectable facilities. As a consequence, only 115 separate inspections were required to cover the 133 Soviet INF facilities elaborated in the MOU (figure 1–3). The Soviets—who had a somewhat easier task because of the smaller numbers of U.S. INF facilities—required just 21 inspections to cover the 31 U.S. facilities contained in the MOU (figure 1–4).

The INF Treaty provides that the inspecting party notify the other sixteen hours in advance of its inspection team's arrival at the point of entry. Following arrival but no sooner than four to forty-eight hours later, the team declares the specific facility it intends to visit. Once declared, the escorts of the inspected party have nine hours to transport the inspection team to the site. Upon arrival at the facility, the actual inspection is initiated after a short orientation briefing on safety and related procedures. The inspection team then has twenty-four hours to complete the inspection (although it can be

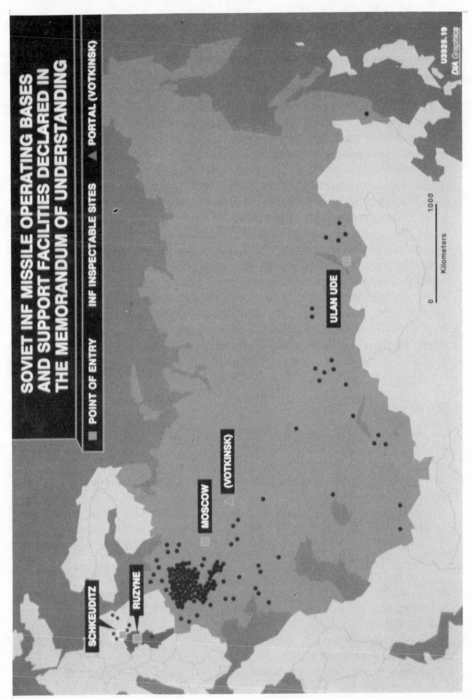

Figure 1–3.

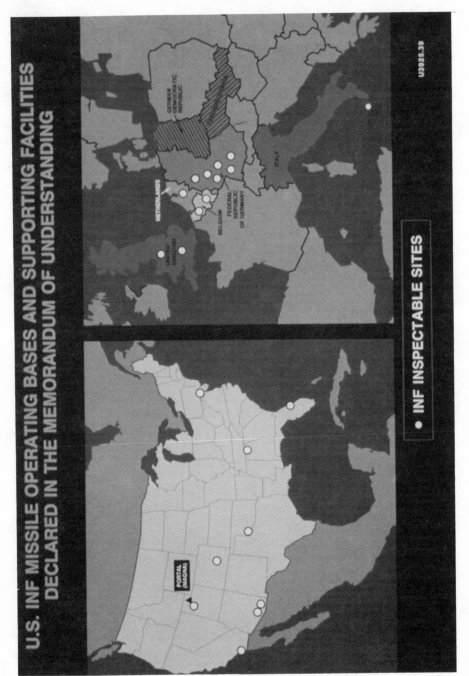

Figure 1–4.

extended by an additional eight hours if the inspected party agrees). Neither U.S. nor Soviet inspection teams required such an extension during the baseline period.

During the actual inspections, every structure and vehicle within a facility capable of holding a treaty-limited team was subject to inspection. Following the inspection, a joint report was prepared in both the English and Russian languages detailing the missiles and the INF equipment identified at the facility. In this manner, the OSIA accounted for the approximately 6,000 Soviet treaty-limited teams listed in the MOU, and Soviet inspection teams accounted for the almost 2,000 MOU-specified items of the United States.

The baseline inspections were completed by August 31, having involved 146 inspections in nine countries. In addition to inventorying the treaty-limited items detailed in the MOU, the process institutionalized on-site inspections and established the working-level relations between OSIA and the Soviet inspection authority that are crucial to successful implementation of the INF Treaty inspection regime.

Closeout Inspections

Closeout inspections are conducted after one of the parties to the treaty declares that a facility is free of INF equipment and no longer supports intermediate- or shorter-range missile operations. Within sixty days of the declared closeout date, the other party has the right to visit the facility to confirm its new status. Some facilities on both sides actually achieved this status prior to the June 1, 1988, entry-into-force date of the treaty but after the treaty signing in December 1987. For these facilities, the closeout inspection was combined with the baseline inspection. The remaining INF facilities will be closed out over the three-year elimination period of the treaty.

Quota Inspections

The INF Treaty provides an annual quota of short-notice inspections for a period of thirteen years. These inspections are conducted along the same lines as the baseline inspections, with only minor differences; all of the facilities elaborated in the MOU are subject to these inspections for the entire thirteen-year period.

Like the other inspections called for by the treaty, the quota of annual short-notice inspections is front-end loaded. For the first three years of the treaty regime, each side can conduct twenty short-notice inspections per annum. During the next five years, fifteen such inspections are permitted annually. The annual quota for the final five years is ten inspections.

Elimination Inspections

The INF Treaty requires that the elimination of certain treaty-limited items—intermediate- and shorter-range missiles, launchers, and associated support equipment—be monitored on-site by the other side. The Soviets began eliminating these missiles and equipment in August 1988. The United States began the following month. By early 1989, OSIA had conducted some forty elimination inspections in the Soviet Union, and the Soviets had completed about thirty such inspections. By that time both sides had eliminated over 30 percent of their INF missiles and a slightly higher percentage of their INF support equipment (figure 1–5).

The United States is conducting treaty-mandated eliminations at three facilities in the United States and one in the Federal Republic of Germany. Intermediate-range Pershing II and shorter-range Pershing IA missiles are being eliminated at U.S. Army facilities in Longhorn, Texas, and Pueblo, Colorado. The Pershing rocket motors are static fired, eliminating the solid propellant. Thereafter, the spent motor cases and the missile front sections are crushed or flattened. The BGM-109G ground-launched cruise missiles (GLCMs) and their support equipment are being eliminated at Davis-Monthan Air Force Base in Arizona. After allowable components, such as the fuel and the guidance package, are removed, the GLCMs are cut longitudi-

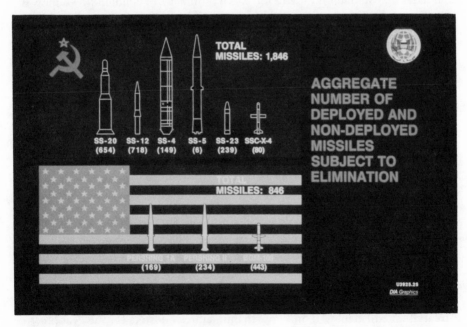

Figure 1–5.

nally in half with titanium-steel bladed power saws. Pershing II missile launchers based in the Federal Republic of Germany are being eliminated at the U.S. Army Equipment Maintenance Center Hausen, near Frankfurt. The treaty provides that the launch vehicles be disassembled and cut into pieces, a process accomplished with hand-held torches.

The Soviet Union has more than twice as many missiles and roughly three times as many other treaty-limited items that must be eliminated under the terms of the INF Treaty than the United States. Certain items, such as SS-20 missiles, are being destroyed at the Kapustin Yar Missile Test Center by explosive demolition. Their front sections are crushed in a similar manner to the U.S. missile front sections. In addition to the explosive demolition method, seventy-two SS-20s were launched to destruction from missile facilities at Kansk and Chita in the eastern Soviet Union. (The treaty allowed each side to destroy up to one hundred intermediate-range missiles in this manner during the first six months of the treaty regime. The United States decided against exercising this option.) The SS-20 launcher and transport vehicles are being eliminated at a separate facility in Sarny. The older SS-4 and SS-5 intermediate-range missiles are being cut into pieces at a facility in Lesnaya.

The Soviets' shorter-range missiles—the SS-12 and SS-23—are being eliminated at Saryozek, and their launcher and transport vehicles are undergoing elimination at Stan'kovo. The process of elimination is identical to that for the intermediate-range systems. The Soviets' intermediate-range GLCM, the SSC-X-4, was eliminated at Jelgava, near the Baltic city of Riga. The SSC-X-4 was never operationally deployed, and all eighty that were declared in the MOU and accounted for in the baseline inspection were destroyed by October 5, 1988.

Portal Monitoring

Unlike the other inspections provided for by the treaty, portal monitoring is a continuous, long-term operation—24 hours a day, 365 days a year for up to 13 years. The treaty allows both sides to establish a detachment of inspectors outside the gates, or portal, of a designated missile production plant. The U.S. detachment is at the Votkinsk Missile Assembly Plant in the Ural Mountains east of Moscow. This is the plant that formerly assembled the intermediate-range SS-20 and shorter-range SS-12 and SS-23 missiles. At present, the plant produces the Soviets' road-mobile, SS-25 intercontinental-range ballistic missile (ICBM).

The Soviet detachment is at the Hercules Corporation's Bacchus Works near Salt Lake City, Utah. This plant once produced rocket motors for the treaty-limited Pershing II and now manufactures boosters for the Peacekeeper ICBM and Trident submarine-launched ballistic missile.

The genesis of portal monitoring in the INF Treaty derives from the fact that the SS-20 has a second stage that is outwardly similar to, but not interchangeable with, the first stage of the SS-25 ICBM. To preclude the possibility that the Soviets could continue producing SS-20s in the guise of missiles that are not covered by the INF Treaty, that is, the SS-25, the United States insisted during the INF negotiations in Geneva upon the right to monitor the Votkinsk plant. OSIA now has thirty U.S. inspectors at Votkinsk, and the Soviets have the same number of inspectors at the Hercules Plant.

The portal monitors have the right to inspect every shipment leaving the plant that is capable of containing an SS-20 (at Votkinsk) or Pershing II (at Hercules) missile stage. Moreover, they have the right to patrol the walled-in (Votkinsk) or fence-enclosed (Hercules) perimeter of the plant at will to ensure that treaty-limited missiles are not clandestinely exiting the plant.

The U.S. portal monitoring detachment consists of six OSIA officials and twenty-four contract personnel. The OSIA representatives supervise the operation and serve as the official U.S. government interface with the Soviets on-site. They report to OSIA headquarters through the U.S. embassy in Moscow. The Soviet detachment at Hercules similarly reports through the Soviet embassy in Washington, D.C.

Conclusion

The INF Treaty's inspection regime at first appears cumbersome and unwieldy (skeptics said "unworkable"). In fact, the regime is imposing. The treaty itself consists of seventeen articles, and the Protocol on Inspections comprises eleven separate sections with eighty-two numbered paragraphs. Despite the fact that some of the finest minds in the United States government had labored mightily to give birth to the INF on-site inspection process, no one knew on December 8, 1987, how it would work in practice. Now, almost two years after the signing of the treaty and more than a year since it entered into force, the experience of the OSIA has shown that on-site inspection can be made to work, and to work effectively.

Far from being unwieldy, the treaty has proved to be an eminently workable document. The mandated inspections are being carried out thoroughly and professionally. The Soviets have been serious and businesslike throughout the process. More important, intermediate- and shorter-range missiles and their launchers and support equipment are being eliminated.

We cannot afford to be complacent, in spite of this good beginning. We are just one year into a three-year elimination and thirteen-year inspection regime. And on-site inspection is not a panacea; it has its limits. In the INF context, it does not provide for anytime, anywhere inspections. We can inspect specific sites for specific items and activities. We cannot inspect beyond the boundaries of those sites nor can we examine facilities not included in the treaty's MOU.

Notwithstanding these limitations, the experience of the OSIA to date gives testimony to the positive role that on-site inspection can play to increase confidence in treaty compliance, thereby contributing to predictability in the superpower relationship. The INF Treaty and OSIA have made on-site inspection a reality. They will provide an important foundation on which U.S. negotiators can build in other arms control forums.

2

The Stockholm Accord: On-Site Inspections in Eastern and Western Europe

Don O. Stovall

> Observations and challenge inspections to date have offered valued insights into the capabilities of the Warsaw Pact Forces, as well as contributed to the general lessening of tension in Europe.[1]

The Soviet Policy Reversal

Within the last several years, there has been a dramatic change in Soviet thinking about on-site inspections. Implicit in Roland Timerbayev's 1983 book on verification of arms limitation and disarmament, for instance, is that on-site inspection is a device of last resort for the Soviet Union.[2] Indeed, academics, government officials, and military officers have often stated, regardless of the subject or the agreement, "The Soviets will never agree to on-site inspections.[3]

This impasse on on-site inspection was broken on September 19, 1986, when the United States, Canada, and thirty-three European nations adopted the Document of the Stockholm Conference on Confidence- and Security-Building Measures and Disarmament in Europe (CDE). In addition to verification provisions, the document provides for an annual exchange of calendars with forecasts of notifiable military activities, a standard format for the notification of military exercises, agreed time and size constraints, and procedures for observation and inspection of such exercises. (Appendix 2A lists the complete compliance and verification provisions.) Underlying the shift in the Soviet position on on-site inspection probably was the conclusion that more comprehensive agreements and treaties were needed to provide the Soviets a breathing space to deal with domestic ills. Acceptance of on-site inspection might facilitate such arm control progress, thereby freeing political and economic resources to tackle domestic problems.

There are vast differences among the types of on-site inspection contained in various recent agreements. The Treaty on the Elimination of Inter-mediate-Range and Shorter-Range Missiles (INF Treaty) contains provisions to establish baseline inventories, monitor the elimination of weapons and associated facilities, monitor production facilities, and conduct follow-on short-notice inspections. In the Strategic Arms Reduction Talks (START) agreement, likely to be the next arms control treaty signed by the Soviets and the United States, there will be additions and revisions to the verification provisions contained in INF. For the conventional arms negotiations,[4] which replaced the now-defunct Mutual and Balanced Force Reduction (MBFR) talks in Vienna, the requirements for on-site or suspect-site inspections[5] will be quite different from those for both INF and START, as is the case for any possible chemical weapons convention or treaty.

This chapter provides a practitioner's view of some of the important events that took place during the first on-site inspection of a Soviet ground force exercise in the Belorussian Military District conducted under the auspices of the Document of the Stockholm Conference and during several later inspections. The analysis is based largely on my personal experiences as the first chief of the U.S. CDE on-site inspection team based at Headquarters, U.S. European Command, Stuttgart, Germany. I led the first four U.S. on-site inspections and also participated in several of the first Soviet and other Warsaw Pact inspections where U.S. forces were involved. (A complete list of CDE on-site inspections that had been conducted at the time of writing appears in appendix 2B.) The events leading up to these first on-site inspections and the lessons learned from them are instructive for future arms control negotiations.

The Stockholm Accord

After over two years of deliberations, the document of the Stockholm Conference was adopted by the delegates of the thirty-five member states on September 19, 1986. The deliberations had begun inauspiciously under a cloud created by Soviet foreign minister Andrei Gromyko, who used harsh, cold war rhetoric during his address to the opening session in 1984. The final document, however, committed the participants to an unprecedented degree of cooperation and was a significant breakthrough in arms control negotiations. It was the first major agreement in which the Soviet Union and other Warsaw Pact countries permitted on-site inspections on their territory as a means of verification.

The Stockholm Document considerably expands the confidence-building measures of the 1975 Helsinki Final Act, which had reaffirmed a commit-ment "to peace, security and justice and the continuing development of friendly relations and cooperation."[6] Measures included in the 1975 accords encouraged the thirty-five member states to invite other participating states, voluntarily and on a bilateral basis, to send observers to attend military maneuvers. Participating states also were encouraged to notify of major planned military maneuvers and movements.[7]

The objectives of the Helsinki Final Act were reaffirmed in the follow-up session of the Helsinki meeting in Madrid in 1980. The Concluding Document of the Madrid meeting also initiated the agreement to convene the Conference on Confidence- and Security-Building Measures and Disarmament in Europe (CDE).[8]

The Helsinki Final Act and the Concluding Document of the Madrid meeting had proposed the invitation of observers but had made no mention of inspections. The Stockholm Document, by contrast, requires notification and observations for a much broader category of activities and provides for on-site inspections with no right of refusal. The inspections are not necessarily limited to military exercises, moreover, but may be conducted for other, potentially suspect, military activities.

More specifically, the Stockholm Document sets forth the basic rules of engagement for inspecting states. Its major provisions include the following:

- Use of national technical means (for example, photographic reconnaissance satellites and aircraft-based systems such as radar and optical systems) to monitor military activities;
- Compulsory inspections without the right of refusal;
- Provisions for short-notice inspections: allowing twenty-four hours to answer a challenge call for an inspection; an additional twelve hours to facilitate the start of the inspection; a forty-eight-hour period for the conduct of the actual inspection; a right to conduct inspections on the ground, from the air, or both; a maximum of four inspectors on the team; a maximum of three inspections per year from different states (other than members of the same military alliance); and access, entry, and unobstructed survey (with use of dictaphones, cameras, maps, and binoculars), excluding specified restricted areas whose number and extent should be "as limited as possible."

The First CDE On-Site Inspection

In preparation for the first inspection, a rudimentary U.S. on-site inspection regime was organized at Headquarters, U.S. European Command, in Stuttgart, Germany, in March and April 1987. Inspectors were trained during the ensuing weeks, and the first rehearsal of a mock inspection was conducted in May against elements of the U.S. 1st Armored Division. The second, and final, rehearsal was carried out in mid-June against the West German 12th Panzer Division. Both rehearsals cleared the way for the identification and elimination of most operational problems and served as excellent trials of equipment to refine inspection techniques and procedures. The practice inspections also served as a catalyst of cooperation among the various U.S. governmental agencies involved and served to pull these various elements together. Close cooperation also had been achieved among the representatives of several allied nations.

Regardless of the detailed preparations and war gaming of possible problems that might arise during the course of the inspection, however, there still remained numerous unanswered questions and uncertainties that had to be worked out once the actual inspection began. This continued to be true for subsequent on-site inspections conducted by the U.S. CDE On-Site Inspection Team.

The Stockholm Document contains minor discrepancies and a few ambiguous portions but on balance is a good working guide. It is virtually impossible, and possibly unwise, to attempt to anticipate and reduce every possible contingency to the definitive, written word. If intelligent personne with experience and good judgment are in charge, decisions can be made or matters not fully covered in the basic document. In other words, it is im possible to avoid dynamic adaptation during the "military implementatior of a document that essentially was negotiated by our political masters," a: several inspectors of different nationalities have explained it.

In accordance with paragraphs 65 and 66 of the Stockholm Document the U.S. government invoked its right on August 26, 1987, to conduct ar inspection of a Soviet ground force exercise that involved elements of one tank division and one motorized rifle division of 16,500 troops and 425 tanks. As specified in the document, the challenge or request for the inspection had been submitted by the U.S. State Department concurrently to the Soviet Foreign Office in Moscow and the Soviet embassy in Washington, D.C. The Soviets replied to the U.S. authorities within twenty hours (the document permits a maximum of twenty-four hours for an affirmative reply) in both Moscow and in Washington.

The U.S. team's explanation of the reason for the inspection, which it stated in the State Department's request for the inspection, was, "In accordance with paragraphs 65 and 66." At no time during the inspection did the Soviets question that explanation, although paragraph 66 specifies that the participating state requesting an inspection "will state the reasons for such a request."[9] Paragraph 65 states that each participating state "has the right to conduct inspections."

Thus, the first small area of possible confrontation had passed without much notice by either party. This issue of reasons was considerably more important in the eyes of several Western states. Representatives from one of those states declared informally that without a clearly stated reason for an inspection (other than merely in accordance with paragraphs 65 and 66), the request would be denied. A denial is not permitted (paragraph 71). Such negative feelings still exist, however, at least among some representatives of certain Western and neutral or nonaligned States.

In this first inspection, it appeared the Soviets were anxious to proceed and would not raise questions about that ambiguous portion of the document. Informally, a Soviet military officer had mentioned to a Western officer at a social function earlier in 1987 that "someone should inspect in order to complete the final act of fulfillment of the Stockholm Document, and, we [the Soviets] are not going to be first." This indicator, plus the fact that the exercise that had been the subject of Soviet notification, involved 16,500 troops (just under the 17,000 required for compulsory invitation of observers but substantially over the 13,000 required for notification), and 425 tanks (considerably over the 300 required for notification of the exercise) appeared to some to be almost a Soviet invitation for the inspection. During subsequent inspections conducted by the U.S. team, the potential frictions arising from the question of reasons were not an issue. Press releases of these other inspections also have indicated that such a problem does not exist in this respect.

For many outside observers, the Soviet exercise may have seemed to be just another routine military exercise in a major Soviet training area. But for the four U.S. Army officers, all specialists in Soviet affairs, heading for what was most likely to be the first landing by a U.S. military aircraft at the Minsk Civilian Airfield in the Soviet Union since World War II, the exercise was much more.[10] Dealing with the Soviets can be a trying and frustrating experience, and this first on-site inspection was perceived by all concerned as having the potential to set the tone for the future. In essence, policy would be determined by a handful of U.S. and Soviet military officers carrying out provisions of a document that had been negotiated and agreed to by representatives of thirty-five nations. It was not a responsibility to be taken lightly.

It also was significant for several senior military officers and other governmental officials at Headquarters, U.S. European Command, in the Pentagon, and at the U.S. State Department. As an official commented after the first CDE on-site inspection: "We were very keen to do it right the first time, to set the right precedent. That was achieved."[11]

The State Department's request for the inspection had specified the Soviet Machulushche Military Airfield (southwest of Minsk) as the touchdown point in the Soviet Union. The Soviets had denied that request, however, and had substituted the civilian airfield at Minsk.

At Minsk, a small welcoming party was on hand. The Soviets stood a short distance from the airport reception hall, near the four helicopters that were to be placed at the disposal of the inspection team. Two helicopters had been requested, and the other two were determined to be spares. Back-ups also were provided for the two ground vehicles requested.

As the American inspectors exited the aircraft, the Soviet Air Force colonel greeting them requested that they remain near the aircraft for a few minutes while the final touches to the assembly of the welcoming party were accomplished. One of the Soviet generals was a few minutes late, and the inspectors agreed with the colonel that it would be best to let the Soviet party get completely organized prior to the introductions. The delay did not present a problem for the inspectors; their planning had allowed for sufficient time to inspect portions of the specified area by helicopters and by ground vehicle prior to nightfall. This was extremely important to allow time for aerial reconnaissance, to gain familiarity with the terrain, and to locate the major troop dispositions during daylight hours. While the inspectors waited, visas were stamped in the diplomatic passports.

Once the receiving line was in order, the chief inspector introduced the team to the members of the welcoming party: two major generals, the air force colonel, and two interpreters introduced as civilians. The Soviet colonel was well known to the inspectors since he and the chief U.S. inspector had been together for three days during an observation of a Soviet–East German exercise in the Letzlinger Heide main training area in the German Democratic Republic under the auspices of the observation of the Stockholm Document in July 1987.[12] One of the interpreters introduced as a civilian, Mr. Popov, was known to have been a Soviet major eight years earlier when he had worked with one of the inspectors, Lieutenant Colonel Michael Crutcher, during the Strategic Arms Limitation Talks negotiations in Geneva.[13] Following the introductions, the group chatted cordially for a few minutes, and then the inspectors were led to the reception hall. The event appeared to be off to a good start. It was fairly obvious that this was going to be a convincing Soviet display that there would be complete compliance with all pertinent provisions of the Stockholm Document. By the same token, the inspectors wanted to accomplish as much as possible in applying agreed measures and in testing those that were not clear in the document.

During the next one and one-half hours, discussions ensued about administrative and logistical arrangements. A first step was to provide a flight plan for the helicopters to the inspection area and for the initial overflights of it. The Stockholm document specifies that "after the flight plan . . . has been filed with the competent air traffic control authority the inspection aircraft will be permitted to enter the specified area."[14] That was the reason for selecting the initial touchdown point outside of the specified area. There was a common desire to work precisely in accordance with the document.

During the discussions in the receiving hall of the airport, the Soviets were told that the team would split into two subgroups and that each group would overfly and inspect major portions of the specified area. At first the

Soviets were dismayed; one of the Soviet generals explained that there was no military activity in that area, especially in the northern portion. "Why do you want to go there [pointing to the northern half of the map]?" he asked. "That is merely farming area with absolutely no military activity. The exercise will be conducted here [again pointing to the map], in the Borisov training area and no place else."[15] After brief discussion, both Soviet generals accepted the fact that the two subteams initially would fly over as much of the specified area as they deemed necessary although avoiding any sensitive points.

The specified area, delineating the area in which the inspectors would be permitted "access, entry, and unobstructed survey," encompassed 20,000 square kilometers. The document states in paragraph 73 that the specified area should "not exceed that required for an army level military activity."[16] Access to such a large expanse of terrain had been requested by the team so as to judge better the strength of units moving to and from the exercise area. Also, the overflight of much more than the immediate main training area west of Borisov was required to ensure that this was in fact a training exercise. One of the objectives, of course, was to determine if the exercise was militarily threatening in any way. Notably, no receiving state has ever questioned the requested size or location of a specified area. Representatives of some participating states, however, have expressed grave concern over the possible inclusion of certain territory within a specified area.

In accordance with paragraph 74 of the document, the inspectors were entitled to "access, entry, and unobstructed survey, except for areas or sensitive points to which access is normally denied or restricted."[17] Determination of exactly what are sensitive points prompted most of the questions about implementation of the verification provisions—during this first inspection and also during subsequent inspections conducted by the U.S. team.

The U.S. team failed several times to gain entry to certain areas that should not have been declared sensitive points. In one case, the area denied was a railhead where the extent of the tracked-vehicle trackage leading to and from the point showed that it had been used as a loading and unloading point, probably for the exercise. Access to one road within the training area also was denied, with no reason given. During two attempts to count columns of vehicles in the training area, the interpreters (purported to be from the Ministry of Foreign Affairs) continually insisted that the vehicles had been previously counted and special permission from the major general in charge was required before the inspectors could go there again. Those columns of vehicles were not declared to be sensitive points; thus, valuable time was wasted.

It would be difficult not to accept an escort officer's declaration of a command post, a permanent encampment, or some other such item as a sensitive point. A column of vehicles involved in the exercise, however, cannot be considered a sensitive point by any stretch of the imagination. In this case, the vehicles were removed and could not be relocated after the major general had been found and permission had been granted to count them. According to the Stockholm Document, the Soviets were unjustified in delaying this part of the inspection.

None of the problems with associated sensitive points were critical to the accomplishment of the mission, however, and none warranted the kind of serious incident that probably would have accompanied an official protest. Consequently, although a strong vocal protest was lodged, an official one was not deemed appropriate. But the incidents did demonstrate the inflexibility of certain Soviet officers (and the interpreters) and indicated that they too were learning from this first experience. Since then the Soviets have become more flexible in their interpretations of the verification provisions, and the U.S. inspection teams have been better able to work with them to bring about a good deal of mutual understanding and cooperation during actual inspections.

Paragraph 75 states, "Within the specified area, the forces of participating States other than the receiving State will also be subject to the inspection conducted by the inspecting State." Minor problems arose in this regard during the Soviet inspection of Exercise Iron Forge in the Federal Republic of Germany, October 28–30, 1987, and also during the U.S. inspection in Poland, July 25–27, 1988. Both times several military units jointly occupied portions of the large training areas and were actively involved in unit training. Although these were not part of the notified exercises, it was difficult to explain this to inspecting officers, particularly since the guidelines that pertain are not clear in the Stockholm Document. Generally it is assumed that the receiving state must prove that a particular military unit, located within the specified area and actually out of garrison, is not directly involved in the exercise or activity being inspected. This has not been a serious problem, but it is an area that requires careful explanation and coordination on the ground during an actual inspection. No such problem was encountered during the first inspection.

Another issue concerned at what point the inspection—and the prescribed forty-eight-hour period—actually started. Paragraph 78.5 of the Stockholm Document specifies that the inspecting state will notify the receiving state of the exact starting point of the inspection within the specified area. For the inspection in Belorussia, a point on the map was selected close to the Minsk airfield where the edge of the specified area intersected a major road. The intent was to begin the inspection as the helicopters flew over that point and entered the specified area. That point on the ground turned out to be a landfill, which was not indicated on the U.S. maps. The Soviet assumption was that all participants had to identify the starting point on the ground. In characteristic fashion, the Soviets led the way to that point in

Volga sedans, following a rather high-speed dash through downtown Minsk. The column arrived in a cloud of dust. Everyone exited the vehicles and verified that it was, in fact, the exact starting point selected by map reconnaissance. Because of the terrain and safety requirements, the helicopters could not land in or near the landfill.

Both parties then agreed that the starting time of the inspection would be the precise moment at which the helicopters lifted off from the heliport. Consequently everyone returned to the sedans and headed for the heliport nearby. Again the Soviets were intent on proving their compliance with the document provisions, in this case by positively identifying the specified starting point. The ground between strict compliance and reasonable variation through flexibility and agreement at the scene seemed to be lost somewhere in the activity.

As Lieutenant Colonel Wagner's helicopter lifted off, the chief inspector in the second helicopter and the Soviet escort officer agreed on an official starting time of 0845 hours, GMT, though their helicopter experienced minor mechanical problems and was delayed a few minutes. The Soviets offered to start the inspection time officially after the second helicopter lifted off. In the interest of cooperation and in an attempt to reduce the exactness and great formality that might otherwise stifle meaningful inspection precedents, however, the Americans declined the offer. (A subsequent reference to exactness near the completion of the inspection will make it clear why I emphasize this point.)

Actually starting the inspection immediately was not so important since the inspectors had arrived early enough to become familiar with the terrain and the major troop and equipment locations before dark. On a subsequent inspection in the German Democratic Republic, however, the team arrived too late to conduct an aerial reconnaissance at the beginning and that turned out to be a disadvantage.

Paragraph 86 requires the receiving state to provide the inspection team with "appropriate board and lodging in a location suitable for carrying out the inspection." The Soviets selected the leading hotel in Minsk to meet this requirement. Although the hotel was only 70 kilometers from the Borisov training area, a great deal of time was consumed moving back and forth during the actual inspection because of poor road conditions, one-way traffic sections of the main road, heavy civilian truck traffic, and livestock that occasionally strayed onto the highway. Adverse weather conditions, and the fact that the Soviets declined to fly at night even if the weather had so permitted, precluded the use of the helicopter for this purpose, so that alternative was not available.

It was not necessary for the team to return to the hotel during the inspection. The members, however, had determined that the Soviets probably would be unnecessarily offended if their room and board offerings were not accepted. Protocol plays a role in inspections, and the team attempted to cooperate with the hosts whenever possible.[18] After a detailed search of the training area, moreover, team members had determined that probably no additional military activity would take place that first night, and the army rule of "rest while you can" became the deciding factor.

Access to appropriate telecommunications of the receiving state, including the opportunity for continuous communication between members of an inspection in an aircraft and those in a land vehicle during the conduct of an inspection, is stipulated in paragraph 88. The official U.S. government report on the inspection provided to the other participating states declared that radio communications between the two subgroups was generally excellent. Although true, that statement should be qualified. First, little flying was done because of the safety requirements imposed while the exercise play (attack, defend, and meeting engagement) was taking place and also because of high winds and poor visibility on the second day, which made flying too dangerous. Flying was not permitted over the exercise area after the exercise began because of low-flying Hind helicopters and Flogger and Frogfoot aircraft. Also, when the aircraft or ground vehicles were out of range (because of the distance limitations of the tactical radios provided), attempts to communicate by radio were not made. Thus, during this inspection, and several subsequent ones, communications proved inadequate. During U.S. inspections, tactical radios without added relay capability have not proved satisfactory. Better planning can help alleviate most problems that could occur as a result of poor communications. In certain situations, the subdivision of the specified area for the subgroup inspection teams is a simple but effective way to react when communications are known to be inadequate or nonexistent.

Paragraph 90 states that "directions to crews will be given through a representative of the receiving state on board the aircraft involved in the inspection." In all cases during this first inspection, that rule was followed. On several subsequent inspections conducted by the U.S. team, however, it was possible to give directions directly to the pilot on certain occasions because of the cooperation of the escort officers of the receiving state. In most cases, this was accomplished by giving arm and hand signals to the pilot. An average of ten minutes was required during the Belorussian inspection in order to alter flight directions, whereas only seconds were needed during the later inspections in Hungary and Poland. Again, most of these procedural improvements can be attributed to the experience of working together over a period of time, which has increased the understanding and cooperative spirit during inspections.

The Soviet officers had placed a great deal of emphasis on the exact starting time of the inspection. On the final day of the inspection, while on the main observation post in the Borisov training area, the chief inspector casually mentioned that he estimated the flying time from that point to the edge of the specified area was thirty minutes, and by road, it was probably considerably more than one hour away. One of the Soviet colonels who had accompanied the team during most of the inspection was asked, "What happens if the weather closes in, and we cannot fly? Is it absolutely essential that the inspectors are out of the specified area at the termination of the forty-eight-hour periods?" Immediately one of the individuals in civilian clothes who had been observing the activities leaped forward and, tapping his finger firmly on the chief inspector's chest, announced in a loud voice: "Colonel Stovall, you know the document as well as I, and it states that you must be out of the specified area within forty-eight hours, so do not attempt to stay longer and violate the document!" Later, one of the Soviet interpreters and another Soviet officer apologized for the rudeness.

In fact, paragraph 83 states that "within 48 hours after the arrival of the inspection team at the specified area, the inspection will be terminated." No words in the document state that inspectors must be out of the specified area upon termination of the inspection. Among professionals applying a fair interpretation of the document, cameras and dictaphones would have been put away after forty-eight hours had the team remained in the specified area after official termination of the inspection. It was obvious to the inspectors that the Soviet colonel was wrong, but they saw that nothing would be gained by raising an official protest.

As the time neared for departure from the observation point by helicopter and for the termination of the inspection, a Soviet air force lieutenant general arrived. He accompanied the chief inspector on the flight "out of the specified area" and pointed out, at the precise moment when the helicopter exited the specified area, that exactly forty-eight hours had transpired since the inspection began. (Actually, the helicopter exited the specified area exactly six seconds early. Exactness and flexibility have a strange relationship when dealing with some Soviets.)

CDE Inspections of a Nonexercise

Twenty-two of the twenty-four CDE on-site inspections conducted through July 1989 have been of notified exercises, that is, exercises that a Stockholm party is required to notify in advance because of size. The U.S. inspection carried out in the German Democratic Republic, April 10–12, 1988, was of a different nature. Here, there was no prior notification of an exercise within the Stockholm limits for the specified area which the U.S. challenge asked to inspect. The purpose of the visit was to exercise the right to inspect or challenge military activities to determine if they were in fact within the threshold agreed under CDE to require advance notice. The U.S. inspection team was sent to inspect what eventually was determined to be end-of-cycle training of a Soviet tank division based in Riesa.

As the inspection progressed and the number of positively identified tanks began to accumulate, it was apparent that there was some concern on the part of the senior East German escort officer and the senior Soviet liaison officer. On one occasion, those officers mentioned that "It might possibly happen *some day* [my emphasis] that an overzealous commander would order more than 300 tanks out of garrison for end-of-cycle or some other type of training activity that would not actually be an exercise *per se.*" Implicit in their statements was the "fact" that if more than 300 tanks were identified during this "activity," it certainly would not be in violation of the Stockholm Document.[19] In other words, there was no question that concern about accidentally exceeding the Stockholm limits had gotten the attention of the East German and Soviet officers with whom the inspectors had come in contact. This experience suggests that at least in the case of ground force exercises and activities, surprise or suspect-site inspections have utility. The Soviet inspection in Italy (May 28–30, 1989) also was an inspection of a non-notified exercise. It is not known what motivated the Soviets to call for an inspection.

The First Soviet CDE On-Site Inspections

The third CDE on-site inspection was carried out in Turkey, October 5–7, 1987, by the Soviets. One of the members of the Soviet team had been present as an observer in civilian clothes during the U.S. inspection in Belorussia in August. (In fact, he was the colonel who had answered the question about the timing of exiting the specified area rudely. He subsequently was in several different inspections during the course of the next year, and he remained aggressive and forceful, a posture the Soviets probably believe is effective.)

The dress and equipment of the four Soviet inspectors were almost identical to that worn and utilized by the U.S. inspectors in Belorussia. The specially designed shoulder patches worn by the Soviet inspectors were professionally done, however, the U.S. inspectors' arm band had been fabricated in-house in order to meet the August 28 deadline.

A U.S. Marine Corps Amphibious Battalion and elements of the U.S. 24th Infantry Division were part of Exercise Display Determination in Turkey on October 5, so it was particularly important that a U.S. liaison team be available to assist the Turkish escort officers whenever the Soviet inspectors came in contact with U.S. personnel or equipment. That precedent already had been set in many respects by the presence of Soviet inspectors acting as liaison officers during the second on-site inspection, by the United

Kingdom in the German Democratic Republic in September 1987. However, because of late notification of U.S. European Command Headquarters in Stuttgart, the U.S. inspection team arrived in Turkey after the Soviets had started their inspection. Coordination has vastly improved since that inspection, and notification is no longer a problem.

The Soviet inspectors were aggressive during that inspection and stayed on the go during most of the forty-eight hours. The four U.S. liaison officers worked closely with the Turkish escort officers and acted as interpreters for the Soviet officers and for U.S. troops as required. That the Turkish officers spoke excellent English, greatly facilitated the rendering of assistance whenever a request was made. The U.S. liaison officers were the guests of the Turkish forces and understood that they were there only with the blessing of the receiving state, which has final authority over verification matters on its soil. All nations regard sovereignty rights seriously, and both inspectors and liaison officers must be sensitive to that fact. (All of the U.S. Liaison officers found working with the Turkish officers was a pleasure.)

The Soviet inspectors strongly objected to the presence of the U.S. liaison officers in the Turkish inspection. They were far less upset when U.S. officers appeared as liaison officers during the Soviets' inspection in the Federal Republic of Germany, October 28–30, 1987, during Exercise Iron Forge. The U.S. officers were there as guests of West Germany, because the U.S. 1st Armored Division was involved in the exercise. Since that time, the Soviets apparently have determined that the presence of U.S. liaison officers is not threatening to their interests and may even work to their advantage. When a determined U.S. commander or other U.S. military member of a unit feels no obligation to answer the questions of a Soviet inspector, for instance, the U.S. liaison officer, who knows and understands all aspects of the Stockholm Document, can offer advice and assistance on both military-technical matters and interpretation of language.

One of the Soviet officers who participated in the inspection in Turkey also was present on several subsequent inspections in both a passive and an active capacity.[20] Largely as a result of continued association, some cooperation and mutual understanding has evolved among inspectors. An Eastern inspector even suggested, "We should form an inspectors' union, have conferences, and work out the problems we all are forced to face in the implementation of the Stockholm Document." Although the statement possibly was made somewhat in jest, there also was a serious element, which made the suggestion seem plausible.[21]

Since 1987, an additional eleven inspections in the East and eight in the West have taken place. Other participating states also have joined the ranks of inspectors during the course of the past year. The Federal Republic of Germany, Poland, Turkey, and Bulgaria have exercised their prerogatives under the provisions of paragraph 65 of the Stockholm Document during

1988. Italy and Canada also conducted inspections during 1989. Added to the United States, Soviet Union, United Kingdom, and German Democratic Republic inspections of 1987, this raises the number of countries that have conducted inspections to ten—six Western and four Eastern countries. Undoubtedly the Stockholm Document objectives of openness and transparency will continue to be tested. Arms control methods, whether in the form of reductions and eliminations or simply measures for increasing confidence and security building, are here to stay.

The CDE Inspections: A Former U.S. Inspector's View

Several broad conclusions can be drawn from the experience with the CDE on-site inspections concerning the Soviet approach, the outcome and purpose of inspections, the learning process, alliance aspects about how to handle ambiguities, and some technical lessons for future agreements.

The Soviets have determined that the dangers to their national security posed by on-site inspection in the Stockholm conventional force arena were not sufficiently serious to block their agreement. Acceptance not only has propaganda value; it could lead to other arms control agreements, which help the Soviets in their urgent need to build their economy and solve other domestic problems.

From the first inspection, the Soviets have demonstrated a willingness to cooperate and to make the inspections a success. Along with the other countries that have participated in inspections, they have mounted a significant effort to comply with the verification provisions of the Stockholm Document. Soviet openness initially was mitigated by subtle control measures aimed at limiting the effectiveness of the inspectors. This tendency to control the movement and actions of the inspectors, however, has lessened considerably during more recent inspections.

There has been no evidence to date that any of the exercises inspected have been threatening to any nation. Nor has there been evidence that any country has cheated. The inspections have increased transparency of Soviet activities. All Warsaw Pact exercises inspected have been standard force-on-force exercises. And there has been no noticeable change in past Soviet training practices. Offensive and defensive tactics are both alive and well, regardless of the inferences in the statement made by a senior Soviet military officer during the U.S. inspection in Poland to "let the defensive battle begin" [*davai, oboronitel'nyi boi*]. And for whatever reasons, the participating states involved directly in the CDE on-site inspections conducted thus far have come to accept and support the purpose of the inspections: to promote more openness and transparency.

There has been a learning process on both sides. Initially aggressive, Soviet inspectors have mellowed in their actions and words after repeated contact with U.S. inspectors. Cooperation has facilitated the handling of problems on the ground during the actual conduct of inspections. A give-and-take atmosphere has become more possible.

For the United States, initial practice inspections greatly helped prepare for the actual inspections, a lesson with applications to other agreements. U.S. inspectors also had to learn when to push hard on a point and when to back off to avoid creating an incident. Detailed knowledge of their rights as inspectors proved essential.

Soviet inspectors were able to discern even minor differences between Western allies with respect to implementation of verification provisions of the document. They also were quick to exploit those differences to their advantage. Western unity regarding the document and its implementation is essential.

Among Soviet allies, escort officers in Eastern Europe deferred to Soviet liaison officers concerning questions of access. In matters concerning the Stockholm Document, disunity among Warsaw Pact nations has not been apparent.

Inspection teams have had to deal with ambiguities in the document. The lack of a complete definition of sensitive points remains perhaps the most serious problem in the current wording of the verification provisions of the Stockholm Document. Any future attempts at rewording will have to be done carefully so as not to make the problem worse. Indeed, a rigid definition may not be possible and probably should not be sought.

Another area of concern has been the distance permitted between inspectors in a subgroup as they walk through an area of troop and equipment deployment. This is important because of the need to keep track of Soviet inspectors. The document states in paragraph 84 that "the inspection team may divide into two parts" but specifies no allowed distance between the two individuals. Generally it has been agreed during the conduct of inspections that inspectors within the subteam must have visual contact. To attempt to increase the distance beyond visual contact probably would be inadvisable.

Several technical lessons also have emerged for verification of future agreements. In the conventional area, recording by dictaphones and/or camera tank turret numbers, armored personnel carrier side numbers, aircraft side numbers, vehicle registration numbers, or other identifying markings will be necessary to preclude double counting weapons and equipment. Second, reduction in the number of hours (thirty-six) after the request and the time "the inspection team will be permitted to enter the territory of the receiving state" in the future should limit opportunities for the receiving state to cover up exercise activities in violation of the Document or any other accord. Improved communications also may be needed for extensive conventional arms control inspections.

Finally, an important lesson learned is that the inspections have not been used for the overt collection of intelligence. It is obviously in everyone's best interest to adhere to that principle. Gathering information for verification and confidence should not be construed as collecting intelligence.

Looking Ahead

It is encouraging to note the spirit of cooperation shown by many of the Soviet and East European military officers, senior and junior, and enlisted men with whom the U.S. inspectors have been in contact during the course of CDE on-site inspections. These inspections have contributed to the objectives of openness and transparency and have become an integral part of the Confidence- and Security-Building Measures regime.

When considering future agreements in the conventional force arena, both on-site and suspect-site inspections will be essential. Paragraph 64 of the Stockholm Document states that "national technical means can play a role in monitoring compliance" Truer words were never agreed upon. National technical means can play *a* role but cannot do the entire job. And not all of the thirty-five participating states have these means available to them.

The events that have unfolded since General Secretary Mikhail Gorbachev's speech before the United Nations on December 7, 1988, indicate that the Soviets, and several East European countries, will cut back the physical size of their conventional armed forces. All of the cards have not yet been played, but should an agreement result on conventional forces, on-site inspections will be an important part of a cautious and studied approach to its verification. It should be informed by and benefit from the experiences and lessons of the Stockholm CDE inspections.

Appendix 2A: Compliance and Verification Provisions of the Stockholm Document

(63) According to the Madrid Mandate, the confidence- and security-building measures to be agreed upon "will be provided with adequate forms of verification which correspond to their content."

(64) The participating States recognize that national technical means can play a role in monitoring compliance with agreed confidence- and security-building measures. [CSBMS]

(65) In accordance with the provisions contained in this document each participating State has the right to conduct inspections on the territory of any other participating State within the zone of application for CSBMs [confidence and security building measures]

(66) Any participating State will be allowed to address a request for inspection to another participating State on whose territory, within the zone of application for CSBMs, compliance with the agreed confidence- and security-building measures is in doubt.

(67) No participating State will be obliged to accept on its territory within the zone of application for CSBMs, more than three inspections per calendar year.

(68) No participating State will be obliged to accept more than one inspection per calendar year from the same participating State.

(69) An inspection will not be counted if, due to force majeure, it cannot be carried out.

(70) The participating State which requests an inspection will state the reasons for such a request.

(71) The participating State which has received such a request will reply in the affirmative to the request within the agreed period of time, subject to the provisions contained in paragraphs (67) and (68).

(72) Any possible dispute as to the validity of the reasons for a request will not prevent or delay the conduct of an inspection.

(73) The participating State which requests an inspection will be permitted to designate for inspection on the territory of another State within the zone application for CSBMs, a specific area. Such an area will be referred to as the "specified area." The specified area will comprise terrain where notifiable military activities are conducted or where another participating State believes a notifiable military activity is taking place. The specified area will be defined and limited by the scope and scale of notifiable military activities but will not exceed that required for an army level military activity.

(74) In the specified area the representatives of the inspecting State accompanied by the representatives of the receiving State will be permitted access, entry, and unobstructed survey, except for areas or sensitive points to which access is normally denied or restricted, military and other defense installations, as well as naval vessels, military vehicles and aircraft. The number and extent of the restricted areas should be as limited as possible. Areas where notifiable military activities can take place will not be declared restricted areas, except for certain permanent or temporary military installations which, in territorial terms, should be as small as possible, and consequently those areas will not be used to prevent inspection of notifiable military activities. Restricted areas will not be employed in a way inconsistent with the agreed provisions on inspection.

(75) Within the specified area, the forces of participating States other than the receiving State will also be subject to the inspection conducted by the inspecting State.

(76) Inspection will be permitted on the ground, from the air, or both.

(77) The representatives of the receiving State will accompany the inspection team, including when it is in land vehicles and an aircraft from the

time of their first employment until the time they are no longer in use for the purpose of inspection.

(78) In its request, the inspecting State will notify the receiving State of:

(78.1)—the reasons for the request;

(78.2)—the location of the specified area defined by geographical co-ordinates;

(78.3)—the preferred point(s) of entry for the inspection team;

(78.4)—mode of transport to and from the point(s) of entry and, if applicable, to and from the specified area;

(78.5)—where in the specified area the inspection will begin;

(78.6)—whether the inspection will be conducted from the ground, from the air, or both simultaneously;

(78.7)—whether the inspection will be conducted using an airplane, a helicopter, or both;

(78.8)—whether the inspection team will use land vehicles provided by the receiving State or, if mutually agreed, its own vehicles;

(78.9)—information for the issuance of diplomatic visas to inspectors entering the receiving State.

(79) The reply to the request will be given in the shortest possible period of time, but within not more than twenty-four hours. Within thirty-six hours after the issuance of the request, the inspection team will be permitted to enter the territory of the receiving State.

(80) Any request for inspection as well as reply thereto will be communicated to all participating States without delay.

(81) The receiving State should designate the point(s) of entry as close as possible to the specified area. The receiving State will ensure that the inspection team will be able to reach the specified area without delay from the point(s) of entry.

(82) All participating States will facilitate the passage of the inspection teams through their territory.

(83) Within 48 hours after the arrival of the inspection team at the specified area, the inspection will be terminated.

(84) There will be no more than four inspectors in an inspection team. While conducting the inspection the inspection team may divide into two parts.

(85) The inspectors and, if applicable, auxiliary personnel, will be granted during their mission the privileges and immunities in accordance with the Vienna Convention on Diplomatic Relations.

(86) The receiving State will provide the inspection team with appropriate board and lodging in a location suitable for carrying out the inspec-

tion, and, when necessary, medical care; however this does not exclude the use by the inspection team of its own tents and rations.

(87)The inspection team will have use of its own maps, own photo cameras, own binoculars and own dictaphones, as well as its own aeronautical charts.

(88) The inspection team will have access to appropriate telecommunications equipment of the receiving State, including the opportunity for continuous communication between the members of an inspection team in an aircraft and those in a land vehicle employed in the inspection.

(89) The inspecting State will specify whether aerial inspection will be conducted using an airplane, a helicopter or both. Aircraft for inspection will be chosen by mutual agreement between the inspecting and receiving States. Aircraft will be chosen which provide the inspection team a continuous view of the ground during the inspection.

(90) After the flight plan, specifying, inter alia, the inspection team's choice of flight path, speed, and altitude in the specified area, has been filed with the competent air traffic control authority the inspection aircraft will be permitted to enter the specified area without delay. Within the specified area, the inspection team will, at its request, be permitted to deviate from the approved flight plan to make specific observations provided such deviation is consistent with paragraph (74) as well as flight safety and air traffic requirements. Directions to the crew will be given through a representative of the receiving State on board the aircraft involved in the inspection.

(91) One member of the inspection team will be permitted, if such a request is made, at any time to observe data on navigational equipment of the aircraft and to have access to maps and charts used by the flight crew for the purpose of determining the exact location of the aircraft during the inspection flight.

(92) Aerial and ground inspectors may return to the specified area as often as desired within the 48-hour inspection period.

(93) The receiving State will provide for inspection purposes land vehicles with cross country capability. Whenever mutually agreed taking into account the specific geography relating to the area to be inspected, the inspecting State will be permitted to use its own vehicles.

(94) If land vehicles or aircraft are provided by the inspecting State, there will be one accompanying driver for each land vehicle, or accompanying aircraft crew.

(95) The inspecting State will prepare a report of its inspection and will provide a copy of that report to all participating States without delay.

(96) The inspection expenses will be incurred by the receiving State except when the inspecting State uses its own aircraft and/or land vehicles. The travel expenses to and from the point(s) of entry will be borne by the inspecting State.

(97) Diplomatic channels will be used for communications concerning compliance and verification.

(98) Each participating State will be entitled to obtain timely clarification from any other participating State concerning the application of agreed confidence- and security-building measures. Communications in this context will, if appropriate, be transmitted to all other participating States. . . .

*　　*　　*

(99) The participating States stress that these confidence- and security-building measures are designed to reduce the dangers of armed conflict and of misunderstanding or miscalculation of military activities and emphasize that their implementation will contribute to these objectives.

(100) Reaffirming the relevant objectives of the Final Act, the participating States are determined to continue building confidence, to lessen military confrontation and to enhance security for all. They are also determined to achieve progress in disarmament.

(101) The measures adopted in this document are politically binding and will come into force on 1 January 1987.

(102) The Government of Sweden is requested to transmit the present document to the follow-up meeting of the CSCE in Vienna and to the Secretary-General of the United Nations. The Government of Sweden is also requested to transmit the present document to the Governments of the non-participating Mediterranean States.

(103) The text of this document will be published in each participating State, which will disseminate it and make it known as widely as possible.

(104) The representatives of the participating States express their profound gratitude to the government and people of Sweden for the excellent arrangements made for the Stockholm Conference and the warm hospitality extended to the delegations which participated in the Conference.

Stockholm, 19 September 1986

Under the terms of the Madrid mandate, the zone of application for CSBMs is defined as follows:

> On the basis of equality of rights, balance and reciprocity, equal respect for the security interests of all CSCE participating States, and of their respective obligations concerning confidence- and security-building measures and disarmament in Europe, these confidence- and security-building measures will cover the whole of Europe as well as the adjoining sea area* and air space. They will be of military significance and politically binding and will be provided with adequate forms of verification which correspond to their content.

As far as the adjoining sea area* and air space is concerned, the measures will be applicable to the military activities of all the participating States taking place there whenever these activities affect security in Europe as well as constitute a part of activities taking place within the whole of Europe as referred to above, which they will agree to notify. Necessary specifications will be made through the negotiations on the confidence- and security-building measures at the Conference.

Nothing in the definition of the zone given above will diminish obligations already undertaken under the Final Act. The confidence- and security-building measures to be agreed upon at the Conference will also be applicable in all areas covered by any of the provisions in the Final Act relating to confidence-building measures and certain aspects of security and disarmament.

---

*In this context, the notion of adjoining sea area is understood to refer also to ocean areas adjoining Europe.

Whenever the term "the zone of application of CSBMs" is used in this document, the above definition will apply.

Appendix 2B: CDE On-Site Inspections

Location	Dates	Conducted By
Soviet Union	August 28–30, 1987	United States
German Democratic Republic	September 10–12, 1987	United Kingdom
Turkey	October 5–7, 1987	Soviet Union
Federal Republic of Germany	October 29–30, 1987	Soviet Union
Federal Republic of Germany	November 11–13, 1987	German Democratic Republic
Hungary	February 4–6, 1988	United States
Norway	March 13–15, 1988	Soviet Union
Soviet Union	April 9–11, 1988	United Kingdom
German Democratic Republic	April 10–12, 1988	United States
Italy	May 1–3, 1988	Bulgaria
Poland	July 25–27, 1988	United States
German Democratic Republic	August 12–14, 1988	Federal Republic of Germany
Soviet Union	August 23–25, 1988	Turkey
Federal Republic of Germany	September 7–9, 1988	Soviet Union
United Kingdom	October 5–6, 1988	Soviet Union
Soviet Union	October 14–16, 1988	United States
Federal Republic of Germany	November 7–9, 1988	Poland
Federal Republic of Germany	November 28–30, 1988	German Democratic Republic
German Democratic Republic*	April 9–11, 1989	Federal Republic of Germany
Soviet Union*	April 15–17, 1989	Italy
German Democratic Republic	May 19–21, 1989	United States
Italy	May 28–30, 1989	Soviet Union
Czechoslovakia	June 14–16, 1989	Canada
Denmark	June 21–23, 1989	Soviet Union

*Observers were invited to these exercises. None of the previous inspections required acceptance of observers under the terms of the Stockholm Document since they involved fewer than 17,000 troops.

Notes

1. U.S. Congress, Senate, *National Defense Authorization Act for Fiscal Year 1989*, S. Rept. 100–326 to Accompany S.2355, 100th Cong., 2d sess., 1988, p. 133.

2. Roland M. Timerbayev, *Kontrol' za ogranicheniem vooruzhenii i razoruzheniem* [Verification of arms limitation and disarmament] (Moscow: Mezhdunarodnye Otnosheniia, November 1983), p. 18.

3. MBFR refers to Mutual and Balanced Force Reduction talks, recently terminated, which had been ongoing in Vienna for the past fifteen years without major consequence. INF is the acronym for intermediate-range and shorter-range missiles. START stands for Strategic Arms Reduction Talks, which probably will be resumed in Geneva late in 1989.

4. These talks previously were referred to as the Conventional Stability Talks. As mandated by the closing sessions of the Conference on Security and Cooperation in Europe (CSCE) in January, 1989, the new talks, which began in March 1989, are called the Conventional Armed Forces in Europe talks. The U.S. Government has declared that the talks will be referred to by representatives of the U.S. as the Conventional Forces in Europe (CFE) talks; they run parallel to the Conference on Security Building Measures (CSBM) negotiations, also located in Vienna. Both negotiations take place within the framework of the CSCE processes.

5. With reference to the inspection of ground force exercises and activities under the auspices of the Stockholm Document, it is understood these inspections refer to short-notice, intrusive, challenge inspections of exercises or any other activity involving ground forces. These are generally considered anyplace, anytime inspections, and their requests would be tempered by an intelligent application of what is reasonable, fair, and responsible. In this chapter, that definition is applicable.

6. *Conference on Security and Co-Operation in Europe Final Act, Helsinki 1975* (Stockholm: Minab/gotab, 1984), p. 77 (hereafter, *CSCE Final Act*). For a definitive account of the negotiations leading to the Helsinki Final Act, see John Maresca, *To Helsinki* (Durham, N.C.: Duke University Press, 1985).

7. *CSCE Final Act*, p. 86.

8. *Concluding Document, Madrid 1983* (Stockholm: Minab/gotab, 1983), p. 37.

9. For additional details on request for inspection see paragraphs 65, 66, 70, and 72 in appendix 2A.

10. In addition to the four inspectors (Colonel Don Stovall, Lieutenant Colonels Warren Wagner and Michael Crutcher, and Major James Silva) and the two-man U.S. air crew, two Soviet Air Force officers (a pilot and a navigator) also were on board the aircraft during the flight from Stuttgart to Minsk. Their presence was required in accordance with Soviet regulations, not as a result of any Stockholm Document requirement.

11. U.S. State Department official comment during a press conference covering the results of the inspection. See Michael R. Gordon, "U.S. Praises Soviet for War Games' Role," *New York Times*, September 22, 1987, p. A3.

12. "Observations" under the Stockholm Document are very different from "inspections," and the modus operandi of the two should not be merged. For details

relating to observations, see *Document of the Stockholm Conference 1986* (Stockholm: Gotab, 1986), pp. 26–32 (hereafter, *DSC 1986*).

13. Popov also acted as the chief interpreter for Soviet Marshal Sergei Akhromeyev during his visit to the United States in 1988. He wore a Soviet army officer's uniform with the rank of colonel during that visit. The point is not whether Popov is a civilian or a military man; it is that the Soviets wanted this first CDE on-site inspection to proceed correctly and without incident. Popov is fluent in English and is extremely knowledgeable on military matters and the Stockholm Document. For whatever reasons, the Soviets place a great deal of emphasis on the importance of the Stockholm Document. The Soviet press reported this first CDE on-site inspection in considerable detail. See "O provedenii inspektsii" [Concerning the Conduct of the Inspection], *Krasnaia zvezda,* August 30, 1987, p. 1; Moscow TASS, "Petrovskiy on U.S. Observers [Inspectors] at "Priverzhennost' novomy myshleniiu" [Adherence to the New Thinking], *Krasnaia zvezda,* September 10, 1987; and, Moscow TASS 1301 and 1502 GMT, September 24, 1987. In general, the Soviets are trying to buy time [peredyshka] in order to bring about domestic reforms. Arms control is a major means for their achievement of that goal. Implementation of the Stockholm Document is a definite means of establishing confidence and reducing tensions, thereby enhancing the atmosphere for arms control agreements. The connection here seems obvious. See David Hoffman, "Gorbachev Seen as Trying to Buy Time for Reform," *Washington Post,* January 23, 1989, p. A29.

14. *DCS 1986,* p. 35. Also see paragraph 90, appendix 2A.

15. The two Soviet generals also mentioned several times that the exercise director, Colonel General Shuralov (also the Commander of the Belorussion Military District), was at the main observation point in the Borisov main training area and was ready to present briefings on the exercise and to answer any questions the inspectors might have. The Soviets did not insist that the U.S. inspectors go there first; however, it was obvious that it was their desire that they do so. By so doing, the team would have been following the prescribed outline of an observation; thus, they elected for the overflight of the specified area as the first priority. Throughout all inspections conducted by the U.S. team, there has been a tendency for the receiving states—the Soviet Union, German Democratic Republic, Hungary, and Poland—to guide the inspections toward the observation format. The U.S. team has resisted this for obvious reasons.

16. See paragraph 73, appendix 2A. During the negotiations in Stockholm, a more definitive agreement as to the size of the specified area could not be reached. Prior to this inspection, there was concern among some Western authorities that the Soviets would question the request for such a large area. However, that issue was never raised.

17. See paragraph 74, appendix 2A.

18. On several occasions during this first inspection and also during subsequent inspections, the U.S. team paused during the inspection to partake of refreshments with their hosts. In the case of the Soviets, this always was nonalcoholic. At least one of the subgroup inspection teams normally returned to the hotel for a few hours of sleep during each inspection. It could be stated that this was

valuable inspection time ill spent, but I differ with that assessment. "Rest while you can" and "do not lose sight of your obligation to be friendly and cooperative" were deemed important. During the most recent U.S. inspection in the Soviet Union, the Soviets became more cooperative in providing hotel accommodations closer to the training areas where military activities were scheduled to take place. That may have been due to low-level, tactful suggestions made to the Polish colonel in charge of CDE affairs and to Soviet liaison officers during the inspection conducted in Poland in July 1988.

19. Paragraph 31.1.1 of the Prior Notification of Certain Military Activities section of the Stockholm Document states that the "military activity will be subject to notification whenever it involves at any time during the activity: . . . at least 300 battle tanks." See *DSC 1986*, p. 26.

20. "Passive" indicates that the officer is present as a liaison officer to the receiving state in order to assist escort officers of the receiving state as required whenever the inspectors come in contact with forces or equipment from the liaison officers' state. "Active" means that the officer is an inspector actually conducting the inspection.

21. An impetus for such meetings could come from recent Soviet pronouncements. Shortly before he was replaced by Colonel-General Moiseev in December 1988, the Chief of the General Staff of the Soviet armed forces, Marshal Sergei Akhromeyev, commented that "contracts between representatives of the military establishments of the USSR and the US . . . are a result of positive changes in Soviet-American relations . . . this [these contacts] will allow each side to know the other better, understand more correctly their military undertakings, and will, if only partly, help to remove mutual suspicion and mistrust." See "Soviet View— Interview with Marshal of the USSR Sergei Akhromeyev," *Defense Science* (October 1988): 63. Also, "The meetings between defense minister Dmitri Yazov and Frank Carlucci, and Chief of the General Staff of the Soviet armed forces Sergei Akhromeyev and Chairman of the U.S. Joint Chiefs of Staff, Adm. William Crowe, have laid down the beginning of post-war contacts and cooperation between the two countries in the military sphere." See Makhmut A. Gareyev, "The Revised Soviet Military Doctrine," *Bulletin of the Atomic Scientists* (December 1988): 34.

3
Lessons of the IAEA Safeguards Experience for On-Site Inspection in Future Arms Control Regimes

Archelaus R. Turrentine

T o understand the rationale behind the safeguards system of the International Atomic Energy Agency (IAEA) and how it evolved into its present form, one must step back in time briefly to the beginning of the atomic age.

The potential dangers associated with nuclear activities were recognized early. In his famous letter to President Roosevelt on August 2, 1939, Albert Einstein noted the prospect that a chain reaction of fissions in a large mass of uranium would generate "vast amounts of power" and that this new phenomenon would lead to bombs, "extremely powerful bombs of a new type."[1] In response, President Roosevelt appointed the Advisory Committee on Uranium. In June 1940 he gave instructions that the committee be reconstituted as a subcommittee under the National Defense Research Committee. In November 1941, the National Academy of Sciences reviewed the U.S. nuclear program and concluded that it was possible to build a fission bomb of "superlatively destructive power" and that a crash program with all possible effort could produce such bombs within three or four years.[2] Subsequently control of the program was transferred to the U.S. Army in 1943 and became the Manhattan Project, with the objective of developing and producing an atomic bomb in the shortest possible time. The Manhattan Project was carried out with great emphasis on secrecy and security to restrict access to the new bomb technology.

After the dramatic ending of World War II with the use of nuclear weapons for the first time, the United States began to consider ways to deal internationally with the problems posed by nuclear energy. There was a realization that the basic scientific aspects of nuclear physics could not be contained effectively; however, it might be possible to restrain military programs directed toward acquiring atomic bombs by restricting access to nuclear technology and fissionable material. In March 1946, the Acheson Report on the International Control of Atomic Energy, submitted to the secretary of state, concluded in part that "the facts preclude any reasonable reliance upon inspection as the primary safeguard against violations of conventions prohibiting atomic weapons, yet leaving the exploitation of atomic energy in national hands." Furthermore, "only if the dangerous aspects of atomic energy are taken out of national hands and placed in international hands is there any reasonable prospect of devising safeguards against the use of atomic energy for bombs."[3]

The Acheson Report was modified slightly and presented to the United Nations later in 1946 as the Baruch Plan. The Baruch Plan proposed that no nation would have veto power to stop the international agency controlling atomic energy from taking action in case of a violation. The United States proposed to place all of its nuclear facilities and nuclear weapons under control of an International Atomic Development Authority after "an adequate system for control of atomic energy, including the renunciation of the bomb as a weapon, has been agreed upon and put into effective operation."[4] The Soviet Union rejected the Baruch Plan, however, so no such system was established.

During this same period, the U.S. Congress was taking action to put severe restrictions on nuclear material and nuclear technology. In 1946, the first Atomic Energy Act was passed, creating the U.S. Atomic Energy Commission, under civilian control. The Atomic Energy Act of 1946 required U.S. government ownership of all U.S. nuclear source material and facilities capable of producing any significant quantity of fissionable material. It stated:

> That until Congress declares by joint resolution that effective and enforce-able international safeguards against the use of atomic energy for destructive purposes have been established, there shall be no exchange of information with other nations with respect to the use of atomic energy for industrial purposes.[5]

For the next eight years the United States practiced a policy of almost total restriction with regard to its nuclear programs. A key policy shift was revealed by President Eisenhower in his address, "Atomic Power for Peace," which he delivered to the United Nations General Assembly on December 8, 1953. President Eisenhower proposed that an international atomic energy agency be established under the aegis of the United Nations and that "the governments principally involved" should "make joint contributions from their stockpiles of normal uranium and fissionable materials." Further, "This fissionable material would be allocated to serve the peaceful pursuits of mankind." The president concluded by indicating that he was prepared to submit to Congress a plan that would allow the United States to make nuclear material available for "worldwide investigation."[6]

The Atomic Energy Act of 1954 contained provisions to permit the implementation of international cooperation by the United States. Over the next several years, a number of bilateral agreements for peaceful nuclear cooperation were concluded between the United States and various allies and friends. Under many of these agreements, the United States provided small research reactors. These agreements contained provisions that permitted the United States to apply bilateral safeguards to ensure that any material or nuclear equipment it provided under the agreements was not being misused.

Following President Eisenhower's "Atoms for Peace" proposal, a conference was convened at the United Nations to work out the details for the new atomic energy agency. After lengthy negotiations, the Conference on the Statute of the IAEA reached agreement in October 1956. The IAEA Statute came into force on July 29, 1957.[7]

The IAEA Mandate for Safeguards

From the outset, the IAEA had a dual mandate: to facilitate the peaceful use of nuclear energy and to provide safeguards against misuse of materials and nuclear equipment, such as reactors. Article II of the IAEA Statute states:

> The Agency shall seek to accelerate and enlarge the contribution of atomic energy to peace, health and prosperity throughout the world. It shall ensure, so far as it is able, that assistance provided by it or at its request or under its supervision or control is not used in such a way as to further any military purpose.[8]

Article III of the Statute authorizes the IAEA to

> establish and administer safeguards designed to ensure that special fissionable and other materials, services, equipment, facilities, and information made available by the Agency or under its supervision or control are not used in such a way as to further any military purpose. The IAEA is given the authority to apply safeguards, at the request of the parties, to any bilateral or multilateral arrangement, or at the request of a State, to any of that State's activities in the field of atomic energy.

Article XII outlines the agency's rights and responsibilities with respect to safeguards. The IAEA is given the right

> to examine the design of specialized equipment and facilities, including nuclear reactors, and to evaluate it only to assure that it will not further any military purpose, that it complies with applicable health and safety standards, and that it will permit effective application of safeguards.

The IAEA also is authorized

to require the maintenance and production of operating records to assist in ensuring accountability for source and special materials used or produced in a project or arrangement.

In addition, the agency is given the right to approve the means to be used for "the chemical processing of irradiated materials solely to ensure that this chemical processing will not lend itself to diversion of materials for military purposes and will comply with applicable health and safety standards."

The agency may require that "special fissionable materials recovered or produced as a by-product" be used for peaceful purposes under continuing agency safeguards for research or in reactors specified by the "member or members concerned."

The Statute gives the IAEA authority "to require deposit with the Agency of any special fissionable materials recovered or produced as a by-product which exceed what is needed for [permitted uses] in order to prevent stockpiling of these materials, provided that thereafter, at the request of the member or members concerned special fissionable materials so deposited with the Agency shall be returned promptly to the member or members concerned for use" in specified peaceful activities. It is given authority

to send into the territory of the recipient State or States inspectors, (designated by the Agency after consultation with the State or States concerned,) who shall have access at all times to all places and data and to any person who by reason of his occupation deals with materials, equipment, of facilities which are required . . . to be safeguarded, as necessary to account for source and special fissionable materials and to determine whether there is compliance with the undertaking against use in furtherance of any military purpose . . . , and with any other conditions prescribed in the agreement between the Agency and the State or States concerned. Inspectors designated by the Agency shall be accompanied by representatives of the authorities of the State concerned, if that State so requests, provided that the inspectors shall not thereby be delayed or otherwise impeded in the exercise of their functions.

In the event of non-compliance and failure by the recipient State or States to take requested corrective steps within a reasonable time, the Agency is authorized to suspend or terminate assistance and withdraw any materials and equipment made available by the Agency or a member. . .

Paragraph C of Article XII of the Statute contains the provisions for actions to be taken when a question regarding compliance arises:

The inspectors shall report any non-compliance to the Director General, who then transmits the report to the Board of Governors. The Board shall call upon the recipient State or States to remedy any non-compliance which it finds to have occurred. The Board is to report the non-compliance to all members and to the Security Council and General Assembly of the United Nations. In the event of failure of the recipient State or States to take fully corrective action within a reasonable time, the Board may take one or both of the following measures: 1) direct curtailment or suspension of assistance being provided by the Agency or by a member, and/or 2) call for the return of materials and equipment made available to the recipient member or group of members. The Agency may also suspend any non-complying member from the exercise of the privileges and rights of membership.

In 1961 the board of governors approved the First Safeguards Document, which established the initial IAEA safeguards system. The document applied only to reactors with outputs of up to 100 megawatt (tons), which meant that it did not include large-scale power reactors.[9]

In 1962, the United States initiated a policy of converting its bilateral agreements into trilateral agreements that included the IAEA as the third party. The IAEA assumed the responsibility for carrying out safeguards. An exception was made for the EURATOM (European Atomic Energy Community) countries, which were subsequently encouraged to subsume their bilateral agreements with the United States into the U.S.-EURATOM agreement, with EURATOM assuming safeguards responsibilities.

In 1964, the IAEA safeguards procedures were extended to cover reactors above 100 megawatt (tons). After considerable technical work, a revised safeguards system was approved by the board of governors in 1965 and outlined in the agency's Information Circular 66, INFCIRC/66/Rev.2. Subsequent safeguards agreements were based on INFCIRC/66, and previous agreements were updated when they came up for renewal. To this day, a number of the IAEA's older safeguards agreements, with nonparties to the Treaty on the Non-Proliferation of Nuclear Weapons (NPT), continue to be based on INFCIRC/66.[10]

In 1967, the IAEA was given a special safeguards role in the Treaty for the Prohibition of Nuclear Weapons in Latin America, the Treaty of Tlatelolco. Article 13 of the treaty requires:

Each Contracting Party shall negotiate multilateral or bilateral agreements with the International Atomic Energy Agency for the application of its safeguards to its nuclear activities. Each Contracting Party shall initiate negotiations within a period of 180 days after the date of the deposit of its instrument of ratification of this Treaty. These agreements shall enter into force, for each Party, not later than eighteen months after the date of the initiation of such negotiations except in case of unforeseen circumstances or *force majeure*.[11]

During this same period, the NPT was under negotiation. It was signed on July 1, 1968, but did not enter into force until March 5, 1970. Under the NPT, the IAEA was given a major safeguards role.

Under Article II of the NPT, each non-nuclear-weapon state party to the treaty undertakes not to receive the transfer of any nuclear weapon or other nuclear explosive devices and "not to manufacture or otherwise acquire nuclear weapons or other nuclear explosive devices." The commitment to safeguards is contained in Article III, which states that

each non-nuclear weapon State Party to the Treaty undertakes to accept safeguards, as set forth in an agreement to be negotiated and concluded with the International Atomic Energy Agency in accordance with the Statute of the International Atomic Energy Agency and the Agency's safeguards system, for the exclusive purpose of verification of the fulfillment of its obligations assumed under the NPT. This is intended to prevent diversion of nuclear energy from peaceful uses to nuclear weapons or other nuclear explosive devices. Procedures for the safeguards required [by the NPT] are to be applied with respect to source or special fissionable material, whether it is being produced, processed or used in any principal nuclear facility or is outside any such facility. The safeguards required by the NPT applied to all source or special fissionable material in all peaceful nuclear activities within the territory of each non-nuclear weapon State Party, under its jurisdiction, or carried out under its control anywhere.

Each State Party to the Treaty undertakes not to provide: (a) source or special fissionable material, or (b) equipment or material especially designed or prepared for the processing, use or production of special fissionable material, to any non-nuclear-weapon State for peaceful purposes, unless the source or special fissionable material shall be subject to IAEA safeguards. . .

The NPT requires that non-nuclear-weapon states party to the treaty

conclude agreements with the International Atomic Energy Agency . . . either individually or together with other States in accordance with the Statute of the International Atomic Energy Agency. Negotiation of such agreements [were required to be initiated] within 180 days from the original entry into force of . . . [the NPT]. For States depositing their instruments of ratification or accession after the 180-day period, negotiation of such agreements will begin not later than the date of such deposit. [It is required that such agreements] . . . enter into force not later than eighteen months after the date of initiation of negotiations.[12]

Immediately after the NPT entered into force, the IAEA established a committee under the chairmanship of Kurt Waldheim to advise on the agency's responsibilities with regard to safeguards required by the NPT, as well as on the content of the agreements on safeguards that would have to be negotiated. The committee completed its work in March 1971. (Ironically, it was his success in chairing the committee on NPT safeguards that subsequently facilitated Waldheim's election as U.N. secretary general.) The board of governors considered the committee's report and authorized the use of this material as the basis for negotiating agreements required by the NPT. The material was published as Information Circular/153 and is known as INFCIRC/153.[13]

In sum, the legal bases of the IAEA safeguards system are the agency's statute, the Treaty of Tlatelolco, the NPT, INFCIRC/66/Rev.2, INFCIRC/153, and the various safeguards agreements with member states and EURATOM.

The IAEA Safeguards Organization

The 1988 budget for the IAEA is $137 million, which includes $45 million for the Department of Safeguards. In addition to the regular budget, the IAEA safeguards program will receive approximately $12 million to $14 million from extra budgetary support programs including $6.4 million from the U.S. support program, Program on Technical Assistance for Safeguards (POTAS). Currently the thirteen support programs outside the regular budget focus on high-priority tasks that the agency has identified, including the development of specialized safeguards equipment. Thirty-two safeguards experts are being provided to work with the agency at no cost through these support programs.

The IAEA has five departments, each headed by a deputy director general who reports to the director general of the agency. The Department of Safeguards is organized into seven divisions. Three divisions are involved with safeguards operations and are assigned responsibilities on a regional basis.

Division A covers the Far East and South Asia, including Japan, Korea, India, and Pakistan. Division B is responsible for North America, Latin America, Africa, Scandinavia, and Eastern Europe. Division C is responsible for EURATOM. The four support divisions include the Division of Safeguards Development and Technical Support, which is responsible for developing and supporting the instruments and equipment used in safeguards. The Division of Safeguards Evaluation reviews the safeguards reports and activities. Each year this division prepares the Safeguards Implementation Report (SIR) that permits the director general and the board of governors to evaluate the safeguards effort. The Division of Safeguards Information Treatment is responsible for computerizing the safeguards data from the inspection reports and from reports on facilities submitted by states. The Division of Safeguards Administration, Training, and Standardization provides the administrative and personnel support for the Department.

The Department of Safeguards has 277 professional and management personnel, in addition to the 32 experts. It also has 199 personnel providing clerical, secretarial, and personnel support services. Depending on the number of experts serving at any given time, the size of the department runs from 500 to 510. There are about 180 safeguards inspectors, with an additional 15 inspection assistants (who tend to have a particular specialty such as accounting, data handling, or equipment maintenance). In general, the inspectors have broader experience in the nuclear field and more education in nuclear science and engineering than the inspection assistants. Over the past few years, the number of inspectors has not increased, given the tight budgets that the IAEA has faced. The annual turnover rate has been less than 10 percent. While this means that the level of experience with inspections has increased, it also means that the system has settled into established ways to a far greater degree. In the future, the agency is likely to face a significant loss of experience as the current generation of inspectors begin to retire more or less as a group. It requires about one year for a new inspector to be trained and to gain sufficient experience to become fully effective.

Safeguards Inspections

The IAEA carries out safeguards based on several different legal regimes, those governed by INFCIRC/66/Rev.2, those governed by INFCIRC/153, and those covered by special arrangements (such as the agreements based on the voluntary offers of the nuclear weapon states). In the case of INFCIRC/66 safeguards, the agency and a member state conclude an agreement that covers specific material and/or facilities. In accordance with the agreement, the IAEA accounts for the nuclear material and ensures that the material and facilities being safeguarded are not "used in such a way as to further any military purpose." A state with material and facilities covered by an INFCIRC/66 type of agreement may have other material and facilities completely outside of safeguards. In other words, INFCIRC/66 safeguards do not necessarily provide full-scope safeguards. In the case of INFCIRC/153 safeguards, an agreement is concluded with the IAEA based on the NPT obligations of a member state or a group of member states. In non-nuclear-weapon states, the safeguards are applied to all source or special fissionable material in all peaceful nuclear activities "for the exclusive purpose of verifying that such material is not diverted to nuclear weapons or other nuclear explosive devices."

While most of the agency's safeguards efforts are devoted to carrying out INFCIRC/153 safeguards in NPT countries, most of the countries that represent the greatest risk in terms of nuclear proliferation are covered by INFCIRC/66-style agreements. Although INFCIRC/66 predates INFCIRC/153, the procedures and approaches developed for IAEA safeguards for the most part have been based on 153 rather than 66. In truth, the potential actions that could be taken under 66 have never been exploited fully. The objection from those who might be subjected to more stringent safeguards applicable under INFCIRC/66 agreements is that it is "discrimination!" As in most other multilateral undertakings, the tendency has been for the IAEA to seek to avoid controversy and to rely on established procedures.

Safeguards for nuclear material are influenced by a number of considerations, including the following:

1. Nuclear materials have utility for both peaceful purposes and nuclear explosive applications. There is considerable overlap in the facilities and infrastructure needed for either purpose.

2. The most sensitive fissionable materials that could be used directly for a nuclear explosive, highly enriched uranium and plutonium, are valuable and dangerous. Therefore, anyone holding or handling such material is expected to keep careful records and provide security.

3. Since fissionable material is radioactive, it can be monitored with equipment that detects the radioactive events. For example, a scan with a gamma ray spectrometer can detect the isotopes contained in a fresh fuel element and provide a rough approximation of the level of enrichment contained in the element (but not the exact amount of nuclear material).

4. Nuclear fuel elements that have been irradiated in a reactor and contain plutonium are normally held for a long period of time (a number of years) in static storage.

5. In most types of reactors, fuel is loaded and remains in place for an extended period of time until the reactor is shut down. Reactors that have an on-line fueling capability that permits the removal of irradiated fuel during operations present a more difficult safeguarding problem.

6. The handling of irradiated fuel to recover the plutonium requires special facilities and equipment.

7. With bulk quantities of nuclear materials, frequent sampling by the process manager is routine to ensure quality control and safety. This provides opportunities for simultaneous safeguards sampling without disrupting the material processing.

8. The nuclear safeguards system was developed over a long period of time. As new and more complex facilities have been planned, there has been considerable lead time to design safeguards, develop new monitoring equipment that might be necessary, and train new inspectors who may be needed. In the past, the IAEA has not always taken advantage of the lead time.

9. Cooperation by the party being inspected is required in order for IAEA safeguards to be carried out effectively. In an adversarial atmosphere, IAEA safeguards can be thwarted. However, a breakdown of safeguards for any reason will be brought to the attention of the director general and the board of governors.

The primary approach to IAEA safeguards has been to track and account for nuclear material, increasing the intensity of inspection as the material approaches a condition where it could be used directly in a nuclear explosive. The safeguards do not control the material or prevent it from being misused; however, they are intended to detect in a timely fashion if any material is being diverted and to provide warning. After receiving a warning from safeguards, it is up to the board of governors and the individual member states to take appropriate political action.

At the front end of the nuclear fuel cycle, not much attention in terms of safeguards is given to uranium until it is processed for enrichment or natural fuel. In the past, the enrichment services were provided by one of the nuclear weapon states, and no safeguards were applied until the enriched material was transferred to another state. However, with the spread of enrichment technology, this will change before long. The safeguards resources required to deal with a large-scale enrichment facility, in terms of both personnel and equipment, will be considerable.

The safeguards approach for fuel fabrication for power reactors has been to check shipping records to ensure that the quantity of material sent to a fabrication facility is the quantity actually received. The process is monitored to ensure that the isotopic content of the fuel is correct and that the output quantity matches the input, minus any waste. When the fuel elements are shipped, the containers may be sealed to ensure that there has been no diversion.

At the reactor, an IAEA inspector observes the removal of the seal and verifies that the fresh fuel element is placed in the reactor. After the reactor is loaded and closed, it might also be sealed to prevent removal of the fuel. In addition, cameras might be installed to monitor paths from the reactor through which a fuel element cask might pass. When the reactor lid is again opened for maintenance or refueling, an inspector typically is present.

Normally the spent fuel from a reactor is moved to a nearby storage pool to cool off for an extended period of time. The racks in the storage pool might be sealed by the inspector to prevent movement without detection, and the pool might be monitored by cameras to detect activity.

If the spent fuel is then reprocessed, it is shipped to a chemical reprocessing plant in a cask, under seal, and again placed in a storage pool. When the reprocessing is initiated, normally IAEA inspectors are at the facility full time. The chopping up of the fuel is observed and the process of its' being dissolved in acid monitored. The separation of the plutonium and its conversion into oxide are monitored and samples taken. The finished product is placed in a container and sealed by the IAEA inspector. It is inspected frequently in storage until it is again placed in use. The inspection effort required for a chemical reprocessing plant and a plutonium fuel fabrication plant is considerable.

At every stage of the fuel cycle, the IAEA inspectors review the records of a facility to account for the types and quantities of material and make measurements as needed to confirm the numbers. Cameras and other detectors may be used to monitor static areas or possible diversion paths. Samples taken by inspectors are sent to the IAEA's laboratory for analysis to confirm proper content. The entire system is based on containment, surveillance, and the probability of detection of diversion in time to react politically.

As in any other human endeavor, the IAEA inspectors discover many discrepancies in the course of administering safeguards. These events are called "anomalies." Some may be caused by human error in recording data, some by miscalibration of scales or other instruments, and some by the loss of material during processing. Anomalies that cannot be resolved and are considered serious are reported by the director general to the board of governors. As has been noted by senior U.S. officials in testimony before Congress, the United States does not have routine access to the inspectors' safeguards reports, which are treated as confidential by the agency. However, since the director general is required to report to the board any serious anomalies that have not been resolved and the United States has a governor on the board, the United States and other board members would know promptly of any serious problem.[14]

Lessons Learned from the IAEA Safeguards Experience

In many ways, the IAEA safeguards experience has been unique and may have little relevance for other safeguards or related verification activities; in other ways, it may provide a valuable model of how to carry out some multilateral verification activities in the future.

The dual role that the IAEA has sought to play from its inception—promoting peaceful use of nuclear energy and administering safeguards—has made it difficult to ensure that safeguards receive adequate funding. Members of the IAEA from the developing world have insisted that the IAEA budget allocations for development programs and safeguards be kept in balance. In other words, as the safeguards program expanded to deal with a growing number of facilities (especially in the developed countries), the development programs for peaceful nuclear applications in the developing countries were expanded as well. To some extent, the linkage between development programs and safeguards has probably facilitated the acceptance of safeguards in the Third World; however, it has also meant that it costs twice as much each time an additional inspector is hired. To avoid this type of linkage, it would be desirable in any future inspectorate to have its tasks dedicated solely to the verification mission.

The fact that most of the safeguards effort is devoted to states that pose little or no risk in terms of proliferation represents a weakness in the legal bases of the IAEA system that future arms control regimes should attempt to avoid. In terms of allocating safeguards or inspection effort, a portion will always have to be used for routine activities. However, it would be desirable to have a significant part available to use on problems and on a random basis. If all inspections are routine, the inspected party is able to predict when inspections will occur and has the potential to carry out certain diversion activities with little fear of detection.

In drawing conclusions with respect to a state's meeting its obligations, having access to all peaceful facilities, as in the case with non-nuclear-weapon states that are NPT parties, permits the IAEA to gain a meaningful picture. But since the IAEA inspects only declared facilities and does not attempt to uncover any facilities that may not have been declared, the entire system has a basic flaw as a model for any other arms control verification system. There is even less knowledge with respect to countries that have some important facilities not under safeguards. For example, the world was caught by surprise when Argentina announced in 1983 that it has mastered uranium enrichment technology and had built an unsafeguarded enrichment facility in secret.

IAEA safeguards are directed toward specific objectives. The acceptance of safeguards permits countries that have significant peaceful nuclear capabilities to demonstrate that these capabilities are not being used to acquire nuclear explosives or for other prohibited purposes. IAEA safeguards alone are not sufficient to verify the treaty obligations under the NPT and the Treaty of Tlatelolco. While safeguards contribute to confidence on the part of interested states that the state with its facilities under safeguards is complying with its obligations, the United States uses its own national means to monitor nuclear activities and draw its own conclusions. From a national security perspective, the key questions are related to nuclear proliferation and intentions rather than whether safeguards have been implemented according to plan. In cases where nuclear proliferation may have occurred, it does not appear that diversion of safeguarded material has played a significant role.

The value of collecting data and confirming previously reported data through safeguards inspections conducted on site increases as inspections are repeated and inspectors become familiar with a facility. By the same token, when an inspector falls into an established routine, his or her pattern of behavior becomes predictable, and it may be easier to circumvent detection of diversion. This suggests that there should be a balance between experienced and fresh inspectors, particularly in facilities where resident inspectors may be assigned for extended periods.

In some instances, the IAEA has become locked into an agreement on a specific facility that has made it difficult to use new monitoring equipment and to relocate installed equipment such as cameras. While it is important to protect safeguards activities necessary to ensure effectiveness, it is also important to preserve flexibility that will permit the use of new techniques and equipment.

Since the outset of IAEA safeguards, high standards have been maintained with regard to the technical qualifications of inspectors. While an effort has been made to ensure broad regional and national representation among the inspectors, the major emphasis has remained on the educational qualifications and technical experience of candidates. In other multilateral inspectorates that may be established in the future, it will be important to ensure that the technical competence of inspectors be considered as the essential consideration in selection and that a regional balance be taken into account as long as it is kept subordinate to competence.

With respect to IAEA safeguards, there is a firm technical basis for the general approach. When quantities of nuclear material that may be used directly in nuclear explosives exceed an amount sufficient to construct a basic nuclear explosive (8 kilograms of plutonium or 25 kilograms of fissile quantity of uranium-235), particular attention is directed toward the activity in question. Safeguards are directed toward detecting the most likely type of diversion that might occur involving a significant quantity of material. Other possible diversion scenarios are considered and are guarded against. However, too much effort may be directed toward the more exotic diversion schemes that are unlikely to be used, especially when large quantities of material are processed in a national program.

Having a solid technical basis for its safeguards activities has permitted the IAEA to justify the safeguards portion of its budget. Any future verification system should contain the technical underpinnings that justify the cost of the on-site inspection activity. Inspection activity carried out at an arbitrary intensity cannot be sustained. In the case of the United States, the Congress must be convinced of the value of a verification system if funding is to be provided over the long term.

After an inspector has served for several years and the inspection tasks have become routine, it becomes increasingly difficult to motivate individuals to be alert in identifying potential problems. Training and rotation of duties are useful measures to stimulate inspectors and provide a change of pace. It is also important to review the performance of all inspectors against established standards to maintain quality control.

As in most other organizations, a certain internal political dynamic has developed over time in the IAEA Department of Safeguards. In dealing with the safeguards system in the IAEA, or with any other international organization, it is important to take into account the internal political landscape when seeking any particular course of action. It is particularly important to pay close attention to the selection of managers, both in terms of their competence and compatibility.

The Relevance of Safeguards to Other Arms Control Regimes

Hans Blix, the director general of the IAEA, has promoted the notion that the agency's experience with nuclear safeguards might be useful in working out verification arrangements for arms control agreements in other areas. He has even suggested that the IAEA might be given a role to carry out additional verification tasks.

While some of the agency's experiences with safeguards should be taken into account in designing future multilateral verification regimes, it would be very difficult, and probably undesirable, to assign the IAEA any additional verification mission beyond its statute. Nuclear safeguards would almost certainly suffer if the IAEA were to take on such additional responsibilities. Also, it would be preferable to have the organization carrying out verification of some future treaty composed only of states party to the treaty. Some of the members of the board of governors whose countries are not party to the NPT conduct a relentless sniping campaign against the NPT at every opportunity. This is a strong argument to avoid assigning the IAEA any additional treaty verification activities beyond nuclear safeguards, especially if all states represented on the board were not party to the treaty.

It is difficult to see how the IAEA could play any role in the context of any bilateral agreements involving nuclear arms reductions, nuclear testing, or space arms. In considering bilateral verification arrangements, however, it would be prudent for the United States to take advantage of the experience of U.S. safeguards experts who have insights that could be useful in suggesting solutions to some of the bilateral verification problems.

Some future arms control areas where the lessons learned from the IAEA should be taken into account include possible bans or limitations involving chemical weapons, radiological weapons, removal of nuclear material from military programs, and conventional force reductions.

While the experience gained with the IAEA can provide a number of useful insights in the current negotiations on a comprehensive chemical weapons ban, nuclear safeguards are not a good model for a future chemical weapons verification regime. First, the volume of material involved in a chemical weapons ban is so great that the material balance approach used in nuclear safeguards would be unmanageable. Second, there are no choke points in the production of toxic chemicals that compare to enrichment and processing in the nuclear fuel cycle. Third, the most important element of the chemical weapons verification regime will be the inspection of undeclared suspicious activities. Nuclear safeguards deal only with declared facilities.

While safeguards may be a poor model for the verification regime for a chemical weapons ban, some of the safeguards technologies will have considerable relevance. For example, the cameras used to monitor material in a static condition under safeguards could be used in the same way in chemical weapons verification. Seals used in safeguards could be adapted for use in confirming that equipment inside chemical weapons facilities has remained in an inactive status. Some safeguards sampling techniques might be adapted for use in verifying the destruction of chemical agents or the permitted production of limited quantities of chemical agents. The experience gained through safeguards in the shipment of radioactive samples could be useful in working out procedures for shipping highly toxic chemicals for analysis.

In sum, the safeguards experience can provide important lessons and technologies for future multilateral arms control agreements. It will not, however, provide solutions to all of the verification challenges presented by a comprehensive chemical weapons ban or conventional force reductions.

Notes

1. "Stopping the Spread of Nuclear Weapons," Report of a National Policy Panel established by the United Nations Association of the USA (UNA) (1967).
2. Henry DeWolf Smyth, "A General Account of the Development of Methods of Using Atomic Energy for Military Purposes under the Auspices of the United States Government: 1940–1945" (Washington: Government Printing Office, 1945).
3. Report on the International Control of Atomic Energy," prepared for the Secretary of State's Committee on Atomic Energy (Washington: Government Printing Office, 1946).
4. U.S. Department of State, *Documents-on-Disarmament—1945–1959* (Washington: Government Printing Office, 1960), I.
5. U.S. Congress, Joint Committee on Atomic Energy, *The International Atomic Policies and Programs of the United States,* 86 Cong., 2d sess., 1960, I.
6. Ibid.
7. *Statute,* International Atomic Energy Agency (Vienna: IAEA, 1980).
8. Ibid.

9. Mason Willrich and Theodore B. Taylor, *Nuclear Theft: Risks and Safeguards* (Cambridge, Mass.: Ballinger, 1974).

10. Stockholm International Peace Research Institute (SIPRI), *Safeguards against Nuclear Proliferation* (Cambridge, Mass.: MIT Press, 1975).

11. U.S. Arms Control and Disarmament Agency, *Arms Control and Disarmament Agreements* (Washington: Government Printing Office, 1982).

12. Ibid.

13. SIPRI, *Safeguards*.

14. U.S. Congress, Subcommittee on International Security and Scientific Affairs, House Foreign Affairs Committee, *Nuclear Proliferation: Future U.S. Foreign Policy Implications*, 94th Cong., 1st sess., 1975.

4

On-Site Inspection for Nuclear Test Verification: Past Research and Continuing Limits

Carl F. Romney

F undamental differences between the United States and the Soviet Union about the need for technical verification measures for a possible nuclear test ban treaty were clearly in evidence as early as the mid-1950s. U.S. proposals at the time were for "limiting and monitoring" nuclear tests. The Soviet Union, by contrast, believed there was no need for special verification measures. Premier Bulganin wrote to President Eisenhower in 1956, "The discontinuation of such tests does not in itself require any international control agreements, for the present state of science and engineering makes it possible to detect any explosion of any atomic or hydrogen blast wherever it may be set off."[1]

While Bulganian's conclusion was probably an accurate reflection of the perspective of a closed society looking at an open society, the reverse was not true. The United States would have required sophisticated monitoring systems to gain even approximate parity with the Soviet Union in its ability to verify compliance with testing limitations. Thus, the task of developing technical monitoring systems and capabilities fell largely to the United States, as did the task of negotiating suitable provisions for the application of these systems.

A number of underlying technical problems are associated with on-site inspection as an element of a comprehensive nuclear test ban monitoring system, and the United States has engaged in major research and development efforts to solve them. These problems are inextricably linked to the limitations of seismic monitoring capabilities. In particular, the number of detected seismic events that cannot be identified by the seismic monitoring system largely determines the number of candidate events for on-site inspections. Also, the size of the area that would have to be inspected is directly related to the magnitude of the estimated seismic location uncertainty.

The Geneva Conference of Experts

The initial discussion between East and West on technical means for verifying compliance with nuclear testing limitations took place in Geneva during the summer of 1958. For seven weeks, scientists from four Western countries met with scientists from four Eastern countries to study methods for detecting possible violations of a comprehensive test ban treaty. This Conference of Experts, as it became known, was convened at the urging of President Eisenhower and set the stage for formal treaty negotiations later in the year.

During the intense and often tense discussions, the Experts:

- Agreed on the definition and description of observable phenomena resulting from nuclear explosions (acoustic waves in the atmosphere and oceans; radioactive debris, especially from low-altitude atmospheric explosions; seismic waves, especially from explosions detonated underground; radio signals from atmospheric explosions; and high-altitude phenomena such as atmospheric florescence).
- Defined the apparatus required to detect and measure observable phenomena.
- Described a hypothetical worldwide network of 160 to 170 control posts and ten ships equipped with the appropriate apparatus to detect subsurface and low-atmospheric nuclear tests, supplemented by aircraft sampling for radioactive debris, and described the estimated capabilities and limitations of that system.

Evasive testing practices were not considered in the final report, and specification of the means for monitoring high-altitude explosions was left as unfinished business.

The Experts did not advocate the hypothetical system as one designed to meet the specific test ban monitoring objectives of any particular nation represented at the meeting. Such objectives were not discussed and, indeed, have not been completely defined by the United States to this day. The report indicated what the effect of increasing or decreasing the number of control posts would be, implicitly leaving it to governments to decide whether greater or lesser capabilities should be the negotiating objectives of the political conference to come. However, the control system was recommended for "consideration by governments." When the nuclear test ban treaty negotiations began in October, the Experts' report was accepted as the technical basis for negotiation, and the Experts' control system became, de facto, the monitoring system for consideration.

Among the conclusions in the report were the following:

I.I. A basic difficulty in detecting and identifying small explosions arises because many natural phenomena (earthquakes, thunderstorms, and others) give signals which are similar to those produced by explosions, or which by their presence hinder the detection of the signals sought. . . .

IV.6   When the control posts detect an event which cannot be identified by the international control organ and which could be suspected of being a nuclear explosion, the international control organ can send an inspection group to the site of this event in order to determine whether a nuclear explosion had taken place or not. The group would be provided with equipment and apparatus appropriate to its task in each case.

For the first time, the technical basis for on-site inspection to aid in nuclear test monitoring was enunciated in an agreed document between East and West. At the time, this was considered by many to be the most important contribution of the Conference of Experts. However, the phrasing of conclusion IV.6 was indicative of a deep difference of opinion that would emerge as to what circumstances would call for on-site inspection.

A linkage between the required number of on-site inspections and the number of control posts also was indicated clearly in the Experts' report:

IV.2.   A network of control posts is characterized by three main parameters:

(a)   The minimum yield adopted for the nuclear explosion or the natural events giving equivalent signals;

(b)   The number of control posts;

(c)   The probability of correction identification of natural events, particularly earthquakes.

The dependence between these parameters is such that with an increase in the yield of the explosion or the number of control posts the probability of detection and especially identification increases, and the number of unidentified events suspected of being nuclear explosions decreases. On the other hand, for the identification of the increased number of unidentified events resulting from a smaller number of control posts it would be necessary to increase the number of on-site inspections.

That unidentified seismic events would be the primary reason for requiring on-site inspection was clear enough in the report. What was perhaps not so clearly revealed by their conclusions is why. Basically it is because of the relative ease of identifying explosions in the atmosphere compared to underground events. This derives from the former's detectability by several methods, which together provide complementary capabilities. For instance, both acoustic signals and radio signals are generated by atmospheric nuclear explosions, and this helps to eliminate false alarms that might be caused by natural events. The relevant detection methods for atmospheric events were well understood in the late 1950s, moreover, having been thoroughly tested on large numbers of atmospheric explosions. Most important, radioactive debris, which is usually detectable, could provide unequivocal evidence of the nuclear nature of a detected event.

By contrast, deep underground nuclear explosions are detectable at long range only by seismic waves, as are earthquakes. No other types of signals can be used to discriminate between earthquakes and explosions. Furthermore, detection and identification methods for underground explosions were less well understood than for atmospheric events since there had been only one underground nuclear explosion prior to the Experts' Conference. On-site inspection offered the possibility of acquiring proof of a nuclear event, the underlying objective of on-site inspection provisions for a test ban.

There may be circumstances, of course, when the seismic data alone establish a strong presumption of a nuclear event, such as seismic signals originating within a seismic region and equivalent in size to an explosion of 10 kilotons or so. Given the typically highly charged political atmosphere surrounding any suspicion or accusation of a treaty violation, however, technical data are likely to be ignored or explained away absent a single unambiguous interpretation.

In practice, valid questions of interpretation of seismic data arise frequently. They would be even more likely to emerge in the case of an attempted clandestine test where the would-be treaty evader could exploit knowledge of seismic detection and identification capabilities to obscure the evidence. Thus, a secondary rationale for on-site inspection is to help solve problems related to seismic identification, such as to establish that an event was actually an earthquake or at least that a nuclear origin was unlikely.

Treaty Negotiation and Objective Criteria for On-Site Inspection

Initial Positions on On-Site Inspection

The Conference on the Discontinuance of Nuclear Weapon Tests, among the Soviet Union, the United Kingdom and the United States, was convened in Geneva on October 31, 1958. Each participating country observed a moratorium on nuclear testing beginning after the Soviet test on November 3 and continuing until the Soviets resumed testing in 1961.

The United States and the United Kingdom initially took the position that an international control organization for a test ban treaty would analyze each seismic event, using "agreed seismic criteria" to identify earthquakes.[3] Remaining unidentified events, including explosions, would be subject to automatic on-site inspection. According to the U.S. and British view, conclusion IV.6 stipulated that there be inspections at any time that seismic data were inconclusive. In other words, since seismic signals were expected to be the only available source of evidence of a clandestine underground explosion detectable by the control posts, seismic events not identified as earthquakes were automatically considered suspicious. The number of inspections would be governed by the level of seismic activity and the quality and number of control posts in the monitoring network.

The Soviet Union took the position that unidentified seismic events of concern to other parties would be the subject of consultations, with on-site inspection to follow only if agreed to by the party on whose territory the event had taken place. The Soviets interpreted the conclusion IV.6 as requiring causes for suspicion beyond the ambiguity of seismic data before an on-site inspection could be conducted. They argued that each country would naturally want to permit inspection in instances where there were valid grounds to suspect that an event might have been a nuclear explosion. Neither of these positions, however, was based on sound technical grounds. This became apparent during Technical Working Group II (TWG II) in December 1959.

New Seismic Data and TWG II

During the early days of the political conference in Geneva, U.S. seismologists were completing analysis of new seismic data from the Hardtack II test series, acquired after the conclusion of the Conference of Experts.[4] These data substantially increased the available knowledge about the detection and identification of underground nuclear explosions. In the interagency reviews that quickly followed the data analysis, the United States decided that the conclusions of the Conference of Experts had been unduly optimistic about the estimated capabilities of the control system for underground explosions. This resulted in two subsequent actions:

1. The new seismic data were tabled at the conference in Geneva on January 5, 1959, along with the new U.S. assessments and a proposal that experts should be convened to reassess the conclusions of the Conference of Experts. The Soviets refused to consider the data or convene a new experts' group.

2. In the United States, a panel of scientists, which became known as the Berkner Panel after its chairman, Lloyd Berkner, was convened under the aegis of the special assistant to the president for science and technology to develop recommendations about how to improve seismic capabilities. The panel's report, together with the report of Technical Working Group I (on monitoring of high-altitude explosions) subsequently became the basis for a vigorous new program of research in nuclear verification technology sponsored by the Advanced Research Projects Agency of the Department of Defense, and known as the Vela

program. Vela started in 1959 and included the U.S. research effort for on-site inspection technology, along with the other relevant nuclear monitoring technologies.[5]

In Geneva, the United States and the United Kingdom continued to exert pressure on the Soviet Union to convene a working group to consider problems associated with underground testing. Ultimately the Soviet Union agreed. The terms of reference for the group of experts were to

> consider the question of the use of objective instrument readings in connection with the selection of an event which cannot be identified by the international control organ and which could be suspected of being a nuclear explosion, in order to determine a basis for initiating on-site inspections. As part of their work, the experts, proceeding from the discussions and the conclusions of the Geneva Conference of Experts, shall consider all data and studies relevant to the detection and identification of seismic events and shall consider possible improvements of the techniques and instrumentation.[6]

The group met twenty-one times between November 25 and December 18, 1959, but failed to reach agreement on objective instrument readings or the requisite criteria to initiate on-site inspection. Numerous disagreements about details connected with the new seismic data contributed to disagreement about identification criteria, but the major difficulty stemmed from differences over the desired approach to verification.

Soviet scientists took the view that the criteria had to be formulated so as to restrict as many events as possible from eligibility for inspection. Any that remained unexplained could then be regarded as suspicious. Unfortunately, as both the U.K. and U.S. scientists pointed out, the Soviet criteria would have misclassified as earthquakes the Hardtack II nuclear explosions, which ranged up to 19 kilotons and made them ineligible for inspection.

The United States formulated criteria, by contrast, so that explosions would rarely be misclassified as earthquakes. The associated requirements for accuracies and signal-to-noise ratio would have resulted in identification of only the larger earthquakes, leaving large numbers of events unidentified and eligible for inspection. The Soviet experts labeled these criteria as being "on the brink of absurdity" in the subsequent report of the working group.[7] In the report, which contained an agreed portion along with separate comments from the three delegations, the United States argued:

> In the view of the U.S. Delegation, the problem of the formulation of criteria is a strictly technical problem. If technical knowledge permits one to identify a large fraction of seismic events as earthquakes then it is clearly a great advantage to the control system. If technical knowledge does not permit this, then seismic events must remain eligible for inspection.

The result was that the U.S. position requiring the use of "agreed seismic criteria" to initiate on-site inspection proved to be unattainable in any practical sense. The Soviet Union, on the other hand, was unable to describe clear technical grounds for establishing that one unidentified event was more suspicious than another, without misclassifying explosions as natural earthquakes. These problems underscored the challenges faced by the Vela program, both to improve seismic identification capability significantly and to establish the technical basis for effective on-site inspection.

On-Site Inspection in the Vela Program, 1960–1963

The Vela program's research into on-site inspection methods was initiated under a contract with the Stanford Research Institute on September 2, 1960.[8] By mid-1961, $2,175,000 had been committed to research and development by the Advanced Research Projects Agency, and eleven contractors or governmental laboratories were participating in the research.[9] The technical parameters of on-site inspection in this area that it set remain basically unchanged.

On-site inspection was conceived of in three phases: aerial, surface, and subsurface activities. The size of the area to be inspected was defined by uncertainties in the seismic methods for locating the epicenter of a suspicious event.[10] This area was estimated to be about 500 square kilometers. An essential first step therefore was to reduce greatly the target area for inspections.

Aerial sensing techniques appeared to offer the best means of reducing the target area for on-site inspection. This phase of the inspection would employ visual and photographic techniques, airborne magnetometry, spectrometry, and scintillometer measurements. The objective was to define an area of 1 or 2 square kilometers where inspection teams might continue to search on the ground.

Surface survey techniques were intended to reveal evidence that the suspicious event was of natural origin, as was usually the case, or that nuclear testing actually might have occurred, and if so, where. This phase would begin with visual inspection, followed by a series of geophysical inspection procedures, such as seismic monitoring for aftershocks, use of gamma ray detectors, and searching for evidence of soil density changes.

Subsurface surveys would use methods to obtain sufficient samples of nuclear debris deemed necessary to prove that a test ban violation had taken place. These would include the search of mine tunnels, seismic refraction profiling, geochemical surveys, and drilling and logging of bore holes to drill into the explosion cavity.

In accordance with this general concept of how an on-site inspection would proceed, a number of technologies were identified for investigation under the Vela program. The following projects were underway or authorized as of August 1961 to address these techniques:

Handbook for on-site inspection techniques.
Seismic profiling Rainier Mesa and Lollipop site.
Stereophotogrammetric techniques.
On-site geochemical and gamma ray spectral measurements.
Mine environment study.
Visual and photographic inspection.
Seismic noise monitoring and surface-subsidence measurements.
San Andreas aftershock investigation.
Techniques for measuring soil differences.
Correlation of reflectance properties of midlatitude vegetation.
Analysis of data for on-site inspection.
Shock-induced solid state effects.
Aerial spectral reconnaissance systems.
Airborne magnetometer survey.
Vertical survey at Orchid.
Radon studies.
Resistivity and self-potential.
Marine environment study in Eurasia.

The main technical elements of the program were classified as follows:

Changes in the surface of the earth. Work in this category sought to detect fracture patterns, landslides, craters, evidences of unusual human activity, changes in soil density (and hence absorption of solar heat), and damage to vegetation from disturbance of root systems. Technologies included multispectral photography, photogrammetry, and visual inspection.

Aftershock monitoring. Detection of aftershocks, which often follow a large earthquake, can help in more precise location of the original event. Lack of recent human activity at a location could help alleviate concern the event was a nuclear test. Aftershocks may also follow underground nuclear explosions as a result of relaxation of strain induced in the surrounding rock by the explosion and by rock falling into the cavity created by the explosion. Again, detection of these characteristics might help pinpoint the explosion site. There was also some hope that the seismic signals from underground explosions might differ from those generated by earthquakes.

Seismic exploration techniques. Conventional seismic oil exploration methods were to be tested for their ability to locate cavities or crushed zones on the rock surrounding an explosion site.

Geophysical exploration techniques. Electrical, magnetic, and gravity surveys were to be evaluated as tools to locate cavities and crushed zones.

Ground inspection. A wide variety of verification techniques were potentially applicable if parties of inspectors could be placed in proximity to a nuclear test site. Possibilities considered included searching for crevices or similar discontinuities resulting from ground shaking, sampling for radon or other gases to detect levels in excess of what was normal for the region, changes in luminescence of certain minerals as a result of ground shock, and changes in plant and animal microecology.[11]

The research program started with considerable optimism based in part on the experience of the Hardtack II underground explosions, which had each left conspicuous traces. Furthermore, there were many apparently promising technical avenues of approach.

Vela Seismic Program

In parallel to the on-site inspection research, the Advanced Research Projects Agency initiated a vigorous and much larger program of research into seismology. The program was comprehensive in scope, covering sensor and detection system development, basic research in the generation and propagation of seismic waves, marine detection techniques, and evasive testing methods. An ambitious program of large chemical and nuclear explosions was formulated, and portable seismic detection and recording stations were built to record seismic waves from these explosions. These were soon used to record seismic data from underground nuclear weapons development tests conducted by France, the Soviet Union, and the United States after 1961 when the testing moratorium ended.

From the standpoint of on-site inspection, the two most important areas of seismic research concerned the development of seismic identification criteria and studies of seismic location capabilities.

Identification Criteria

At the Conference of Experts, identification of earthquakes relied principally on the determination of focal depth and the direction of first motion. Confident determination that a selected seismic event originated at a depth inaccessible by drilling provided proof of natural origin. Methods for improving depth determination were soon developed within the Vela program. This method became—and remains—the most effective means of discrimination.

Earthquakes are usually caused by slippage along a fault or fracture in rock. In the direction of the slip, the earth will be pushed away from the epicenter, but in the opposite direction, the earth will be pulled in toward the epicenter. When several seismic stations detect an initial seismic motion of the ground toward the epicenter, the event can be positively identified as an earthquake. (Explosions cause the earth initially to move away from the source in all directions.)

On the other hand, the converse is not true. When only outward first motion is recorded, it may simply mean that none of the stations was located where the first motion was inward toward the fault. Seismic recordings from underground nuclear explosions, which became abundant after the testing moratorium ended, continued to confirm the U.S. experts' conclusion at TWG II that this technique was an unreliable discriminant except at very high signal-to-noise ratios. As a consequence, the first motion criterion was of limited utility in identifying suspicious events.

Various criteria based on the spectra of explosions and earthquakes, or on the relative partitioning of energy among the different kinds of seismic waves, were developed in the Vela program. The most effective of these is the so-called $M_s:m_b$ ratio, which uses measurements of the amplitude of very-low-frequency Rayleigh waves and of higher-frequency body waves. This criterion has been widely accepted and is the second most effective method of discrimination. Whether it will be effective for explosions under all possible testing conditions is uncertain since no firm theoretical understanding has been established.

The improvements in the effectiveness of discrimination techniques have been impressive. Currently it is estimated that the United States can discriminate almost all events as small as magnitude 4.5 (equivalent to 5–25 kilotons) inside the Soviet Union. This may be compared with estimates made in 1960 that, even with twenty-one stations inside the Soviet Union, and with more sophisticated equipment than specified by the Conference of Experts, more than fifty unidentified events equal to or larger than magnitude 4.75 could be expected annually.[12]

Epicenter Location Accuracy

Research on seismic event location accuracy became an important part of the Vela program because of its great importance to on-site inspection. Epicenter locations are determined from the times of arrival of seismic waves at detecting stations around the event, together with knowledge of the time required for the seismic waves to travel a given distance. Thus, the accuracy with which epicenters can be determined depends on how well the travel times of seismic waves to various distances are known. In the early 1960s, these travel times had been estimated from seismic recordings or earthquakes, but the exact time and location of the earthquakes could not be independently known; hence errors in these parameters propagated into the travel time curves, and estimation accuracy suffered.

Underground nuclear explosions provided a new source of data from events whose location and time of occurrence were often precisely known. Several explosions outside the Nevada Test Site were conducted under Vela, in large part to investigate location accuracy. Such explosions allowed direct measurements of travel time to be made. In addition, for the first time, the accuracy of the seismically determined epicenter could be tested by comparing it with the actual site of the explosion.

The results of the seismic location tests were not encouraging for on-site inspection. Research showed that scatter in the travel times of seismic waves would result in location uncertainties well above 500 square kilometers unless the event occurred in a region that had been calibrated by a prior explosion or was large enough to be recorded by twenty or more seismic stations. Research also demonstrated location biases due to crustal and deep mantle structural features of the earth that systematically offset the calculated location up to 20 kilometers or more from the true location, even when the explosion was recorded by scores of seismic stations. Research on location accuracy faded in importance when the Limited Test Ban Treaty was signed in 1963 because underground tests were not limited by the treaty, but it is clear that the problems of bias and travel time scatter remain for any future monitoring system.

The Vela Final Report on On-Site Inspection

Funding for on-site inspection research grew to more than $5 million per year by 1966. The program continued through federal fiscal year (FY) 1968, and some residual work in gas sampling continued into FY 1970. After the conclusion of the program, a summary of various lines of investigation was presented to Congress by Stephen Lukasik, the director of the Advanced Research Projects Agency (table 4–1). Some of the topics were the subject of only a single investigation, but others, such as radiochemical sampling, have been the subject of extensive research involving several independent investigations.

In addition to these research efforts, the work included the development of atlases, manuals, and handbooks to guide inspectors in the field. These were used in exercises at the sites of U.S. underground tests. There was also a substantial effort in developing clandestine test scenarios to evaluate the feasibility and costs of such tests; results are not reported here because of classification.

Lukasik reported the following conclusions of the Vela effort to Congress:

1. Research has shown that visual inspection and radiochemical analysis are the only useful techniques.

2. Deep burial of the explosion will prevent surface disturbances and see-page of radioactive gases to the surface.

3. Nevertheless, on-site inspection could be a deterrent because of the evader's fear of miscalculations and mistakes.

4. Search rates will probably be slow—Reconnaissance: 14 unit-days to find 90 to 100 sites in 250 km
   Detailed search: 8.4 unit-hours per site

5. Gas sampling is slow—
   3 Samples per site
   12 Samples per day per two-man team

6. Because search and sampling rates are low, accurate seismic location would be needed to reduce the size of the area to be inspected, and to insure that the epicenter lies in area to be inspected.

These conclusions remain essentially valid.

Some Observations

The disappointing conclusions of the on-site inspection research program resulted to an important degree from inaccuracies in the seismic estimates of location. This remains the major constraint on the usefulness of on-site inspection to verify comprehensive testing limits. Generally location accuracy is not expected to improve greatly, absent improbably dense seismic moni-

Table 4–1
Effects Produced by Underground Explosions
Investigated for On-Site Inspection

Physical	Radioactivity
Explosion-formed cavity	Puddle
Aftershocks	Drill-back cuttings
Solid state changes in minerals	Groundwater
Incipient sink	Soil
Fractures	Atmosphere
Artifacts	
Surface disturbances	Anomalies
Soil puffing	Temperature
Stable fission product gases	Near-surface water
Water flow into cavity	Magnetic
	Radon
Biological effects	Lead
Shock to flora and fauna	Mercury
Effect on human activity	Soil gas
Water table changes	

toring networks and major efforts to calibrate them with large explosions. Given the large search areas that need to be explored due to epicenter uncertainties, geophysical techniques designed to pinpoint the explosion cavity would be unacceptably expensive, time-consuming, and uncertain. Anomalies would be found, but they would be too numerous. Techniques designed to produce nuclear proof would be subject to the same problems, and, in any case, they would most likely not be persuasive in determining an actual treaty violation.

Negative conclusions—proof that the event was an earthquake—are unlikely to result from on-site inspection. Not only do technical methods suffer from location uncertainties, but the evidence of a small natural source is even more subtle than that from an explosion. Nevertheless, from a political point of view, there may be some benefit from such technologies if they strengthen overall confidence that there was no deliberate violation.

The United States continued to press for compulsory on-site inspection during the comprehensive nuclear test ban treaty negotiations between 1977 and 1980 but eventually acceded to voluntary inspection. A wide range of technical methods was proposed for application during inspection, though they have been revealed by research to be relatively ineffective. Considering the wide range of testing options available to a potential treaty violator, having a variety of inspection tools available is probably justified. The primary deterrent, however, continues to rest on fear of a mistake, as Lukasik stated in his testimony to the Congress.

Finally, the wisdom of advocating agreed seismic criteria for initiating a request for on-site inspection—either mandatory or voluntary—is questionable. Ambiguities in seismic data are common. Codification of empirical criteria is still possible but runs the risk that explosions conducted in new geological and geophysical settings may produce signals that do not fit the empirically determined model. Furthermore, suspicion concerning an event may well result from other sources and may not be susceptible to resolution through application of rigid seismic criteria.

Notes

1. Premier Bulganin to President Eisenhower, as reported in U.S. Department of State Document 7258. (See note 6). September 11, 1956.
2. *Report of the Conference of Experts to Study the Methods of Detecting Violation of a Possible Agreement on the Suspension of Nuclear Tests,* August 21, 1958, EXP/NUC/28 U.N. Secretariat Document. (See notes 6 and 9).
3. This reflected the seismological understanding of the time. Earthquakes could be identified as such when they could be shown to originate at an inaccessible depth or when the initial detected motion of the earth moved inward toward

the event, as may happen in some directions from motion along a fault. There were no known positive identifiers of explosions.

4. The Hardtack II test series, hastily conducted prior to a moratorium proposed to commence with the start of the impending treaty negotiations, included five underground nuclear explosions at the Nevada Test Site. Mobile seismic stations were installed at a number of locations in the United States to record seismic signals from these explosions.

5. *Report of the Panel on Seismic Improvement,* U.S. Department of State, March 31, 1959, and *Report of Technical Working Group on the Detection and Identification of High-Altitude Nuclear Explosions,* DNT/63, July 10, 1959.

6. *Geneva Conference on the Discontinuance of Nuclear Weapons Tests, History and Analysis,* U.S. Department of State Publication 7258 (Washington, D.C.: Government Printing Office, 1961).

7. *Report of Technical Working Group II on Seismic Problems,* DNT/TWG, 2/9, December 18, 1959.

8. *Technical and Management Handbook, Vela-Uniform Program,* Advanced Research Projects Agency (ARPA), August 1961.

9. Hearings before the Joint Committee on Atomic Energy, July 25, 26, 27, 1961.

10. The Conference of Experts had concluded that an epicenter can be localized within 100–200 square kilometers when signals are recorded at several surrounding stations. The 500 square kilometers reflected an assumption that stations would not surrounding the epicenter.

11. Charles Bates, Hearings before the Joint Committee on Atomic Energy, March 5, 6, 7, 8, 11, 12, 1963.

12. Richard Latter, Hearings before the Joint Committee on Atomic Energy, April 19, 20, 21, 22, 1960.

13. Stephen Lukasik, Hearings before the Joint Committee on Atomic Energy, October 27, 28, 1971.

5
Proposals for On-Site Inspection over the Years: From the Baruch Plan to the Reagan Initiatives

Timothy J. Pounds

From the Truman administration's call for international control of atomic energy to the Reagan proposal to eliminate ground-launched intermediate-range missiles, on-site inspection has been a key part of many postwar U.S. arms control and disarmament proposals. An examination of the shifting political and technical prominence of on-site inspection during the postwar period makes clear that proposals for it have served many, and sometimes conflicting, purposes. An understanding of these many purposes, and the trends they reveal, helps provide a needed framework for a detailed review of postwar on-site inspection proposals.

Thinking about On-Site Inspection

At face value, on-site inspection most often has been proposed as a means to monitor Soviet or other countries' compliance with specific arms control agreements. Even after the advent of space-based sensors for remote reconnaissance, or so-called national technical means, on-site inspection has offered an ability to check inside facilities, to monitor sites continuously, and to take a closer look at sites not possible with national technical means.

On-site inspection, and especially an on-site presence in the form of observers, also has been viewed as a means to increase the transparency of Soviet and Eastern bloc military activities. As such, its purpose was to test Soviet intentions and to build confidence as a stepping-stone to agreements reducing or controlling U.S. and Soviet forces. Some of these proposals in the early years also reflected attempts to compensate for U.S. intelligence deficiences. If accepted, on-site inspection probably would have improved U.S. knowledge of Soviet military capabilities.

Proposals for on-site inspection have served more political purposes as well. The U.S. government has frequently called for intrusive on-site inspection as a means to put the Soviet Union on the political defensive and to garner domestic and international support. Especially in the early postwar years, proposals were used to focus world attention on what was viewed as intransigent Soviet behavior. The United States, knowing that the Soviets were likely to reject on-site inspection, could purposefully insist on it as a means to undercut Soviet disarmament proposals and to take the high ground politically. In effect, on-site inspection proposals were means of political confrontation.

Conversely, in some situations, proposals for on-site inspection have played a more positive political role. They have helped on occasion to establish a political consensus for particular arms control initiatives. Some on-site inspection proposals have served as well to strengthen alliance solidarity and U.S. political relations with other key countries in achieving consensus in multilateral arms control initiatives.

In addition, on-site inspection has figured in the bureaucratic maneuvering that surrounds arms control and disarmament negotiations. In some instances, on-site inspection's main purpose in the eyes of its bureaucratic proponents has been to reduce the chances of an agreement constraining U.S. forces, if not to block it altogether. At the same time, this tactic still would allow these opponents, or for that matter the United States, to appear to support the agreement.

During the past four decades, these basic purposes for on-site inspection in U.S. arms control and disarmament diplomacy have remained relatively constant. But in different arms control or disarmament proposals, at different times, one of these purposes has often predominated. The relative emphasis or prominence among these purposes has reflected the broader state of U.S.-Soviet relations.

Finally, despite the ups and downs of on-site inspection, the past decades also have seen a steady trend to more reliance on on-site inspection in arms control agreements. From creation of the International Atomic Energy Agency (with safeguards on peaceful nuclear activities) to implementation of the Intermediate-Range and Shorter-Range Nuclear Forces Agreement (INF), practical applications of on-site inspection have grown in prominence and significance.

For purposes of analysis, it is useful to distinguish four periods of on-site inspection proposals in postwar U.S. arms control and disarmament diplomacy. Characterized by their most prominent landmarks, these are as follows:

1. 1946–1953: Baruch Plan controls to Truman transparency proposals.

2. 1953–1962: Atoms for Peace to the nuclear testing stalemate.

3. 1963–1979: National technical means for nuclear testing and strategic arms control verification.

4. 1979–1988: The Reagan on-site inspection proposals and the Soviet reversal.

These periods reflect the varied purposes of on-site inspection proposals, as well as differing balances among them, the impact of changing U.S.-Soviet relations, and the trend toward agreements with provisions for it.

1946–1953: Baruch Plan Controls to Truman Transparency Proposals

Immediately following World War II, on-site inspection played a central role in many U.S. disarmament and arms control proposals. The Baruch Plan's provisions for international control of atomic energy relied heavily on on-site inspection for verification. Later U.S. disarmament proposals under Truman also included comprehensive on-site inspection as a means to increase transparency on the slight chance that the Soviets would allow foreign inspectors into their territory. The Soviets rejected these proposals, arguing that inspection and control regimes should be preceded by actual reductions in atomic and conventional weapons and that unlimited inspection was an infringement against national sovereignty.

In the highly competitive environment of immediate postwar U.S.-Soviet relations, U.S. proposals for on-site inspection served as part of a broader political strategy that aimed to put the Soviets on the defensive concerning disarmament. In turn, U.S. diplomats hoped that an anti-Soviet consensus could be achieved in the newly created United Nations as a means to reduce Soviet influence outside Eastern Europe.

The Baruch Plan, 1946

In what became known as the Baruch Plan, the United States in June 1946 proposed to the newly established United Nations that an international atomic development authority be created to provide direct oversight and control of atomic energy through ownership of all fissionable materials production and distribution.[1] For its part, the U.S. government offered to destroy its nuclear weapons once the authority was in place.

One cornerstone of the Baruch Plan was the establishment of continuous monitoring and rights for unlimited on-site inspection of all atomic energy–related facilities by personnel from an international inspection organization. By raising the likelihood that illegal activities would be detected, the plan sought to deter illegal behavior. The Baruch Plan called as well for unspecified penalties for such illegal activities, without the right of veto in the Security Council.

Even at this early stage, however, the anticipated effectiveness of on-site inspection was a matter of debate. In the Acheson-Lilienthal Report—the precursor to the Baruch Plan—U.S. officials acknowledged that on-site inspection was a vital element for establishing international control of atomic energy. At the same time, the report recognized the limits of on-site inspection. In it, American officials explicitly stated, "We have concluded unanimously that there is no prospect of security against atomic warfare in a system of international agreement to outlaw such weapons controlled only by a system which relies on inspection and similar police-like methods."[2] For that reason, the report, and later the Baruch Plan, called for complete international ownership of, mangement of, and control over fissionable materials.

Politically, however, more was involved in the U.S. proposal (including on-site inspection) than a farsighted attempt to establish international control over atomic energy production and head off growing U.S.-Soviet nuclear arms competitions. At stake was U.S. global prestige and reliability as the leader of the noncommunist world. Both had been called into question as a result of what many saw as a weak U.S. response to Soviet violations of the Yalta accord and establishment of control in Eastern Europe.

The call for unlimited inspections in the Baruch Plan was fully consistent with Truman's new public diplomacy campaign to present the U.S. government in a tougher light at home and abroad.[3] In this regard, the plan played on Soviet sensitivities and presented the Soviets with something they were likely to reject. This approach fostered the perception that the Soviets were the cause of the lack of progress in disarmament, which helped to win U.S. allies abroad and isolate the Soviets in the new United Nations.

For Baruch, on-site inspections also were a potential means to open up Soviet society. This reflected the widespread belief that the West could not trust the Soviet Union until fundamental changes occurred in its political structure.[4]

The Soviets rejected the Baruch Plan. From the start, they objected to the notion of international ownership of fissionable materials and the right of unlimited inspections as infringements against state sovereignty. They also insisted on a right to veto any sanctions in the U.N. Security Council.[5] At most, the Soviets eventually appeared ready to allow in principle limited access to some mining and production facilities, supplemented by submission of statistical data, and the right to request explanations of the host government.[6] But they were not prepared to accept a plan that would have allowed inspectors to go anywhere in the Soviet Union.

U.N. Commission on Conventional Armaments, 1947

Parallel to discussions on international control of atomic energy, U.N.-sponsored discussions took place on conventional disarmament. These too reflected a mix of motivations and purposes of on-site inspection proposals.

In February 1947, the U.N. General Assembly, led by the United States, established the Commision on Conventional Armaments. The commission's mandate stipulated the necessity of

> adequate systems of safeguards which function under international super-
> vision to insure the observance of the provisions of the treaty or convention
> and which is (a) technically feasible and practicable, (b) is capable of de-
> tecting promptly the occurrence of violations and (c) causes minimum in-
> terference with the economic and industrial life of individual nations.[7]

In pursuit of this mandate, the commission, composed of a majority of Western countries, proposed in an August 1949 working paper that each member provide detailed military data on manpower, weapon levels, and deployments for the purpose of an international military census. The report recommended that each country provide its "complete order of battle . . . to the control organ." This plan was to be verified through spot checks and physical counts undertaken by an international inspectorate for the duration of the agreement.[8]

This proposal sought explicitly to promote on-site inspection as an inventory mechanism, one that would increase transparency, promote confidence between the two sides, and perhaps lead to actual reductions later. Its focus was not nearly as intrusive as the Baruch Plan. But though there was the appearance of greater sensitivity to Soviet concerns about intrusion, there was still a confrontational edge in the U.S. position. By pushing for apparently benign—but, to the Soviets, controversial—measures, the United States sought to isolate the Soviet Union further from the majority of the commission and, eventually, the rest of the United Nations.

For their part, the Soviet delegates continued to block any agreement where implementation of control measures and on-site inspection were not preceded by actual disarmament. Expressing to the United Nations a view that would guide Soviet policy for many years, Soviet representative Jacob Malik stated in 1948: "It would be folly for the USSR to disclose everything and then have others invent conditions as a pretext for dropping the whole question of reduction of armaments after they had found out everything they wished to know."[9]

More U.N. commission debate concerning the issue of data verification and conventional arms reductions occurred in October 1949. But soon after, the Korean War broke out, and the Soviet delegation walked out of the commission in protest over the exclusion of the People's Republic of China from it. This move effectively killed any chances for agreement within the commission. The walkout, however, further alienated the Soviet Union from the rest of the United Nations, playing into U.S. strategy to broaden the military role of the United Nations in the Korean conflict.

Truman Speech, Fall 1951

The issue of a military census verified through on-site inspection came up again in a major radio address on the principles of U.S. security policy and its philosophy toward disarmament given by President Harry Truman in fall 1951. Truman called for a "continuing inventory of all armed forces and armaments," saying: "It cannot be a one-shot affair. The fact finder must know not only what the state of armament is on any given day but how it is proceeding . . . whether the armed forces of country concerned are increasing or decreasing."[10]

To accommodate the need for ongoing knowledge, Truman called for disclosure of military inventories in phases, starting with the least vital information and progressing to the more sensitive information as confidence between the parties increased. In addition, he called for the creation of an inspection system to verify declared military arsenals. During the process of disclosure, Truman said, discussion about arms reductions could proceed.

This Truman proposal reflected most of the different on-site inspection objectives. Like its predecessors in the United Nations, it could serve as a device to improve data gathering for monitoring compliance with a later agreement. If accepted by the Soviets, it could build confidence and stability through better transparency. But since the idea of inspection was almost certain to be rejected by the Soviets, the president could also score propaganda points.[11] And if the Soviets had agreed, the United States would have benefited in making up for a lack of accurate information on the Soviet military.

Truman's radio address led to a U.S.-sponsored resolution in the General Assembly that called for the replacement of the by-then defunct U.N. Atomic Energy Commission and the Commission on Conventional Armaments by a new committee to discuss disarmament measures. The resolution contained a call for continual monitoring and disclosure of military capabilities in incremental phases, inspection measures to detect violations promptly, and a provision for minimum interference in internal affairs. It passed despite Soviet opposition, and a new forum was created to discuss disarmament and control issues.

Closing out this first period of on-site inspection proposals, in April 1952, U.S. ambassador Bernard Cohen presented to the new U.N. Disarmament Commission a resolution calling for a five-stage process of conventional and nuclear disarmament, entitled "Proposals for a Progressive and Continuing Disclosure and Verification of Armed Forces." Seeking to extend control as far as possible, he suggested several types of inspection necessary for different stages to verify disclosed information, including aerial inspection and inspection of waterways, railways, all power lines, and all declared atomic installations. Inspection and monitoring in the plan were to be undertaken by international control organ, whose composition and powers would be worked out later.[12]

The Soviets refused this proposal outright, objecting to the plan on grounds that it delayed the disclosure of quantities and design of the weapons that threatened them the most—nuclear weapons. They held to their old arguments, refusing to discuss control and inspection measures that did not involve prior disarmament.

1953–1962: Atoms for Peace to the Nuclear Testing Stalemate

Between the start of the Eisenhower administration and the election of President Kennedy, Soviet and U.S. representatives worked to establish the first international controls, including inspections, on the peaceful uses of atomic energy. On-site inspection for transparency and verification also figured prominently in several U.S.-Soviet discussions, from conventional forces to nuclear testing. But there were no significant substantive breakthroughs in U.S.-Soviet arms control discussions, partly due to continuing disagreement over on-site inspection. In this period, the Soviets moved to accept verification through limited on-site inspection in principle, but they were unwilling to submit to inspections on their territory over which they had little oversight or which they judged to be a risk to vital security and technical developments. Besides, the U.S. government continued to propose on-site inspection in many cases with no expectation that the Soviets would actually agree, reflecting again the narrower political purposes of on-site inspection.

From Atoms for Peace (1953) to the IAEA (1957)

In December 1953, President Dwight Eisenhower proposed in his annual address to the United Nations that the United States and the Soviet Union transfer some of their fissionable material to a new international agency. He predicted that as a result, both sides' nuclear arsenals could be slowed. He suggested that this international agency not only oversee redistribution of U.S. and Soviet fissionable material for peaceful purposes but also take other steps to ensourage and safeguard the peaceful uses of nuclear energy. In stepping away from political uses of on-site inspection, the Atoms for Peace proposal sought explicitly to avoid drawn-out debate on the issue of on-site inspections. Eisenhower's proposal promoted measures "without the irritations and mutual suspicions incident to any attempt to set up a completely acceptable system of world wide inspection and control."[13]

The proposed transfer of U.S. and Soviet materials was rejected by the Soviet Union; however, Eisenhower's proposal to create a new international agency led to establishment of the International Atomic Energy Agency (IAEA) in 1957. The agency's purpose was to foster peaceful nuclear cooperation under safeguards, including the right of on-site monitoring and inspection.

To detect diversions from peaceful nuclear activities, the statute of the IAEA contained provisions for on-site inspection, though their application was dependent on bilateral agreements between state parties and the IAEA. Not least, Article XII, paragraph 6 of the IAEA statute gave the IAEA the right

> to send into the territory of the recipient State or States inspectors, desig-
> nated by the Agency after consultation with the State or States concerned,
> who shall have access at all times to all places and data and to any person
> who by reason of his occupation deals with materials, equipment, or facil-
> ities which are required by this Statute to be safeguarded.[14]

During the decade that followed creation of the IAEA, additional documents were drafted to spell out in detail its safeguards, procedures and rights.[15] Together these documents provided basic guidelines for the negotiation of all safeguard agreements with specific countries. They set up material accounting, materials containment, and inspection procedures for all types of plants, reactors, reprocessing plants, and nuclear material in R&D facilities. The control system allowed for the auditing of nuclear material records, verification of the amount safeguarded by physical inspection, and review of the facilities. As such, IAEA inspections set an important precedent, with states accepting certain limits on their sovereignty. They also have provided useful operational experience in the dat-to-day running of an inspection system.[16]

Soviet Ground Control Posts Proposal

Although the Soviets did not move from their call for comprehensive nuclear and conventional reductions with minimal control, there were signs after Stalin's death in 1953 that they were becoming somewhat more flexible in their position on on-site inspection for verification. Or, at least, the new Soviet leadership was more sensitive to the political disadvantages of opposing proposals for inspections.

On-site inspection figured prominently in a May 1955 Soviet disarmament proposal that came to be known as ground control posts. This three-part proposal called for reductions and eventual prohibition of weapons in two stages, marking a shift from comprehensive reduction proposals to incremental approaches. It also included a first-time proposal for the discontinuation of nuclear tests under supervision of an international commission, in addition to calling for discontinuance of production of nuclear weapons.

It addressed the problem of control, as well as ways to prevent surprise attack through greater transparency.[17]

The Soviet proposal contained two sets of controls, to be implemented in an incremental fashion. In the first stage of reductions, a control organ would be created to establish on the territory of all states concerned on a basis of reciprocity, control posts at large ports, railway junctions, on main motor highways and in aerodromes."[18] In the second stage, the control organ would have the authority to inspect on a continuing basis and to have its own staff of permanent inspectors with "unimpeded access at all times to all objects of control."

If accepted on its face value, this provision was similar to the Western view that extensive rights of inspection were necessary to detect violations in a timely manner and to monitor potential buildups that might lead to a surprise attack. Consequently Western representatives present at the meeting initially praised this proposal.

When the Soviets clarified the operational details, however, the divergence between the two sides became clear. The Soviets proposed the creation of roughly 100 ground posts in Central Europe, with six in each country, and twice as many posts in North Atlantic Treaty Organization (NATO) states as in Warsaw Pact Treaty countries. The Soviets insisted that a majority of the inspectors be host-country nationals, with only one or two observers from the outside. A national from the host country would determine what, when, and how the inspectors could see. Although this proposal would have allowed foreign inspectors on Soviet territory for the first time, it virtually amounted to self-inspection.

Open Skies Proposal

Despite the gaps in the Soviet ground posts proposal, political pressures grew for the United States to come up with a counterproposal. In addition, there were perceived benefits for the United States from more Eastern bloc transparency, at a time of considerable controversy over the lack of accurate information concerning the Soviet production of nuclear weapons and bombers (the so-called bomber gap). These differing purposes were reflected in President Eisenhower's "open skies" proposal to the leaders of France, the United Kingdom, and the Soviet Union at the Geneva Summit in July 1955.

In preparation for the summit, experts from academia and the business sector had met in early June 1955 to discuss military policy initiatives to recommend to the president. Out of this meeting, which became known as the Quantico panel, emerged the idea of mutual aerial inspection on a bilateral basis between the Soviet Union and the United States.[19] Specifically, the Quantico panel proposed that both sides furnish lists of their military installations, with agreement to permit inspection of these installations, as well as undeclared facilities, from the air. Ground inspection would be limited to facilities with no sensitive operations.

American defense experts at Quantico conceived of this proposal mainly as a way to test Soviet intentions at a time when Soviet behavior was sending mixed signals. They reasoned that Soviet refusal of this transparency plan would be evidence of Soviet aggressiveness and also the need for an increase in U.S. defense expenditures. If the Soviets accepted, perhaps there was hope for improved relations in the future.

President Eisenhower liked the idea. Others, however, were worried about collateral intelligence risks, especially if the Soviets asked to examine U.S. nuclear weapons. But overall, there was agreement among Eisenhower's advisers that a proposal for aerial inspection to reduce superpower tensions would produce public diplomacy gains. This proposal, some thought, would lessen the risk that Eisenhower would be upstaged by Khrushchev at the summit. Besides, it would challenge the Soviets to agree to greater transparency with what appeared to be a goodwill gesture.[20]

President Eisenhower included the proposal in his summit address, timing it for the day when Khrushchev was chairing the group. Khrushchev responded to the proposal by calling it a thinly veiled attempt to sanction espionage. But the idea for mutual aerial inspection did not die there.

In fall 1955, the United States submitted to the U.N. Subcommitte on Disarmament an outline plan elaborating on the types of data to be exchanged and procedures for doing so. During 1956, the United States tabled two U.N. proposals to facilitate the exploration of inspection systems. The first called for demonstration area tests whereby the Soviet Union and the United States would establish reciprocally zones of 30,000 square miles, containing military and industrial facilities. Each side would then test and refine aerial and ground monitoring techniques.[21] The second U.S. proposal called for the formation of technical exchange missions, which would be composed of the five members of the Disarmament Committee and would study methods of control, inspection, and reporting.[22]

The Soviets again objected. They argued that the effectiveness of such measures would be minimal since aerial photography could not alter capability for surprise attack; only disarmament could do that. They also charged that the plan left out the armed forces and military infrastructure in other countries outside the United States and Soviet Union.

This impasse continued through 1957. In July 1958, however, Khrushchev agreed to the idea of a conference on preventing surprise attack. In the 1958 Surprise Attack Conference convened on November 10, 1958, by the ten participating members of the U.N. Disarmament Subcommittee, both the Soviet ground control posts and the U.S. open skies proposals were on the agenda. From the beginning, however, this conference foundered, as American technical experts seeking to focus on better early warning and transparency schemes confronted Soviet political officials whose primary purpose was to discuss a denuclearized zone in Central Europe.[23] Moreover, although the Soviets were willing to discuss the issue of inspection in peripheral areas, they remained unwilling to consider on-site inspection on Soviet territory.

In the midst of these continuing differences over on-site inspection, the United States and Soviet Union did reach agreement on the 1959 Antarctic Treaty, which demilitarized Antarctica. The treaty's provisions permitted on-site inspection, including observers to inspect any or all of the stations, installations, and equipment of the nations controlling territory in Antarctica. The treaty marked an initial, halting step toward use of on-site inspection for monitoring activities, if only in a peripheral area. But it was a far cry from the level of transparency proposed by the open skies or ground control posts proposals or from the inspection provisions to be accepted nearly three decades later.

Nuclear Testing and Disarmament Talks, 1955–1963

During this second period, on-site inspection issues also figured prominently in U.S.-Soviet discussions of nuclear testing limits. Suggestions for such a test ban first surfaced in May 1955, followed by talks on an irregular basis. In August 1958, a conference of experts on nuclear testing was held to examine the technical limits of methods for detection and identification of nuclear tests. The report of the Experts' Conference, initially accepted by the Soviet, British, and U.S. governments, concluded that it was technically feasible to set up a system for detecting violations of a nuclear test ban. It also said that without on-site inspection, underground nuclear tests could not reliably be distinguished from seismic tremors.[24] Later American underground explosions indicated that the method of distinguishing earthquakes from underground explosions recommended by the Experts' report was even less effective than previously thought.[25] For the United States and Great Britain, this meant that a future agreement to ban nuclear testing would require inspections for every unidentified seismic event; the Soviets, however, wanted each inspection subject to consultations between the state parties.

By spring 1960, these differences had been partially resolved. Instead of a comprehensive ban, the participants were seriously negotiating an agreement to prohibit atmospheric tests, as well as underground tests that registered greater than 4.75 on the Richter scale. In addition, both sides were talking of a moratorium on smaller underground tests, during which a seismic research program would have been undertaken. Negotiations broke off in May 1960, however, with the downing of an American U-2 reconnaissance plane over the Soviet Union.

Although talks were effectively dead for the remainder of the Eisenhower administration, the new Kennedy administration sought to recover the momentum that had been lost. In April 1961, the United States and Great Britain proposed a ban on all but smaller underground nuclear tests, reviving the offer for a moratorium on those smaller tests and offering to allow Soviet inspectors to see peaceful nuclear explosions on a reciprocal basis.[26] The proposal also suggested that each party accept a number of annual on-site inspections per year. This number was placed at twenty, a figure that administration experts thought high enough to have a good probability to investigate enough ambiguous events to deter the Soviets from cheating.

The Soviets agreed in principle to a quota of annual inspection but would go no higher than three per year. After continuous negotiations, the West reduced its proposed requirements to seven on-site inspections per year but would have been prepared to accept six.[27] The difference was not resolved.

U.S.-Soviet differences on on-site inspection went beyond the matter of numbers; they also disagreed on procedures. First, the Soviets insisted on a right of veto over on-site inspections and demanded that the inspection teams be organized on an ad hoc basis and comprised primarily of nationals of the country to be inspected. In addition, they demanded that personnel of the in-country control posts that would determine whether there was a need for inspection be composed of nationals of the country with only one or two outside observers. As Glenn Seaborg recalls:

> Considering that the procedures were quite rigorous and intrusive—involving, for example, low-flying helicopter flights over up to five hundred square kilometers in each inspection—I share Averell Harriman's view that the Soviets would not have agreed to them even if we had yielded on the number of inspections.[28]

Familiar U.S.-Soviet positions on verification and on-site inspection were also reflected throughout discussions of comprehensive disarmament measures. This period was punctuated by Soviet proposals that ranged from a September 1959 call by Khrushchev for the withdrawal of all foreign troops from the European states to the 1960 call for the elimination of all nuclear weapons, cessation of rocket launches for military purposes, and reduction of military expenditures. The United States, on the other hand, focused mainly on the issue of control and inspections as a precondition for disarmament.

Perhaps the high point of these late 1950s–early 1960s talks on disarmament was the 1961 McCloy-Zorin Agreement by which the United States and the Soviet Union pledged themselves to pursue in principle general and complete disarmament. Both sides agreed that on-site inspection would be applied under the control of an international authority to verify agreed limits and reductions. As soon as the document was signed, however, McCloy and

Zorin disagreed over whether the verification provision was to be applied to verify levels of retained forces or to verify disarmament.[29]

During this second period, on-site inspection proposals frequently reflected the traditional postwar U.S. objective of maximizing transparency. But the role of on-site inspection proposals as a political instrument to make political gains for the United States and to keep the Soviets on the diplomatic defensive continued to be a strong theme as well. Differences over on-site inspection symbolized the continuing lack of progress in arms control, itself reflective of broader U.S.-Soviet political disagreements.

At the same time, there were also certain positive developments. On-site inspection in both the IAEA statute and the Antarctic Treaty provided precedents that foreshadowed the nonadversarial, nonpropaganda use of on-site inspection. They provided experience that could be drawn on later. Further, the Experts' Conferences on Nuclear Testing and Prevention of Surprise Attack entailed serious attempts to assess on-site inspection requirements for verifying nuclear test limits and for increasing strategic stability through enhanced early warning measures.

1963–1979: National Technical Means for Nuclear Testing and Strategic Arms Control Verification

After an initial unsuccessful pursuit of on-site inspection in a 1964 nuclear freeze proposal, from the mid-1960s to the late 1970s, the U.S. government placed less emphasis on on-site inspection in arms control negotiations as the key to verification. With the exception of the Non-Proliferation Treaty (NPT) negotiations, there was a concentrated effort, as the first annual report of the new Arms Control and Disarmament Agency (ACDA) put it, "to see whether technological progress in certain fields might make it possible to develop scientific techniques for verification of treaty obligations which can bypass hurdles which have stood in the path of negotiations."[30] Breakthroughs in satellite and sensor technologies were critical to this shift. On occasion, however, proposals for on-site inspection also performed their earlier function of seizing the political high ground in both domestic and international arenas.

The 1963 Limited Test Ban Treaty

This shift toward U.S. emphasis on national technical means was most evident in the conclusion of the Limited Test Ban Treaty (LTBT) in 1963. In April 1963, President Kennedy sent Ambassador Averell Harriman to Moscow to negotiate a test ban. Khrushchev made it clear that the Soviets would accept no on-site inspections but would agree to ban all but underground testing. In a matter of days, the United States dropped its demand for inspection and accepted this offer. The United States and Soviet Union signed the LTBT in August 1963.

U.S. readiness to compromise on the on-site inspection issue stemmed from several sources. World reaction had been intense to the Cuban missile crisis, with the fear that both sides had been close to the brink of nuclear war. Hostile public protests over radioactive fallout due to atmospheric nuclear testing also had begun to have an effect. Significant advances in land- and spaced-based sensors and reconnaissance technology, backed by other hedges, provided most critics with confidence that the United States could live with this compromise.

The U.S. government continued to develop national means to detect illegal activity under the LTBT, as well as other agreements in the future.[31] It adopted a set of safeguards to hedge against Soviet violation of the treaty and to adjust U.S. capabilities to fit the treaty's requirements: continuation of underground tests, maintenance of laboratory facilities and programs, maintenance of facilities and resources to institute promptly nuclear tests in the atmosphere "should they be deemed essential to our national security or should the treaty or any of its terms be abrogated by the Soviet Union," and improvement of monitoring capabilities.[32]

These safeguards, advanced by the Joint Chiefs of Staff as condition for their support and used by the administration to foreclose opposition in Congress, diminished the focus on on-site inspection in the bilateral context. On the other hand, on-site inspection remained an important element for multilateral arms control discussions, particularly in the move toward a nuclear nonproliferation treaty.

NPT Negotiations

U.S. officials continued to view on-site inspection as a key element in designing a policy promoting the nonproliferation of nuclear weapons. The U.S. government actively campaigned for universal application of IAEA safeguards to all nuclear cooperation agreements in the early 1960s and unilaterally transferred most of its bilateral supply agreements to IAEA coverage in 1962. Further urgency in U.S. policy toward nonproliferation measures came after the Chinese detonated their first atomic weapon in October 1964. In early 1965, formal discussions for an NPT began in the Eighteen Nation Disarmament Conference. Concurrently India and the Organization for African Unity introduced proposals for nonproliferation treaty into the U.N. General Assembly.

In negotiations on a nonproliferation treaty between 1965 and 1968, two key issues emerged with respect to verification in general and on-site inspection in particular. The first concerned U.S. efforts to include under such a treaty IAEA monitoring of all peaceful nuclear activities in declared nonnuclear weapon states (so-called full-scope safeguards). Most countries were supportive of the idea in principle, but some were reluctant to embrace it wholeheartedly. Nonnuclear weapon countries, particularly in the Third World, argued that countries possessing nuclear weapons would be exempt from IAEA safeguards altogether, and parties would have IAEA safeguards applied only to specific peaceful nuclear activities. This, they said, smacked of discrimination and also left a large loophole in the new nonproliferation regime.[33]

The second issue concerning on-site inspection was the persistent resistance of European governments to proposals allowing international inspectors into their nuclear facilities. The European countries preferred to continue reliance on their own collective system of safeguards, overseen by the European Atomic Energy Community (EURATOM) formed in January 1948.[34] They were particularly concerned about undue foreign interference in their commercial activities and the impact of allowing foreign inspectors to observe sensitive facilities. The Soviets objected to exemption of European countries, while the Johnson administration initially wavered on the issue.

The treaty eventually dealt with these issues in several ways. It resolved the EURATOM issue by stating that applicable safeguards could be negotiated by groups of states in accordance with the IAEA statute and the IAEA safeguards system. Regarding concern about intrusion, the treaty defined the exclusive purpose of the safeguards to verify that there is no diversion of nuclear energy from peaceful purposes to military uses, explicitly mentioning the principle of noninterference. The treaty included Article VI, which committed the nuclear weapon states to future nuclear disarmament talks. Finally, the United States and the United Kingdom offered to accept safeguards voluntarily. This, too, addressed the issue of discrimination and equal sharing of burdens.

The U.S. government's position on on-site inspection was key in achieving these compromises. While the issue of safeguards and on-site inspection had posed many obstacles throughout the negotiations, the U.S. offer to accept unilaterally IAEA safeguards on its peaceful nuclear activities was a case where on-site inspection served as a consensus builder. Glen Seabourg recalls: "When the Safeguards issues loomed as an obstacle to acceptance of a nonproliferation treaty . . . the focus of American interest began to change. We now wanted to use our own acceptance of IAEA safeguards as leverage to win such acceptance from others."[35]

What stood out in this gesture was not the technical value of on-site inspection; rather acceptance of on-site inspection was critical in bolstering confidence that safeguards would be applied equitably and that the U.S. government had faith that the safeguards could adequately achieve their objectives.

To the SALT I Limits

By the mid-1960s, U.S. arms control proposals had shifted from schemes for comprehensive disarmament to more limited controls. The new focus on more limited steps was reflected in President Lyndon Johnson's 1964 suggestion to Premier Khrushchev that the two sides liquidate old bombers. Following up, the U.S. representative to the Eighteen Nation Disarmament Committee proposed destruction of an equal number of B-47s and TU-16s at the rate of twenty planes per month over two years.[36] Taking the idea a step further in April 1964, the United States suggested a freeze on the number and characteristics of nuclear offensive and defensive systems and a ban on new systems. In addition, the U.S. government called for continuous on-site inspection for the monitoring of airfields, missile launching sites, and critical production steps for delivery vehicles. Predictably the Soviet reaction was negative. Striking old themes, the Soviets argued that intrusion into secret facilities would endanger security without leading to disarmament.[37]

Beneath this U.S. proposal for on-site inspection was a conflict among bureaucratic interests in the Pentagon, the Arms Control and Disarmament Agency (ACDA), the State Department, and the White House. Since the Soviets were unlikely to accept this proposal, on-site inspection was a way to achieve two objectives: it was a tool to kill the freeze proposal by those who opposed arms control, all the while preserving the appearance that the United States was interested in promoting arms limitations. The Joint Chiefs of Staff in particular wanted to retain their acquisition programs and thus tended to oppose strategic arms control that they thought might give the Soviets further opportunity to gain ground.[38] This pattern would repeat itself in the years ahead.

By the late 1960s, U.S.-Soviet negotiations had come to focus on limits on deployments of ballistic missle defenses and missile launchers. This was partly a means of sidestepping difficult verification issues. For other reasons, however, despite some questions about reliance on NTM for verification, there was broad agreement that the limits in question could be verified without on-site inspection.[39] (Throughout the 1960s, the Joint Chiefs argued that there were important obstacles relying solely on national technical means for verification, among them cloud cover, camouflage, and other Soviet concealment techniques. But the Central Intelligence Agency consistently expressed confidence in its ability to detect militarily significant violations.)

By contrast, on-site inspection played an important part in the debate over whether to seek limits on multiple independent reentry vehicles (MIRVs) as part of an agreement covering strategic offensive forces. The bureaucracy was divided on this question, with the Joint Chiefs and Office of the Secretary of Defense in favor of deployment and ACDA in favor of a ban. The Verification Panel, an interagency group established and led by national security adviser Henry Kissinger, had direct responsibility for resolving this issue. It recommended proposing a ban on testing and deployment of MIRVs, with verification by national technical means. President Nixon later broadened the ban proposal to include verification by on-site inspection.[40]

The move to ban MIRVs was never a serious part of the Strategic Arms Limitation Talks (SALT) process. Moreover, inclusion of a requirement for on-site inspection in the MIRV ban proposal to the Soviets eased U.S. bureaucratic dissension and served as a means to appear to seek a ban while preserving the right to develop and test MIRV technologies. The commonly held belief was that the Soviets would reject such a proposal as long as it contained provisions for on-site inspection.[41]

Nuclear Testing Talks in the 1970s

An exception to the shift toward reliance on national technical means for verification was the main role of on-site inspection in the nuclear testing talks of the 1970s. In particular, the conclusion of the Peaceful Nuclear Explosions Treaty (PNET) in 1976 set an important verification precedent. Although the treaty was never ratified, its provisions represented a significant compromise between the superpowers leading to greater use of on-site inspection for verification and lessened politicization of the issue. In the comprehensive test ban (CTB) negotiations of the late 1970s, the Soviets agreed in principle to on-site inspection under limited conditions. The United States scaled back its demands and agreed to accept challenge inspections with a right of refusal rather than insisting on the right of mandatory inspections as it had in the past.

More specifically, over the years, the Soviet Union had pressed periodically for a CTB. Like his predecessors, President Nixon was reluctant to endorse the idea, arguing that Congress would oppose a complete limit on nuclear testing. Instead he offered to engage in discussions on a threshold test ban.

Several subsequent technical sessions between the United States and Soviet Union made progress toward achieving a threshold limitation on nuclear testing. With little warning, the United States and Soviet Union, over five weeks in June and July 1974, negotiated a bilateral agreement limiting nuclear weapons tests to yields of 150 kilotons. The Threshold Test Ban Treaty (TTBT) was signed at a summit in Moscow.

The treaty provided for verification by national technical means. Using its own seismic network, each party would measure the seismic magnitude of a weapons test explosion carried out by the other and then estimate the yield. To assist verification, the treaty provided for an exchange of scientific and technical data about each test site. However, measures were not provided for independent confirmation of the accuracy of the supplied data.

Implementation of the TTBT was postponed until negotiations could be concluded on a companion treaty to deal with the issue of peaceful nuclear explosions (PNEs). By 1974, the United States was ready to ban PNEs, since its program had effectively been retired. The Soviets, however, had developed an extensive PNE program, and they insisted on the right to continue it within the limitations of the TTBT, including high-yield, multiple-explosion projects. Later negotiations on PNEs began in fall 1974 and ended in late spring 1976. On-site inspection figured prominently in the talks.

One key question dividing the two sides during the negotiations of the peaceful nuclear explosions treaty was whether to allow group explosions that would exceed the TTBT limit of 150 kilotons. The U.S. delegation was concerned that it would be difficult to ascertain whether any one of the group explosions was in excess of the TTBT limits. To deal with this concern, the treaty allowed for American personnel—the Soviets objected to the word *inspectors*—to be present to make necessary measurements under specified conditions. For example, the Soviets remained uneasy about possible use of measuring equipment for U.S. espionage purposes. In turn, the U.S. delegation expressed concern about possible tampering with its monitoring equipment should the Soviets have complete control over its application. To deal with these concerns, the treaty allowed for two identical sets of equipment to be present, one for the Soviets to inspect and the other for use in measuring the explosion.[42]

On-site inspection was also a contested issue during the CTB negotiations held between 1977 and 1980. The major issue was whether on-site inspections should be mandatory or allowed solely on a voluntary basis.

The Soviets sought to leave the question of inspection to the discretion of the testing party. The U.S. delegation, by contrast, wanted a guarantee that its request for inspection would be honored. Ultimately the United States dropped its position, concluding that voluntary inspections would serve as an equal deterrent to cheating if the rejection of a request could be established as a serious matter. It judged that refusal of the inspection by the challenged party would be tantamount to admission that cheating had taken place.[43] Moreover, refusal to allow an inspection would be grounds to withdraw from the treaty.

The slow but undeniable progress toward compromise concerning on-site inspection for a CTB reflected the generally warmer trend in U.S.-Soviet political relations during the 1970s. This trend came to an abrupt end in the second half of the Carter administration, however. A series of Soviet advances in the Third World and questionable Soviet adherence to the SALT I treaty, as well as a crisis in public confidence at home, led to a hasty reassessment of U.S. military strategy and U.S.-Soviet relations. For these and other reasons, negotiation of a CTB was recessed in November 1980. The talks were not resumed by the end of the Carter administration.

SALT II and Its Critics

In the strategic arms control negotiations of the mid- and late 1970s (SALT II), verification of the limits agreed to by the United States and the Soviet Union continued to depend on national technical means. As in the SALT I accord, on-site inspection was not an issue for U.S.-Soviet negotiations in SALT II. Part of the absence of on-site inspection can be attributed to the negative Soviet attitude toward the issue in general. Another reason is that prominent U.S. officials believed that on-site inspection could be easily circumvented.

During the late 1970s, however, critics of the SALT process challenged the overall arms control process, as well as this reliance on national technical means for verification on a number of fronts. Soviet replacement of older missiles with new, more powerful missiles also led to concerns about Soviet activities and the impact on U.S. national security of the SALT II limits. An intense debate resulted about whether SALT II left the United States vulnerable to a Soviet first strike. In addition, concerns increasingly were expressed that not only was there no way to tell with available national technical means whether the Soviets were complying with the agreements but that the Soviets were in fact violating existing agreements.

In this context, calls for on-site inspection, especially on an anywhere, anytime basis, again became part of political confrontation between the United States and the Soviet Union.[44] On-site inspection came to be symbolic of vigilance in arms control and support for a tougher posture, much as it had in the early postwar years. It coincided with a resurgence of emphasis on military buildup as a means to meet the Soviet threat and a greater use of arms control negotiations to put the Soviets on the diplomatic defensive.

Afterword: On-Site Inspection in the Reagan Administration

In virtually all respects, the ups and downs of on-site inspection during the Reagan administration mirrored the same basic elements that have been part of U.S. arms control and nuclear disarmament diplomacy since the days of the Baruch Plan. On-site inspection served many, at times conflicting, purposes. The relative mix among those purposes, especially between the more cooperative and more adversarial aspects, reflected the basic pattern of relations between the United States and the Soviet Union.

The Reagan administration expanded the role of on-site inspection, putting in place new and precedent-setting accords. In part, the U.S. government saw its calls for Soviet agreement to on-site inspections as an essential foundation for a more demanding approach to arms control. This approach, as its proponents stressed, no longer permitted the limits of national technical means to set the boundaries of arms control agreements. Instead on-site inspection was a means to determine verification of reductions of strategic offensive missiles, of elimination of mobile Soviet intermediate-range missiles, and of a ban on production and possession of chemical weapons.

Particularly at the start of the administration, calls for on-site inspections (for example, to verify reductions of strategic and theater nuclear forces) were also a means to demonstrate a tough new approach to verification and relations with the Soviet Union. This served domestic political purposes, helping to set the new administration apart from its predecessor. The need for stringent verification standards and on-site inspection served as well to undercut demands for a nuclear freeze in the early 1980s while supporting military modernization. At much the same time, on-site inspection was part of a strategy to isolate the Soviet Union diplomatically and put it on the defensive in arms control negotiations. Closely related, at least in some quarters, calls for anytime, anywhere, on-site inspection in chemical weapons arms control were designed to block progress toward a complete chemical weapons ban.

But as in the past, with the improvement of U.S.-Soviet relations, the more positive purposes of on-site inspection came to predominate. One element in this shift was the change in the Soviet position concerning on-site inspection in particular and arms control in general.[45] Important as well was the fact that initial U.S. demands for unqualified on-site inspection helped to yield compromises in practice.

As a result of these factors, the second Reagan administration and the Soviet government under the new leadership of General Secretary Mikhail Gorbachev reached agreement on the INF treaty in 1987. Under this treaty, on-site inspection has played a significant but limited role in arms control verification. The 1986 Stockholm Accord, with a right to inspect Soviet and Warsaw Pact exercises, also has set an important confidence-building precedent. Its inspection provisions have provided a step to the type of increased transparency that the United States has sought since the days of Eisenhower's open skies proposal three decades earlier. On-site inspection thus has become less a means of political confrontation and more a measure of confidence building and assurance.

By the end of the Reagan administration, on-site inspection had become an integral instrument of arms control verification. More than 300 inspections had been carried out under the INF treaty, and nearly twenty exercises had been inspected under the Stockholm Accord. Provisions for on-site inspection remain prominent features of the START (Strategic Arms Reduction Talks) negotiations, the chemical weapons convention, conventional arms control talks, and enhancements of the verification protocols of the Threshold and Peaceful Nuclear Explosions treaties. Although there remain unresolved and difficult issues concerning verification and the role of on-site inspection in these different areas, on-site inspection has become virtually a permanent fixture in the U.S.-Soviet arms control process as a whole. Even a future setback in U.S.-Soviet political relations will be unlikely to turn back the clock on the long-term trend toward acceptance of and some reliance on on-site inspection for arms control verification and political confidence building.

Notes

1. U.S. Department of State, *Documents on Disarmament, 1945–1959* (Washington, D.C.: Government Printing Office, 1960), 1:7–15.
2. *A Report on the International Control of Atomic Energy*, prepared for the Secretary of State's Committee on Atomic Energy by a board of consultants, David E. Lilienthal, chairman (Washington, D.C.: Government Printing Office, 1946), pp. 4–5.
3. John Lewis Gaddis, *Strategies of Containment: A Critical Appraisal of Postwar American National Security Policy* (new York: Oxford University Press, 1982), pp. 26–27.
4. For Baruch's views, see Robert L. Beckman, *Nuclear Non-Proliferation: Congress and the Control of Peaceful Nuclear Activities* (Boulder, Colo.: Westview Press, 1985), pp. 45–50.
5. See Andrei Gromyko's remarks, "Statement by the Soviet Representative to the Security Council, March 5, 1947," in *Documents on Disarmament*, 1:64–82.
6. "Soviet Proposals Introduced in the United Nations Atomic Energy Commission, June 11, 1947," in *Documents on Disarmament*, 1:85–87.
7. Department of State, *U.S. Participation in the U.N. Report 1948*, Publication 3437 (April 1949), pp. 34–35, cited by Bernard Bechhoefer, *Postwar Negotiations for Arms Control* (Washington, D.C.: Brookings Institution, 1961), pp. 88–89.
8. "Working Paper of the Commission for Conventional Armaments, August 1, 1943," in *Documents on Disarmament*, 1:200–207.
9. United Nations General Assembly, Third Session, First Committee, *Summary Records*, Part I, 153 Meeting (October 7, 1948), cited by Bechhoefer, *Postwar Negotiations*, p. 150.
10. "Radio Address by President Truman, November 7, 1951," in *Documents on Disarmament*, 1:275–281. Also see Bechhoefer, *Postwar Negotiations*, p. 162.
11. See Gaddis, *Strategies of Containment*, pp. 98–99.
12. See Bechhoefer, *Postwar Negotiations*, pp. 183–188.
13. "United States Atoms for Peace Proposal, December 8, 1953," in *Documents on Disarmament*, 1:393–400.
14. Jozef Goldblat, ed., *Safeguarding the Atom: A Critical Appraisal* (London: Taylor and Francis, 1985), pp. 167–169.
15. See INFCIRC/26, (GC)INF/39, INFCIRC/66, INFCIRC/66.2, and INFCIRC/153 (These documents are discussed at length in Chapter 3).

16. See chapter 3 in this book.
17. "Soviet Proposal Introduced in the Disarmament Subcommittee: Reduction of Armaments, the Prohibition of Atomic Weapons, and the Elimination of the Threat of a New War, May 10, 1955," in *Documents on Disarmament*, 1:456–467.
18. Ibid., p. 466.
19. Walt W. Rostow, *Open Skies: Eisenhower's Proposal of July 21, 1955* (Austin: University of Texas Press, 1982), pp. 26–34.
20. Ibid., pp. 59–62.
21. "United States Working Paper Submitted to the Disarmament Subcommittee: Demonstration Test Area, March 21, 1956," in *Documents on Disarmament*, 1:600.
22. "United States Working Paper Submitted to the Disarmament Subcommittee: Technical Exchange Mission, March 21, 1956," in ibid., p. 599.
23. "News Conference Remarks by the Polish Foreign Minister (Rapacki) Regarding an Atom-Free Zone in Central Europe [Extracts], November 4, 1958," and "Note from the American Embassy to the Soviet Foreign Ministry Regarding Surprise Attack Negotiations, November 6, 1958," in *Documents on Disarmament*, 2:1217–1220.
24. "Report of the Conference of Experts to Study the Methods of Detecting Violations of a Possible Agreement on the Suspension of Nuclear Tests, August 21, 1958," in *Documents on Disarmament*, 2:1090–1111.
25. Warren Heckrotte, "On-site Inspection to Check Compliance," in *Nuclear Weapon Test: Prohibition or Limitation*, Jozef Goldblat and David Cox (New York: Oxford University Press, 1988), pp. 248–250.
26. Glenn T. Seaborg, with Benjamin S. Loeb, *Stemming the Tide: Arms Control in the Johnson Years*, (Lexington, Mass.: Lexington Books, 1987), pp. 201–204. See also Harold K. Jacobson and Eric Stein, *Diplomats, Scientists, and Politicians: The United States and the Nuclear Test Ban Negotiations*, (Ann Arbor: University of Michigan Press, 1966), pp. 268–287.
27. Glenn T. Seaborg, *Kennedy, Khrushchev, and the Test Ban* (Berkeley: University of California Press, 1981), pp. pp. 187–189.
28. Seaborg, *Stemming the Tide*, p. 203.
29. Jozef Goldblat, *Agreements for Arms Control: A Critical Survey* (London: Taylor and Francis, 1982), pp. 153–154.
30. *First Annual Report of the Arms Control and Disarmament Agency, FY 1961* (Washington, D.C.: Government Printing Office, 1962), p. 17.
31. See the discussion on Project Vela in chapter 4 in this book.
32. Seaborg, *Stemming the Tide*, pp. 204–206.
33. The concerns of the nonnuclear weapons countries were formally presented in U.N. Resolution 2008, in *Documents on Disarmament, 1965*, (Washington, D.C.: Government Printing Office, 1966), pp. 532–534.
34. Ibid., pp. 84–97. EURATOM was formed in January 1958 to develop peaceful atomic activities in Belgium, France, Italy, Luxembourg, the Netherlands, and West Germany. These countries agreed that the existence of EURATOM would not affect each member's freedom to use atomic energy for military purposes.

Safeguards were introduced to ensure that nuclear materials declared for peaceful uses would not be diverted.

35. Seaborg, *Stemming the Tide*, pp. 204–206.
36. U.S. Arms Control and Disarmament Agency, *Annual Report, FY 1966* (Washington, D.C. Government Printing Office, 1967).
37. Seaborg, *Stemming the Tide*, p. 393.
38. John Newhouse, *Cold Dawn: The Story of SALT* (New York: Holt, Rinehart and Winston, 1974), p. 70.
39. Ibid., pp. 69–71.
40. Ibid., p. 179.
41. Henry Kissinger, *White House Years* (Boston: Little, Brown, 1979), pp. 543–544.
42. Warren Heckrotte, "Verification of Test Ban Treaties," in *Verification and Arms Control*, ed. William Potter (Lexington, Mass.: Lexington Books, 1985), pp. 67–70.
43. Heckrotte, "On-Site Inspection to Check Compliance," pp. 251–252.
44. For example, see Richard Perle, "What Is Adequate Verification," in Gordon Humphrey, *SALT II and American Security* (Cambridge, Mass.: Institute for Foreign Policy Analysis, 1980).
45. For a description of this shift in Soviet views concerning on-site inspection, see chapter 10 in this book.

II
On-Site Inspection in Arms Control Agreements

6
Contributions and Limitations of On-Site Inspection in INF and START

James R. Blackwell

The scope of the on-site inspection provisions in the Intermediate-Range Nuclear Forces (INF) treaty is unprecedented in the history of arms control agreements. There will likely be strong political pressure for even more broad-ranging inspection provisions in a treaty resulting from the Strategic Arms Reduction Talks (START).

The verification value of on-site inspection has become a widely debated issue. Some U.S. officials believe that the Soviets will permit U.S. inspectors to see only what they want them to see, creating the false impression that the Soviet Union is complying with the accord. Others believe the threat of inspection will help deter illegal activities and that on-site inspection will provide useful information on treaty-related activities that could not be obtained from other sources. Still others, including some members of Congress and corporate executives, are concerned about the potential security risks posed by allowing the Soviets to inspect certain sensitive U.S. facilities. The perception that any type of on-site inspection in the Soviet Union would enhance U.S. security, in short, is being tempered by the realization that the verification benefits may not be as pronounced and the costs greater than originally thought. This poses the fundamental question of whether the types of on-site inspection that are being used in INF and being sought in START contribute more to verification and political stability than they will cost.

The answer requires agreement on what is expected from on-site inspection. Assuming that it is to be used primarily to counter Soviet noncompliance, one must decide whether such cheating is inevitable and, if so, if one has to guard against not only militarily significant levels of cheating but less important isolated cases. Would the threat of inspection effectively deter either cheating scenario? Is on-site inspection the only means of effectively verifying certain treaty provisions? To what extent will on-site inspection compensate for the asymmetries in U.S. and Soviet societies and thereby reduce suspicions and increase trust?

Answers to these questions also require agreement on the costs that on-site inspection might impose on the United States. Will the risks to U.S. national security of intrusive verification measures outweigh the benefits? This question is particularly applicable to provisions allowing for unscheduled inspections of undeclared facilities where covert activities may be occurring, a potentially important element of a START agreement. Are the financial costs associated with the planning, preparation, and maintenance of readiness for possible Soviet inspections, as well as the cost of conducting inspections of Soviet facilities, commensurate with the verification payoffs of these inspections? In short, are the costs of Soviet inspection of defense contract facilities fully understood, acceptable, and affordable?

Role of On-Site Inspection in INF

The outcome sought by the United States in the INF talks was modified several times during the course of the negotiations. Initially the United States had proposed the elimination of all longer-range (1,000–5,500 kilometers) INF missile systems and a cap, at current Soviet levels, on shorter-range (500–1,000 kilometers) INF missiles. When the Soviets resisted, the United States proposed reductions to equal levels of longer-range INF missiles and the cap on shorter-range INF missiles. Several variants of that outcome were offered, and ultimately the United States and the Soviet Union agreed to the elimination of all longer-range and shorter-range INF missiles. Each proposed outcome posed different verification problems, which affected the design of the verification regime. All outcomes had one thing in common: the verification methods required for the reductions being sought exceeded U.S. monitoring capabilities using national technical means alone.

The verification challenges in INF were much greater than in SALT (Strategic Arms Limitation Talks) for several reasons. First, INF missile systems are relatively small and mobile and therefore easy to conceal. Second, many of the missiles are capable of carrying either conventional or nuclear warheads. Third, operational spares (termed *nondeployed missiles* in the treaty) had to be limited in order to constrain the so-called refire threat (a legitimate concern because of the survivability of the mobile launchers). Finally, there was some uncertainty associated with the estimated total of existing Soviet INF missiles.

While national technical means alone were used to verify provisions in the SALT treaty, it was readily apparent that these would not be sufficient to verify INF, for which an additional dimension of cooperative verification would be a prerequisite. The limit on nondeployed missiles contained in INF requires that missile and launcher support facilities be identified and monitored. As such, on-site inspection would be required to monitor buildings where missiles and launchers could be located. For example, Soviet SS-20 bases have single-bay garages for their launchers; it is necessary to confirm that the multibay garages contain missile support equipment and vehicles, not hidden missiles or launchers. Each type of support facility—production, final assembly, depot-level repair and storage, training facilities, and test ranges—poses unique on-site inspection considerations.

Inspection of production and final assembly facilities poses several challenges: identifying the point at which a missile or launcher becomes accountable, whether an inspection of those facilities would be adequate to count the actual number of accountable missiles or launchers (given the dynamic nature of the production and assembly processes), and if stockpiling of missiles or launchers within those facilities might be occurring.

Inspection of depot-level repair or storage facilities is necessary to count the number of missiles and launchers and to prevent the use of depot-level repair facilities to maintain illegal missiles or launchers from covert locations, a task for which national technical means cannot be used. Assessments of accountable missiles based on calculations of floor space capacity cannot be used because of the probable presence of non-INF systems and uncertainties relating to the utilization rate of the floor space. Under normal circumstances, very few missiles and/or launchers are located at training facilities or test ranges. Nevertheless, because of the availability of storage space and the potential to use training and launch activities to maintain an operationally ready covert unit, inspection rights at those locations are worthwhile.

Ultimately the decision on whether to seek on-site inspection at missile operating bases and missile support facilities had to balance the inspection benefits against the risks of compromising sensitive U.S. information at those facilities.

Over time, the INF verification tasks were simplified by agreements to (1) eliminate all shorter-range INF missiles, launchers, missile transport vehicles, and missile support facilities within eighteen months; (2) eliminate all longer-range INF missiles, launchers, launch-related support equipment and structures, and missile support facilities within three years; and (3) ban the production and flight testing of INF missiles and launchers. Thus, the fundamental verification task in INF changed from having to count the number of residual missiles and launchers for the duration of the treaty to having to detect one illegal missile or launcher after the elimination period. The flight test ban, moreover, was an important step in mitigating the potential for violations by reducing the operational usefulness of any illegal missiles.

The INF Treaty had four major verifications tasks: to confirm the initial inventories of missiles and launchers, to ensure their elimination, to monitor the residual levels of these systems during the two elimination phases, and to verify the nonexistence of INF missiles, launchers, and associated infrastructure after three years. The verification regime that is being used to accomplish those tasks has the following key elements:

1. Missiles and launchers may be located only at declared facilities, in designated deployment areas, or in transit between those locations. Any missile or launcher detected outside those locations that is not in notified transit is considered a violation.

2. The number of missiles and launchers at each location must be declared. Movement of missiles and launchers between declared locations must be notified within a specified period.

3. On-site inspection is used to verify the accuracy of the initial data exchange; elimination of missiles, launchers, and launch-related support equipment and structures; residual levels of missiles and launchers until they are eliminated; conversion of missile bases and missile support facilities to other uses; and nonexistence of missiles and launchers for ten years after completion of the elimination phase.

4. Continuous monitoring at the SS-20 and Pershing II production and final assembly facilities to verify the production ban on SS-20 and Pershings.

5. Collateral constraints on missile activities to enhance verification.

The INF treaty provided for six different types of on-site inspection in the United States, the Soviet Union, and countries in which U.S. or Soviet INF systems are based (including the Federal Republic of Germany, United Kingdom, Italy, Belgium, the Netherlands, German Democratic Republic, and Czechoslovakia.)

Baseline Inspections

Article XI, paragraph 3 of the treaty provides for inspections at all missile operating bases, missile support facilities, and elimination facilities specified in the initial update of the Memorandum of Understanding (MOU) in December 1988 and excluding missile production facilities. Production facilities were excluded from any type of interior inspection at U.S. insistence, for reasons of national security: to protect sensitive technologies and manufacturing processes within the facilities, including production activities unrelated to INF missile systems. The inspections were to begin no earlier than thirty days after entry into force of the treaty, on June 1, 1988, and to be completed no later than ninety days after entry into force.

The purpose of the baseline inspection provisions was to verify the number of missiles, launchers and launch-related support equipment, and support structures that were declared in the initial data update. These data also served as the baseline for subsequent updates.

The United States inspected 133 Soviet locations during the baseline inspection period and apparently found that the Soviets' declared data for each location were accurate. Nevertheless, the fundamental question of whether all missiles and launchers were declared will linger, even if it is well understood that the usefulness of any concealed system degrades over time. Furthermore, it is doubtful that the right to inspect anywhere would have removed the underlying uncertainty associated with concealed systems, since any legal items could be moved before the arrival of the inspection time.

Nevertheless, access to the declared sites probably provided more useful information on Soviet activities than Soviet inspectors acquired at U.S. facilities. Because of the relative openness in the West, the Soviets probably used on-site inspection to fill in missing pieces of information rather than to build on a mosaic derived from national technical means.

Short-Notice Inspections

Article XI, paragraph 5 provides the right to inspect missile operating bases and missile support facilities other than missile production facilities and elimination facilities. The purpose of these inspections is to ascertain that the numbers of missiles, launchers and launch-related support equipment, and support structures correspond with the numerical declarations for each inspection site. Inspection of former missile operating bases and former missile support facilities that were eliminated under the treaty is also permitted.

These inspections may begin ninety days after entry into force (subsequent to the baseline inspections) and continue for thirteen years. Each party may conduct twenty short-notice inspections per year during the first three years after entry into force, fifteen such inspections per year during the subsequent five years, and ten such inspections per year during the last five years. The decreasing number of inspections over time is based on their declining utility as the elimination of INF facilities proceeds and the lessened effectiveness and significance of covert systems that are subject to the prohibition on flight testing.

No more than half of the inspections each year may occur in any one basing country. The constraint on the number of inspections that may be conducted in any particular country was introduced primarily to reduce the opportunities for political harassment and to encourage the concept of burden sharing. The fact that U.S. and Soviet INF systems are based in other countries presented a unique negotiating challenge. Separate negotiations were required with the five U.S. basing countries to secure access rights for Soviet inspectors in each country before the United States could table its inspection proposals in Geneva. Since the INF Treaty is a bilateral accord, each basing country had to reaffirm Soviet access rights to its territory in a diplomatic note to Moscow prior to conclusion of the agreement.

One of the key features of short-notice inspection is timing. The objective is to minimize the time between designation of the inspection site and the arrival of the inspection team at the site in order to increase the difficulty of removing any illegal items. The Protocol on Inspection requires that the United States notify the Soviets of its intent to conduct an inspection at least sixteen hours prior to the inspector's arrival at the point of entry, but the United States is not required to specify the inspection site until four hours prior to departure for the site from the point of entry. The Soviets are then obligated to transport the inspection team to the inspection site no later than nine hours after the site has been specified. Thus, unless the Soviets decide to remove illegal items from all declared and formerly declared sites when they receive the initial inspection notification, they would have only nine hours to remove any illegal items from the specified site.

The timing of the specification of the inspection site will presumably be carefully coordinated to afford maximum national technical means coverage in order to complicate the removal of any illegal items. The Protocol on Inspection also requires a preinspection movement restriction, which prohibits the removal of treaty-limited items, to be implemented within one hour after specification of the site. This restriction provides the basis for a charge of violation if illegal movement is detected. Even so, since continuous national technical means coverage is not possible, there is no way of ensuring that no illegal items were at the site when it was specified as the inspection site.

Although the removal of illegal items will be more challenging with short-notice inspections than for baseline inspections given the time constraints, we should not expect that U.S. inspectors will find that the numbers of treaty-limited items at the site are inconsistent with Soviet declarations. Nevertheless, the continuing threat of inspection should prove a deterrent if the Soviets were contemplating illegal activities, and therefore it may influence their behavior to some extent. In sum, the right to inspect former bases and missile support facilities provides a means to confirm that INF activity has not resumed at the site. This may be more valuable than it would first appear because it would be virtually impossible to conceal all evidence of such activity in nine hours.

Continuous Perimeter and Portal Monitoring

The treaty specified that beginning thirty days after entry into force and for thirteen years thereafter, each party has the right to monitor continuously the portals of any facility that assembles a ground-launched ballistic missile (GLBM) with stages that are outwardly similar to a stage of a solid-propellant, longer-range INF GLBM. If a party has no such facility, the portals of an agreed former INF missile production facility may be monitored. A perimeter/portal monitoring system may be established at those sites within six months after entry into force. Furthermore, if, after two years after entry into force, neither party conducts such final assembly activities for twelve consecutive months, continuous monitoring by both parties shall cease. If such final assembly is initiated again, continuous monitoring may be resumed. The Pershing production plant at Magna, Utah, and the SS-20 production and final assembly facility at Votkinsk in the Soviet Union are specified in the treaty as sites to be monitored.

The concept of a perimeter and portal monitoring system at ballistic missile production and final assembly facilities was developed by the United States as a means of monitoring the flow of missiles from those facilities. The original intent was to use the system to improve the U.S. ability to monitor compliance with residual levels rather than a production ban. Even with adequate monitoring of residual levels, the system would not have significantly reduced uncertainties about the number of existing missiles because of the uncertainty of whether all missiles had been declared in the data exchange. However, the monitoring system would have provided an accurate count of new missiles entering the inventory from the monitored site. Thus, as older ballistic missiles were retired and eliminated, U.S. confidence in the overall inventory would have improved.

Even continuous monitoring of production facilities cannot eliminate the possibility of covert production activities. On the other hand, it would be difficult to disguise solid rocket motor production facilities absent Soviet willingness to compromise safety standards. Solid rocket motor production is a hazardous activity. To reduce collateral damage from possible accidents, pouring and curing of the motors takes place in widely separated building protected by earth revetments. These provide a unique signature for national technical means. This factor, in conjunction with the fact that most new ballistic missiles are solid propellant missiles, convinces most analysts that undetected ballistic missile production is unlikely.

As such, the production ban on all INF missiles removed the primary justification for continuous monitoring. Late in the negotiations, however, the Soviets pointed out that a potential compliance issue could arise because of the similarity of the first stages of the SS-25 and the SS-20. Since the SS-25 and SS-20 (as well as the SS-23) were produced and assembled at Votkinsk, the sides eventually agreed that a perimeter/portal monitoring system would be established to monitor the production ban on SS-20s. Although Pershing stages do not pose a similar problem of distinguishability, the United States agreed to continuous Soviet monitoring at its production plant at Magna to satisfy Soviet demands for equal monitoring obligations.

The Protocol on Inspection specifies detailed monitoring rights, obligations, and procedures. It requires that all vehicles that can contain an SS-20 first stage exit the site through one rail or one road portal. Weight sensors, vehicle sensors, vehicle dimensional measuring equipment, surveillance systems, and inspectors will be used to monitor traffic at those portals. If weight and dimensional measurements of a vehicle (truck or railcar) indicate that it is not large enough or heavy enough to contain the longest stage of an INF ballistic missile, the vehicle is permitted to proceed without further inspection. Otherwise the vehicle is subject to a series of increasingly intrusive inspection procedures to ascertain that an INF missile or missile stage is not contained in the vehicle.

The U.S.-designed perimeter monitoring system, which was explained to the Soviets but not proposed by the United States, would have permitted remote monitoring of the perimeter of the site from a data collection center adjacent to one of the portals. Existing security fencing would have been augmented by a modular fiber optic fence, closed-circuit television cameras, and lighting. Instead it was agreed that inspectors would be used to patrol the perimeter of the site to ensure that missiles or missile stages do not exit the facility through other portals or breaches in the security fence. Although more manpower intensive and subject to adverse weather conditions, the patrols can be as effective as the remote monitoring system with proper planning.

Up to thirty personnel are authorized to operate the perimeter/portal monitoring system around the clock. Understandably, the continuous presence of thirty inspectors causes counterintelligence concerns for both sides. To reduce opportunities for possible intelligence collection, inspectors' travel is restricted to within 50 kilometers of the monitored site, requires official permission, and may involve escorts.

Discussion of perimeter/portal monitoring would be incomplete without mention of one additional and important consideration: costs. Although the system is relatively simple, the installation, logistics, and operating costs are substantial. This may have been one reason that the United States agreed to shift from the remote perimeter monitoring system to perimeter patrols.

Elimination Inspections

Article XI, paragraph 7 requires that inspectors observe the disassembly and destruction process for all INF missiles, launchers, and launch-related support equipment at specified elimination facilities and the elimination of missiles that are launched. Each side is permitted to launch no more than one hundred longer-range INF missiles within six months after entry into force.

Elimination inspections are used to verify numbers and types of missiles, launchers, and equipment to be destroyed and to verify that the disassembly and destruction process is carried out in accordance with the procedures specified in the Protocol on Elimination. During elimination of missiles by launching, inspectors are required to verify the type of missile prepared for launch and to observe the launch. No more than twenty inspectors may be used on an elimination inspection team. A party that is eliminating treaty-limited items may request as many elimination inspections as it wishes.

Elimination inspections are the only type of inspection that the inspecting party is required to carry out. The other types of inspection in INF may be carried out by the inspecting party, if desired.

The inspected party is required to notify the other party of its intention to destroy a specific number of items and the location of the elimination facility at least thirty days prior to the scheduled elimination or ten days in advance of a scheduled launch.

The Protocol on Elimination contains detailed procedures for the disassembly and destruction of each type of missile, launcher, launch canister, and missile transporter vehicle. Destruction methods include cutting, crushing, flattening, burning, and explosive demolition. Ignition of all missile stages is required for missiles eliminated by launching.

The United States called for the destruction of support equipment required to launch a missile rather than all unit equipment since the destruction of readily available, general purpose vehicles would not deter the formation of covert units. It would also be illogical to destroy equipment that could be used for non-INF purposes.

The combination of on-site inspection and the detailed destruction procedures in the protocol permits the United States to effectively verify the elimination of all declared INF missile systems.

Closeout Inspections

Article XI, paragraph 4 establishes the right to confirm by on-site inspection that all INF activity has been terminated at missile operating bases and missile support facilities, except missile production facilities, within sixty days after the scheduled elimination date. A party is required to notify the other party of the scheduled date of elimination at least thirty days in advance. If a baseline inspection is conducted after the scheduled date of elimination of a facility, a closeout inspection would be unnecessary at that facility and is not permitted. No more than ten inspectors are permitted on a closeout inspection team.

The elimination of missile support facilities requires the total absence of INF activity. The elimination of missile operating bases requires the removal of the missile unit and its equipment plus Pershing II launch pad shelters and SS-20 single-bay garages. Launch pad shelters at Pershing II bases and single-bay garages at SS-20 bases must be dismantled or demolished and removed from their base or foundation, and the base or foundation must be destroyed by excavation or explosion.

The United States did not call for the dismantlement and destruction of all structures at Soviet missile bases because it made no sense to tear down buildings and construct new ones for non-INF units that will occupy its INF missile bases. Furthermore, the right to inspect former missile bases provides a means to verify that SS-20 units have not been moved covertly into a base. It is also unlikely that a covert unit would be located at a former base, which would be a priority target for monitoring by national technical means, rather than at an unidentified site.

Optional Elimination Inspections

Article XI, paragraph 8 provides the right to conduct inspection to confirm the elimination of missiles, launchers, and launch-related support equipment that are lost (destruction with an assumed location), destroyed as a result of an accident, or placed on static display. Paragraph 8 also provides the right to conduct inspections to confirm the completion of elimination procedures for training missiles, training missile stages, training launch canisters, and training launchers. No more than twenty inspectors may be used to conduct these inspections.

The elimination provision relating to loss originated in the SALT treaty and was intended primarily for heavy bombers and missile-carrying submarines (SSBNs). It is unlikely, though theoretically possible, that a launcher or missile will disappear during field training or transit. It is also doubtful that either side will exercise its right to search for a launcher or missile.

Accidental destruction may be worth confirming, particularly if several missiles and/or launchers are destroyed in an accident. Regardless of whether the inspection rights are exercised, a means of removing such items from the inventory of accountable items is necessary and is provided for in the Protocol on Elimination.

The Protocol on Elimination permits each party to place up to fifteen missiles, fifteen launch canisters, fifteen launchers, and any number of training missiles, training launch canisters, and training launchers on static display. Prior to being placed on static display, the missile, launch canister, or launcher must be rendered unusable. Inspections may be conducted within sixty days of notification that any of the items has been placed on static display.

Training missiles, training missile stages, training launch canisters, and training launchers may be destroyed at specified elimination facilities or at their current location. At least thirty days in advance, the party must provide the location and the date for an inspection to confirm the completion of the elimination procedures. In contrast to elimination procedures for operational systems (which require that the elimination process be observed), elimination procedures for trainers must be completed prior to the date of inspection. Furthermore, this type of inspection is optional; the items may automatically be removed from accountability if there is no inspection on the date specified. Destruction of trainers is required to avoid potential compliance concerns that could arise due to their similarity to actual missiles and launchers.

Inspections of SS-4 Silos

In addition to the inspection rights provided for in the treaty documents, the two sides agreed in an exchange of letters on December 7, 1987, that the United States could conduct up to six inspections of former silo launchers of SS-4 missiles. Such inspections and the inspection procedures are to be arranged through the Special Verification Commission, the consultative body for the treaty.

Conclusions

In summary, the INF treaty made a number of contributions to on-site inspections; it set some limitations too:

1. Baseline inspections and short-notice inspections at declared facilities provide a better understanding of Soviet activities but improve confidence in compliance only at the inspection site at the time of the inspection. These inspection should not be relied upon to detect a violation but may provide indications of significant levels of illegal activities. They are, however, unlikely to deter militarily significant levels of cheating since the Soviets could be expected to expend the effort necessary to remove any illegal missiles before the arrival of an inspection team. Lack of incentive to cheat (6,000 remaining strategic warheads with a START agreement) will more than likely be the overriding consideration.

2. Short-notice inspections of former missile operating bases and missile support facilities will effectively deter resumption of INF activities at those facilities because it would be virtually impossible to remove all evidence of such activity with only nine hours warning.

3. Continuous monitoring of the SS-20 production and final assembly facility will permit the United States to verify effectively that SS-20 stages or missiles are not leaving the facility. Without periodic, interior inspection of the facility, the only real constraint on illegal production will be the amount of storage space within the facility.

4. Inspection at elimination facilities will permit the United States to verify effectively the elimination of all declared missiles, launch canisters, launchers and missile transporter vehicles.

5. Closeout inspections will provide high confidence that there is no INF activity at the facility at the time of the inspection.

6. Inspection rights for accidental destruction will be useful for verifying accidents involving several missiles or launchers.

7. Inspection rights to confirm the elimination of training missiles, launchers, and so forth will be effective if the inspectors are able to correlate the pieces with a declared number of trainers.

The complete inspection package will yield more information on Soviet activities and behavior than the sum of the information derived from individual inspections. Regardless of the contributions of on-site inspection to effective verification and its limitations and risks, however, political realities suggest that on-site inspection will be part of the verification regime of most arms control accords in the foreseeable future.

Role of On-Site Inspection in START

As in INF, on-site inspection will be used primarily in START to improve the ability of the United States to verify compliance with the numerical limits of the treaty. This task will be more challenging than in INF because of the requirement to verify residual levels of treaty-limited items for the duration of the treaty, as compared to the ban on INF systems and associated infrastructure after three years. Verification also will be more important because of the greater military significance of cheating under START. Moreover, some argue that the incentive to cheat will be enhanced if there are substantial cuts in strategic systems.

Compliance with certain limits on START systems can be effectively verified with national technical means and counting rules, so on-site inspection will be unnecessary for those systems. Numerical limits on deployed (operational) silo-launched intercontinental ballistic missiles (ICBMs) and submarine-launched ballistic missiles (SLBMs) and heavy bombers fall into this category. On the other hand, national technical means cannot be relied upon to effectively verify numerical limits on nondeployed ICBMs and SLBMs or the permitted number of operational spares at each ICBM deployment area. Verification of numerical limits on deployed reentry vehicles (RVs) on ICBMs and SLBMs also probably will require the use of on-site inspection. In addition, on-site inspection may be required to distinguish heavy bombers that carry air-launched cruise missiles (ALCMs) from heavy bombers that do not carry ALCMs, particularly if the same model of aircraft (for example, the B-52H) is counted in both categories. The role of on-site inspection in verifying numerical limits on long-range, nuclear-armed submarine-launched cruise missiles (SLCMs) (probably the most intractable verification problem) cannot be determined until the United States decides how to define desirable limits. Numerical limits, rather than a ban on road-mobile and rail-mobile ICBMs, seem to be inevitable, and on-site inspection will be part of the verification regimes for those systems as well. The regimes will have to be strengthened by improved national technical means capabilities and coverage for START to be adequately verifiable.

Many of the verification tasks requiring the use of on-site inspection in START and INF are identical. Most of the inspection rights, obligations, and procedures that were agreed to in INF are likely to be adopted in START. Moreover, INF will provide operational experience, and that may be useful to improve the inspection procedures for START.

In some cases, however, the inspection rights, obligations, and procedures for START may have to be expanded or modified to cover different types of systems and facilities. There are, of course, a number of uncertainties about the role of on-site inspection for verifying limitations that are still under development. The use of on-site inspection in verifying SLCMs, for instance, is still highly speculative.

Agreed Inspection Provisions

In their joint summit statement in December 1987, President Reagan and General Secretary Gorbachev "agreed to instruct their negotiators to accelerate resolution of issues within the Joint Draft Treaty (JDT) text including early agreement on provisions for effective verification." Among other things, they also agreed to the following relevant provisions:

> Building upon the provisions of the treaty on the Elimination of Intermediate-Range and Shorter Range Missiles, the measures by which the provisions of the Treaty on the Reduction and Limitation of Strategic Offensive Arms can be verified will, at a minimum, include:

1. Data exchanges, to include declarations by each side of the number and location of weapons systems limited by the Treaty and of facilities at which such systems are located and appropriate notifications. These facilities will include locations and facilities for production and final assembly, storage, testing, and deployment of systems covered by this Treaty. Such declarations will be exchanged between the sides before the Treaty is signed and updated periodically after entry into force.
2. Baseline inspection to verify the accuracy of these declarations promptly after entry into force of the Treaty.
3. On-site observation of the elimination of strategic systems necessary to achieve the agreed limits.
4. Continuous on-site monitoring of the perimeter and portals of critical production and support facilities to confirm the output of these facilities.
5. Short-notice on-site inspection of:
   a. Declared locations during the process of reducing to agreed limits;
   b. Locations where systems covered by this Treaty remain after achieving the agreed limits; and

    c.   Locations where such systems have been located (formerly declared facilities).

6.   The right to implement, in accordance with agreed-upon procedures, short-notice inspections at locations where either side considers covert deployment, production, storage or repair of strategic offensive arms could be occurring.

These provisions are expected to parallel closely the INF inspection provisions when they are translated into treaty text for the Joint Draft Treaty.

Baseline Inspections

The inspection rights, obligations, and procedures and numbers of inspectors for baseline inspections in START are expected to be identical to those in the INF Treaty. START will have additional categories of facilities that will probably be subject to inspection, such as ICBM deployment areas, SSBN ports, and bomber bases. Depending on the number of locations, the inspection period may begin later than thirty days after entry into force and may last longer than the sixty days used for INF baseline inspections. Baseline inspections will be used primarily to help verify the number of nondeployed ICBMs and SLBMs and the number of deployed, mobile (assuming the U.S.-proposed ban on mobiles is dropped).

Baseline inspection of road-mobile SS-25 operating bases would be analogous to inspections of SS-20 operating bases in INF. U.S. inspectors would also be required to count the number of rail-launch cars and SS-24s at several rail-mobile garrisons. By contrast since missile silos can be effectively monitored with national technical means, the only reason to conduct a baseline inspection of silo-launched ICBM deployment areas would be to confirm that there are no excess operational spares at each missile complex.

If the Soviets declare that their nondeployed SLBMs located in the vicinity of their SSBN ports to be located at the ports rather than at nearby SLBM repair or storage facilities, the United States would need to inspect the ports; or, conversely, should the Soviets declare the nondeployed SLBMs to be located at nearby repair or storage facilities, the baseline inspection would be conducted at those facilities instead. A baseline inspection at SSBN ports also may be necessary to confirm that any dockside missiles that had been removed from an SSBN were not extra missiles (that is, to verify that the SSBN launch tubes were empty). Since SSBN launch tubes are considered to contain deployed SLBMs, on-site inspection would be the only effective means to avoid double counting a missile that was not in its launch tube and had been observed at the port facility by national technical means.

Other than a desire for consistency, there is no reason for a baseline inspection or short-notice inspection to verify the number of heavy bombers that are declared ALCM carriers because this can be accomplished by national technical means.

Based on its position in INF, the United States is likely to insist that production facilities be excluded from any type of intrusive inspection in START. It thus forfeits the right to use inspections to detect illegal missile stockpiles in Soviet production facilities.

Although strategic missiles are larger and more difficult to move and conceal than INF missiles, it would be unrealistic to expect that baseline inspections will reveal discrepancies in the Soviets' declared data. The extent of concern about undeclared missiles will depend on the intelligence community's confidence in its production estimates for each type of Soviet strategic missile, in conjunction with the Soviet declarations.

Whereas detection of any undeclared missile would cause political concerns, the military significance of undeclared silo-launched ICBMs and SLBMs is debatable. First, there is the question of whether there would by any surviving silos to reload or any remaining ports for SSBN reconstitution to make such missiles militarily usable. Another question concerns whether the concealed missiles could be moved to and loaded into any surviving silos or SSBNs prior to the termination of hositilities. Obviously illegal ICBMs within an ICBM deployment area would be more threatening than ones in storage. On the other hand, undeclared mobile ICBMs, particularly road-mobiles, could be militarily significant (depending on the number) because of the improved survivability of the launcher and its ability to move to a concealed reload missile.

Short-Notice Inspections

The short-notice inspection rights in the joint summit statement are applicable to all declared and formerly declared locations. Nevertheless, because of U.S. objections to inspections of production facilities and separate visits to elimination facilities, the Joint Draft Treaty text will likely exclude missile production facilities and elimination facilities from short-notice inspections, as in INF. The inspections are likely to be conducted after completion of the baseline inspections and to have no more than ten inspectors on a team. An annual quota of inspections, perhaps decreasing during the seven-year reduction period, will apply for the duration of the treaty.

In START, short-notice inspection rights to verify the number of missiles at a location are expected to apply to mobile missile operating bases and rail garrisons, ICBM deployment areas that include the support base, SSBN ports, test ranges, and training facilities. If depot-level repair and storage facilities are not subject to continuous perimeter/portal monitoring, those facilities would also be subject to short-notice inspection.

Short-notice inspection rights, obligations, and procedures used in INF will more than likely be adopted in the START Protocol on Inspection. The problems involved in removing illegal missiles or missile stages prior to the arrival of the inspection team—within nine hours of notification—would differ only in the size of the missile. Thus, U.S. inspectors can expect to find that the number of treaty-limited items at an inspection site is consistent with Soviet declarations.

The number of former START bases and missile support facilities will probably be small. Nevertheless, the right to inspect those facilities should deter illegal activity there because of the difficulty of removing all evidence of such activity in nine hours—or perhaps even a longer period if reasons given for delays are plausible.

Suspect Site Inspections

In the joint summit statement, the sides agreed to "the right to implement, in accordance with agreed-upon procedures, short-notice inspections at locations where either side considers covert deployment, production, storage or repair of strategic offensive arms could be occurring." The United States had sought similar inspection rights for an INF outcome that would have left residual levels of INF systems. This requirement was dropped when both sides agreed to eliminate all INF missiles within three years and to impose a production ban and a ban on flight testing upon entry into force of the treaty. The United States is advocating short-notice inspection rights at undeclared locations (or suspect sites) for START because of the requirement to verify residual levels of strategic systems, particularly if mobile ICBMs are permitted.

The primary purpose of suspect-site inspections is to provide access to undeclared locations to confirm that illegal activities are not occurring. It is also hoped that the continuing threat of short-notice inspection will help to deter cheating at undeclared locations.

It would be reasonable to expect that the Soviets will ensure that U.S. inspectors merely confirm that illegal activities are not occurring at the designated inspection site. One should expect that the Soviets would remove any illegal missiles prior to the arrival of an inspection team. Whether illegal activities were occurring prior to the inspection or whether they will occur after the inspection will always be an unanswerable question. At best, U.S. inspectors may gather circumstantial evidence suggesting that illegal activities had been occurring but should not count on finding a "smoking gun".

Whether the threat of inspection will help to deter cheating is widely debated in the arms control community. Most agree that the threat of inspection is unlikely to dissuade a determined Soviet effort to conduct illegal activities. It may have a positive influence if the payoff of a contemplated illegal activity is small; however, militarily significant levels of cheating are the real concern. This suggests that the political importance of suspect-site inspection is much greater than its verification value.

While congressional views on on-site inspections are still in the formative stage, there is a growing awareness that it is not a panacea for effective verification. There is a realization that it will pose unanticipated operational, economic and political difficulties. Corporations subject to INF inspection or even in the vicinity of facilities subject to inspection have called for compensation for the potential loss of business, loss of proprietary information, and contract discrimination. The complaints raised by INF provisions, which affect relatively few private contractor facilities, may rise to a groundswell when the impact of suspect-site inspection for START is fully understood in the corporate world.

The Soviets reportedly added the phrase "in accordance with agreed-upon procedures" to the suspect-site inspection rights in the summit statement. Some believe that the phrase was added to provide a veto for an anywhere, anytime provision similar to the U.S. proposal in its draft chemical weapons treaty. Although the Soviets have agreed to the concept of suspect-site inspection, they are likely to insist on reasonable bounds on the types of undeclared facilities that may be inspected.

The scope of suspect-site inspections is one of the more controversial issues that must be resolved in START. There is an inherent tension between broad-ranging inspection rights and the requirement to protect highly sensitive national security information at facilities unrelated to START. Furthermore, the Fourth Amendment restriction on the unlawful search of private property would have to be overturned or modified by the Supreme Court to permit Soviet inspection of facilities that are not government owned or operated by companies under contract to the government.

Both sides have sensitive military and intelligence activites at nonstrategic facilities that they are unwilling to expose to inspectors. Few would argue that the verification payoffs from suspect-site inspection warrant the risk of compromising those sensitive activities. Thus, some means will have to be developed that permits access to undeclared locations where cheating would most likely occur while denying access to locations with sensitive activities unrelated to the START treaty. This seemingly straightforward solution has proved elusive.

In October 1988, President Reagan approved a suspect-site inspection proposal that has two basic elements. The first provides the right to request short-notice inspection of any facility in the other's territory that is government owned or operated by companies under contract to the government. If the request is denied, the party refusing the inspection would be required to explain why and to take actions to alleviate the other side's concerns over possible cheating.

Under the second provision, each side would have the right to conduct short-notice inspections at a number of agreed-upon sites—primarily facilities used to produce rocket motors for nonstrategic, solid-propellant missiles (such as short-range missiles or space boosters). Inspection requests for the agreed-upon sites could not be refused.[1]

While the new proposal represents a more reasonable balance between the need to inspect suspicious Soviet installations and the requirement to protect sensitive U.S. sites from Soviet spying, considerable work will be required to develop the implementing procedures for the provision with the right of refusal.

The underlying problem of an approach that denies access to any facility will be the contention that the Soviets would use the facility for illegal activities. Unrestricted access, however, would not increase U.S. verification capability in a measurable way. Further, such access could place sensitive national security information at risk.

This, of course, poses the question of who has the most to gain or lose from the right to inspect an undeclared facility. It is obvious that the United States would gain more general information about Soviet activities than the Soviets would about U.S. activities because of the asymmetries of the two societies. On the other hand, the Soviets could gain more useful information on advanced defense technologies because of the U.S. superiority in most areas. The Soviets have consistently copied U.S. design and technology to produce "look alikes" (such as fighters and cruise missiles), although there has been a time lag before their copied technology has emerged operationally. The United States would have to take steps to ensure that this lead time is at least maintained. It would be ironic if the lead time were to be reduced by an arms control measure. On balance, protecting the U.S. lead in defense technology seems to outweigh the potential verification gains that might be realized from the right to inspect any undeclared facility.

Most of the rights, obligations, and procedures for short-notice inspections of declared facilities in the INF treaty are likely to apply to suspect-site inspections. In that the suspect sites would not be strategic facilities, some minor modifications in the rights and procedures may be necessary to minimize access to nonessential information. There may also be separate quotas for suspect-site inspections and short-notice inspections of declared and formerly declared facilities. The size of both types of short-notice inspection teams is likely to be the same—ten inspectors.

Continuous Perimeter/Portal Monitoring

In the joint summit statement, the sides agreed to continuous on-site monitoring of critical production and support facilities to confirm the output of these facilities. This implies that continuous monitoring will be used at missile production and/or final assembly facilities, as in INF, and possibly at other types of support facilities.

It would also be desirable to monitor the output of mobile launchers (if mobile ICBMs are to be permitted). The most effective monitoring location would be mobile launcher final assembly facilities, where the erector-launcher is mounted on the road transporter or the railcar.

Use of continuous monitoring at depot-level missile and launcher repair and storage facilities would prevent the repair or storage of covert missiles or launchers at those facilities, thereby forcing any illegal missiles or launchers into less cost-effective covert facilities. Without continuous monitoring, excess missiles or launchers could be removed prior to the arrival of a short-notice inspection team.

Use of an effective tagging system (simple nonreproducible tags) on legal missiles and launchers would prevent illegal missiles or launchers from obtaining depot-level repair support at declared facilities. Without some type of tagging system, illegal missiles or launchers could be switched with legal ones enroute to a repair facility, and inspectors at the repair facility would be unable to distinguish an illegal missile from a legal one. If the tagging concept is adopted, all new missiles and launchers could be tagged prior to departing production or final assembly facilities, and all existing (declared) missiles or launchers could be tagged during the baseline inspection. Although tagging is already used in industry, several technical problems must be resolved prior to its application in START.

Use of continuous monitoring at test ranges is impractical because of the size of the ranges and the small number of missiles and launchers at test ranges. It could also compromise sensitive information relating to new weapons systems (both strategic and nonstrategic systems) that are routinely tested at the ranges. Continuous monitoring would not be cost-effective at training facilities because of the limited number of missiles and launchers at the facility and very infrequent movement activity.

Continuous perimeter/portal monitoring is manpower intensive and costly and raises counterintelligence concerns, but its increased use nevertheless is expected as part of START. Congressional demands for improved verification capabilities for START will probably overshadow the importance of these considerations in the administration's decision process. In fact, continuous monitoring is likely to be the centerpiece of the U.S. START on-site inspection package.

Whereas continuous monitoring is used in INF to verify the missile production ban, it will be used in the START context to monitor the flow of new missiles (and mobile launchers) into strategic inventories. Over time, this will improve U.S. confidence in assessing missile inventories as older missiles are retired. Although undetected illegal missile production is possible, covert solid-propellant rocket motor production would be difficult to conceal. Illegal mobile launcher production would be much easier to hide, but this is not a reason to drop continuous monitoring at known mobile launcher final assembly facilities. Continuous monitoring at depot-level missile and launcher repair and storage facilities would prevent illegal use of those facilities if tagging is adopted and would provide an accurate count of missiles and launchers in those facilities. Further, use of short-notice inspections at the depots, which would certainly be less effective, would also be unnecessary.

Monitoring rights, obligations, and procedures in the START Protocol Inspection are expected to parallel those in INF closely. The portal monitoring systems, for instance, are likely to be almost identical. Given the unlimited duration of the START Treaty and the potential number of sites, the remote perimeter monitoring system may be more cost-effective than the perimeter patrol system used in INF, given that the number of monitored sites in START may tax U.S. ability to provide the personnel need to staff the perimeter patrol systems. At a minimum, it would be worthwhile reexamining the issue of remote perimeter monitoring versus perimeter patrol monitoring.

Elimination Inspections

The Soviet agreement to on-site observation of the elimination of strategic systems needed to achieve the agreed limits demonstrates their acceptance of the concept. Thus, the elimination measures in the INF Treaty and the rights, obligations, and procedures in the INF Protocol on Elimination are likely to be adopted for similar weapons systems, support equipment, and structures in START. If so, on-site inspection rights for every strategic system and every method of elimination should be expected. Additional elimination procedures will be required for ALCM-carrying heavy bombers, heavy bombers that are not ALCM carriers, SLBM launchers, silo launchers, railmobile launchers, and launch-related support equipment and structures for those three types of launchers.

Decisions about whether heavy bomber and SSBN conversion will be permitted are still pending. If conversions are permitted, verification procedures will need to be developed. Because the stages of some of the larger strategic missiles could be used as space launch boosters, either side may seek the right to convert some ballistic missiles for space launch purposes. Although such conversions would be cost-effective, the possibility that boosters could be reconverted to ballistic missiles is an issue that will require careful scrutiny.

Finally, there is the question of eliminating missiles by launching. Some critics believe that this method of elimination during the first six months of INF was ill advised because it might have provided useful missile reliability data that would have not otherwise have been available due to the flight test ban. Since there is no flight test restriction in START, however, there is no apparent reason that elimination of missiles by launching should be dropped.

Additional Inspection Requirements

Additional on-site inspection provisions that were not covered by the joint summit statement will be necessary to confirm the elimination of bases and support facilities and systems that are accidentally destroyed or placed on static display, as well as, perhaps training missiles, launch canisters, stages, and launchers. Inspection provisions may also be needed to confirm the number of reentry vehicles on deployed ICBMs and SLBMs and for nuclear-armed SLCMs.

Closeout Inspections

The joint summit statement did not provide for closeout inspections of strategic facilities, possibly because these inspections were considered to be of secondary importance. The omission may have been intentional, based on the Soviets' perception that these inspections would have accorded greater legitimacy to the U.S. proposal that mobile ICBM launchers and launch-related support equipment and support structures be eliminated. Alternatively, it may have been unintentional, since START will reduce rather than eliminate all strategic systems; elimination of systems like SS-11s or Minuteman IIs, may not ever have been considered.

Closeout inspection provisions will become necessary over time since various types of strategic systems will be eliminated eventually due to the unlimited duration of the treaty. Obviously if the U.S. mobile ICBM ban is accepted, closeout inspections will be necessary in the early years of the treaty. The INF rights, obligations, and procedures for closeout inspections are likely to be adopted for strategic facilities associated with classes of missiles slated for total elimination.

Other Elimination Inspections

As in INF, it would be desirable to secure the right to conduct inspections to confirm the elimination of missiles, heavy bombers, mobile launchers, and so forth resulting from accidents or loss. The likelihood of a treaty-limited item's being lost, with an assumed location, is more significant in START because of the presence of heavy bombers and SSBNs. This inspection right would also become more important in the eventuality that a number of items are said to be destroyed in a single accident. The right to confirm that treaty-limited items placed on static display are in fact inoperative also is more important in START than in INF because of the use of multiple independently targetable reentry vehicles and the overall destructive capability of strategic missiles.

When all missiles or launchers of a particular type are eliminated from the inventory, it would be desirable also to eliminate trainers for that type of missile or launcher in order to avoid potential compliance problems. If the treaty were to require that training missiles, training missile stages, training launch canisters, and training launchers be destroyed, the parties would be obliged to verify their destruction. The formal right to confirm completion of the destruction process by on-site inspection would be useful, though the United Stated may decide to exercise that right randomly in any case.

Deployed RV Inspections

The START Treaty will list the number of RVs attributed to each type of deployed ballistic missile. As stated in the summit statement, the sides agreed that "procedures will be developed that enable verification of the number of warheads (RVs) on deployed ballistic missiles of each specific type."

Since national technical means cannot be used to determine the number of RVs on ICBMs or SLBMs when they are in their launch tubes, on-site inspection appears to be the only means of accomplishing this task. Neither side wishes to provide visual access to RVs mounted on missiles, however, so verifying the number of RVs while avoiding visual access will require considerable ingenuity.

Random inspection of statistically derived numbers of ICBMs in an ICBM deployment area and of SLBMs in the launch tubes of an SSBN could provide a desirable level of confidence. This would avoid the need for time-consuming inspection of all ICBMs or SLBMs in their respective launchers.

The most obvious method of confirming the number of RVs on a missile without providing visual access to the actual RVs would be to use some type of portable sensor. The sensor would have to be able to identify the number of nuclear warheads without revealing warhead characteristics or disabling any missile components. There are apparently several types of sensors that are worth considering.

SLCM Inspections

In the joint summit statement, it was agreed that

> the sides shall find a mutually acceptable solution to the question of limiting the deployment of long-range, nuclear-armed SLCMs. Such limitations will not involve counting long-range, nuclear-armed SLCMs within the 6000 warhead and 1600 strategic offensive delivery systems limits. The sides com-

mitted themselves to establish ceilings on such missiles, and to seek mutually acceptable and effective methods of verification of such limitations, which could include the employment of national technical means, cooperative measures and on-site inspections.

The fact that "deployed" SLCMs are to be limited, rather than the total inventory of both deployed and nondeployed systems, eliminates one verification obstacle. Because SLCMs can be concealed in virtually any building, it would be impossible to verify effectively limits on nondeployed SLCMs. Thus, the verification challenge will require accounting for long-range, nuclear-armed SLCMs aboard submarines and surface ships. Although this helps to bound the task, a number of verification problems remain.

If long-range is defined as a range greater than 1,000 kilometers, for instance, we would have little assurance that an excluded SLCM with a declared range of 750 kilometers did not have a range greater than 1,000 kilometers. Replacing heavier conventional warheads with nuclear warheads and adding fuel could also extend the range of a shorter-range SLCM beyond the range threshold.

The provision limiting nuclear-armed missiles is a verification nightmare in a world of dual-capable cruise missiles, such as the long-range, land-attack Tomahawk SLCM, which can be armed with either conventional or nuclear warheads. The mix of antiship, land-attack, conventional, and nuclear SLCMs, as well as other nuclear systems aboard many U.S. Navy ships, adds to the problems of verification. The potential number of SLCMs aboard each vessel would be bounded only by its storage capacity, which can be significant on surface ships. Even if the number of nuclear warheads aboard each SLCM-capable vessel were limited and checked prior to departure from port, concerns would remain about covert loading beyond the port.

These verification problems seem to indicate that continuous inspector presence aboard all SLCM capable vessels would be necessary to monitor nuclear-armed SLCM loadings. This is unrealistic. If nuclear warheads were permitted for other weapons systems and conventional long-range SLCMs were aboard, even a continuous presence could not prevent SLCM warhead conversion in time of crisis.

Potential circumvention options undermine the U.S. ability to verify limits on long-range, nuclear-armed SLCMs effectively with any type of inspection regime that has been envisioned thus far. Nevertheless, the sides have agreed that deployed nuclear-armed SLCMs will be constrained in some way. Unless a verification breakthrough occurs, some variation of "each side merely declaring its planned number of nuclear-armed SLCMs," which has been suggested, may be as reasonable as any other approach. Although not an ideal outcome, this approach would acknowledge the need to constrain nuclear-armed SLCMs and the fact that the constraint cannot be effectively verified. Safeguards against breakout could be developed to reduce the risks inherent in this type of declaratory approach.

Conclusions

Verification of START will be more difficult than INF largely because of the residual levels of strategic systems that will remain. Verification and compliance will also be more important because the incentive to cheat could be greater after substantial cuts in strategic forces. At a minimum, the START Treaty must include the types of on-site inspection contained in the INF Treaty if it is to survive Senate scrutiny during the ratification debate.

On-site inspection in START will be used primarily to help verify numerical limits on nondeployed ICBMs and SLBMs. This measure will become more important if mobile ICBMs are permitted under the treaty, given the much greater refire potential of mobile launchers as compared to silo launchers or SSBNs. As is the case in INF, expectations about the benefits of on-site inspection must be realistic. Baseline inspections and short-range notice inspections will provide a better understanding of Soviet activities but will not be able to reveal a smoking gun. The threat of short-notice inspection is unlikely to dissuade a determined Soviet effort to conduct illegal activities at either declared or undeclared facilities. It should effectively deter illegal activities at formerly declared bases and support facilities where all strategic activities had been terminated, however.

The verification payoffs from suspect-site inspection do not warrant the risk of compromising sensitive military and intelligence activities at key U.S. facilities. The U.S. political commitment to securing inspection rights at undeclared facilities in START, however, must be taken into account. The recent U.S. proposal for suspect-site inspection with a right of refusal and mandatory inspection of agreed nonstrategic missile facilities seeks to balance the need for inspection of suspicious sites against the requirement to protect sensitive sites unrelated to the START Treaty.

Despite the costs and counterintelligence concerns, continuous perimeter/portal monitoring will likely be the centerpiece of the U.S. on-site inspection package in START. It will be used to monitor the flow of new missiles (and mobile launchers) into the inventory. Over time, this will improve U.S. confidence in its calculation of the total missile inventory as older missiles are retired. Continuous monitoring may also be sought at depot-level missile and launcher repair and storage facilities to prevent illegal use of those facilities and to provide an accurate count of systems at those facilities.

Observation of the elimination of strategic systems will permit the United States to verify the elimination of declared numbers of systems effectively, but the question of whether the Soviets have declared all their systems will remain uncertain. On-site inspection will probably be needed for heavy bomber and SSBN conversion, as well as the conversion of some number of missiles for space launch purposes if such conversions are allowed. Inspection provisions will be needed to confirm the elimination of bases and support facilities, systems that are accidentally destroyed or placed on static display, and training missiles, launchers, and so forth, if trainers must be destroyed.

On-site inspection is the only apparent means of effectively verifying the number of warheads (RVs) on deployed ballistic missiles. Portable sensors may permit U.S. inspectors to confirm the number of RVs on a missile without actual visual access.

Potential circumvention options undermine the ability of the United States to verify limits on long-range, nuclear-armed SLCMs with any type of inspection regime that has been envisioned thus far. Nevertheless, the sides have agreed that deployed nuclear-armed SLCMs will be constrained. Unless a verification breakthrough occurs, some variation of "each side merely declaring its planned number of nuclear-armed SLCMs" may be as reasonable as any other approach.

There is a synergistic effect among the various types of on-site inspection in START, as well as the inspection packages in START and INF, which increases overall confidence. The two agreements would provide access to the bases and infrastructures for almost all strategic and intermediate-range systems, helping to constrain some of the most likely and feasible cheating scenarios.

Finally, we return to the original question: Will the types of on-site inspection that are being used in INF, and probably will be used in START, contribute more to verification and political stability than they will cost? The political commitment to on-site inspection may change as the benefits, limitations, and costs are more fully understood. Some types of on-site inspection, such as continuous perimeter/portal monitoring, elimination inspections, closeout inspections, and short-notice inspections of former bases, increase the ability of the United States to verify certain treaty provisions. Conversely, the verification value of other types of on-site inspection, such as baseline inspections and short-notice inspections of declared and undeclared facilities, is debatable. Policymakers should fully understand the limitations and costs of those types of inspections prior to any final decisions about alternative verification measures.

Note

1. "Reagan Approves Limited Inspection of Weapons Sites," *New York Times*, October 26, 1988, p. 1.

7

On-Site Observation and Nonnuclear Arms Agreements: Too Short To Sell, Too Long to Throw Away

Christopher J. Makins

Thdots is is a chapter about on-site inspection by an author who has, for the most part, been at best an off-site observer of the subject for several years. It is therefore more consumed with laying out a framework for addressing the subject than with detailed analysis of the issues. Given the apparent paucity of literature on the subject and its inherent complexity, this may be no bad thing.

The first problem is the proper scope. The subject lacks—and may be increasingly subject to confusing and harmful influence from—the relatively precise and accepted notions of on-site inspection related to nuclear or chemical arms agreements. The body of wisdom assembled in the Conference on Security and Cooperation in Europe (CSCE), the Mutual and Balanced Force Reductions (MBFR), and the Conference on Disarmament in Europe (CDE) is certainly helpful in defining the field. That wisdom is, of course, entirely focused on Europe. The potential value of on-site inspections elsewhere in the world in connection with nonnuclear arms agreements seems to have been little studied, with the partial exception of the Middle East, where various schemes for demilitarization have attracted thoughts (and in Sinai the implementation) of on-site observation arrangements. I will follow the pattern of focusing on Europe—and particularly Central Europe—for the usual reasons.

A further question of scope concerns the types of measures to be discussed. Although the assigned topic refers to on-site inspection, there are reasons for using instead the broader term of on-site observation in this context. This alternative term is less tied to the concept of monitoring compliance with specific limitations of some kind and more readily covers possible free-standing measures that are in themselves designed to enhance security.

The first category of measures consists of familiar procedures like baseline and closeout inspections, steady-state observation (such as continuous monitoring of facilities or transit points by humans or unattended sensors), and periodic inspections, whether by invitation or by challenge, intended to ascertain compliance with agreed limits of some kind. The second category consists of two types of measures: those (such as liaison officers with military units or military attachés with expanded mandates) for which the primary purpose is to generate information of certain kinds, unrelated to specific limits, and those that are intended to deter or inhibit certain activities (for example, preparations for surprise attack or the use or movement of certain types of equipment). Most attention seems to have been devoted to the first of these categories, although the second periodically receives a minor spate of interest.

Beyond the categorization of the measures themselves, there is an important distinction concerning the purpose of the regime of which on-site observation measures form a part. In general, most of the ideas advanced for nonnuclear arms agreements in Europe seem to have been designed to serve one or more of three purposes.

1. The prevention, or the reduction of the risk, of surprise attack. This has probably been the most frequently asserted purpose although not necessarily the one most likely to be achieved by the measures periodically proposed by the West.

2. The inhibition of the use of Soviet forces for coercion of the non-Soviet Warsaw Pact countries. This purpose has often been unstated or played down but should not be overlooked.

3. The achievement of greater stability in the military balance in Central Europe, whether or not explicitly linked to a reduction in U.S. forces in the region. Such concepts as "greater security at lower levels of forces" tend to be used to describe this goal, though lower or even more equal force levels would not necessarily lead to greater security (for example, against surprise attack).

The importance and efficacy of different on-site observation measures will vary in relation to which of these, or other, purposes they are intended to serve.

There is a further distinction that bears on this point among the different types of situation in which the measures may have to operate. These vary from peacetime, in which the measures' primary function is to confirm that there is no departure from the normal state of affairs, including compliance with agreed limits, to varying levels of escalation of a crisis and eventual deescalation from it, in which their principal potential value would be to facilitate crisis assessment and response.

One question that has often been raised is whether any on-site observation measures (or other confidence- and security-building measures) should be thought of as being applicable to crisis periods. The most reasonable assumption is that in one way or another, such measures would be suspended as a crisis deepened—at least in the sense that they were no longer allowed to work by one side or both and that whatever value their absence had as an indicator of aggressive intent had been realized. However, they could conceivably be reinstated as part of a deliberate attempt by both sides to strengthen confidence in a step-by-step climb down from crisis.

The importance of these distinctions becomes clearer when one examines the way in which on-site observation measures actually work. With the exception of measures that are in themselves intended to deter or inhibit certain actions, the most frequently touted measures operate by providing the observing country with access to information. This information, obviously enough, supplements other information on the phenomena observed on-site that is already available to some or all of the countries that will receive it. So the value of the additional information gathered by the on-site observation is dependent on whether it has a beneficial or positive effect on the assessments and actions of the observing side.

The question of what constitutes positive value is not quite as easy to answer as it might seem. One can say that information has positive value if it helps the observing side to reach an accurate understanding of the phenomena observed and to take "correct" and timely action (or inaction). This means, of course, that it should help to avoid both false negatives and false positives and that it should generate neither greater ambiguity nor greater certainty in the minds of the observing side than is warranted by the situation. It is fairly obvious, and has been quite widely noted at least in general terms, that information from on-site observation—and indeed the very existence of procedures that enabled such observation to take place—could result in a less accurate understanding of the observed phenomena and a less "correct" and timely response to them on the part of the North Atlantic Treaty Organization (NATO).

One can in theory distinguish nine cases that are relevant to thinking about this problem. These are defined by three possible states of Soviet–Warsaw Pact intentions and three corresponding states of Western perceptions of those intentions. The three states are benign, ambiguous, and malign. For any situation in which actual Soviet–Warsaw Pact intentions are in one of these states, Western perceptions of those intentions could be in any one of the three states, depending on the accuracy of the Western interpretation of what was known about Soviet–Warsaw Pact behavior. The issue for on-site observation in a particular situation is whether the increment of information generated by on-site observation measures would tend to bring Western perceptions more in line with actual Soviet–Warsaw Pact intentions or to create or confirm an inaccurate perception.

This may seem like a rather abstract line of reasoning, but it can lead to some useful insights. A full-scale analysis of this subject would proceed by identifying a range of on-site observation measures and the degree of accuracy and timeliness of information they could be expected to generate in peacetime and crisis. It would take into account the potential for the kinds of spoofing and delay that might be regarded as normal, or at least compatible with a benign intent on the part of the other side. It would then assess the likely value of the information that would be generated by the observations in relation to the other information likely to be available to the allies in those situations and its likely impact on the timeliness and desirability of their response.

Such an analysis is not possible in this chapter for several reasons, only one of which is the classification problems it presents. What can be said is that as national technical means of gathering and processing information have become steadily more capable, the value of incremental information, except perhaps information of certain highly specific kinds, has presumably become much less. To quote a recent House of Representatives Intelligence Committee report:

> the general size and disposition of Warsaw Pact armed forces, as well as their organization and armaments, can be monitored with considerable confidence. Additionally, in a major crisis, our capability is sufficient to detect rather promptly a major mobilization and movement by Warsaw Pact forces to a war footing.

Against this background, I will offer a set of comments on the types of on-site observation measures related to non-nuclear forces that might prove of interest, the contexts, if any, in which they might have positive value for the West, and some issues that arise in considering which, if any, it would be desirable to promote in forthcoming negotiations.

Categories of On-Site Observation Measures

The first and most familiar category of measures is on-site observation related to the monitoring of some kind of agreed limits on nonnuclear forces. At least three types of limits can be distinguished:

1. Manpower limits. These could be expressed in terms of total numbers of men under arms in a defined geographic area or in organizational terms (numbers or types of units). The difficulties associated with this kind of limit have been well explored in the Mutual and Balanced Force Reductions (MBFR) process. But it seems unlikely that such limits can be altogether avoided as part of any militarily significant future nonnuclear arms limitation regime in Europe.

2. Equipment limits. These could be expressed in terms of numerical limits or prohibitions on different categories of equipment in different geographical areas. Thus, zones from which particular types of equipment are banned fall under this category. Equipment limits are the current vogue in the field, although it is not always clear which of the possible purposes of an arms agreement they are designed, or likely, to serve.

3. Operational limits. These could be expressed in terms of the permitted number, size, and/or location of certain types of military activities. The most familiar limits of this type are those agreed at the Helsinki and Stockholm conferences on certain types of military activities. Other ideas of this kind that have been suggested include the agreed storage of certain types or quantities of equipment at designated sites that would be under on-site observation by the other side.

Observation of the first two types of limit and some of those of the third type would require that the observers have access to garrisons.

The second category of measures is on-site observation that is not related to any agreed limit but serves some other purpose of an arms agreement. Among the measures that have been discussed in this category are ones related to:

1. Out-of-garrison activities. These measures could include both the kind of observation agreed to at the Helsinki and Stockholm conferences (to the degree that they were not solely intended to permit the monitoring of agreed numerical limits) and various proposals made for monitoring movements into and out of specified areas either by human observation or by the use of remote monitoring using unattended sensors. One recent proposal makes quite substantial claims for the value of such observation in inhibiting, and presumably therefore deterring, Warsaw Pact preparations for a surprise attack.[1]

2. Other types of military activity. The kind of idea that has been suggested in this category is the attachment of liaison officers with military units of a specified size.

3. Facilities. Measures might be devised to permit the continuous monitoring of certain types of facility, such as storage facilities for equipment of various types, unrelated to any other numerical or operational limits.

In addition to such specific types of observation, there could be a general right of inspection on demand covering more than one type of activity or facility in a specified area.

The purposes of on-site observations in these categories are rather different. The primary purpose of observation related to quantitative or other limits would be to facilitate a decision about compliance or noncompliance with the limits. The primary value of observation not related to specific limits would be to establish an understanding of what constitutes normality and to facilitate the investigation—or direct inhibition—of apparent abnormality.

The most striking characteristic of the types of limits that are being proposed on nonnuclear forces in Europe is the scale of the numbers involved. The manpower numbers are in the hundreds of thousands, the equipment numbers in the tens of thousands. Few of the items of interest are numbered in fewer than thousands. To add to the difficulty, most of the items of interest are inherently hard to count and readily movable, unlike, for example, intercontinental ballistic missiles (ICBMs). It follows that even were cost no object, on-site inspection would be unlikely to contribute greatly to the numerical information necessary to make judgments about compliance. Although efforts might be made (and have been proposed) to develop statistically valid sampling schemes to cross check data gathered from other sources, there are serious methodological problems about doing this with any confidence, and there would probably be serious political and operational problems with any such regime.[2]

Technology may have an impact here in ways that affect the desirable forms of on-site observation. If tagging technology advances to the point at which limits on various categories of equipment can be determined by the number of secure tags given by each side to the other, on-site observation might have a role in confirming that there were no pieces of equipment in the controlled categories without the appropriate tags. While the exact nature of this role would depend on the tagging technology involved (for example, whether the tags could be remotely interrogated), no system of on-site observation seems likely to be able to do more than provide spot checks on compliance. Moreover, while large-scale deception would be difficult to conceal from challenge inspections, the best hope of detecting violations might well be through permanent liaison officers with units or military attachés with expanded access and roles, since their observations would be less easily controlled by the side being observed without giving a clear signal of malign intent.

In sum, on-site observation does not seem to offer a means of solving verification problems associated with quantitative limits on nonnuclear arms agreements as it has done, or might do, for agreements on INF or on nuclear testing or on intercontinental nuclear forces.

A more plausible role for on-site observation in relation to numerical limits is to help to establish a baseline from which other means of observation can proceed in monitoring agreements and to provide a method of investigating suspicious phenomena observed by other means. Precisely what observations would be relevant to the establishment of a baseline is hard to say without a detailed analysis of current intelligence resources. But it is possible that there would be some. The task of investigating suspicious phenomena is more problematical since it would be hard to be sure that by the time observers reached the scene, the phenomena they had come to observe would still be visible. Only if the observation could begin within a very short time of the decision that it was needed could one have confidence that any violation had not been concealed in the interim. The threat of observation might have some deterrent effect, but that is hard to measure.

This point raises again the distinction between the different value these measures might have in peacetime and in crises. At times of low tension, both sides might be presumed to have an incentive to cooperate in removing the suspicion of noncompliance from a suspicious phenomenon (that is, to revert to the schema proposed earlier to ensure that actual benign intention was matched by benign perception). But in a crisis, the situation might be different, with one side or another having reasons to act in ways that would tend to result in on-site observation creating a less correct relationship between actual intention and perception than might otherwise exist.

The second purpose of on-site observation measures—establishing a better understanding of what constitutes normality as a guide to recognizing abnormality—raises rather different considerations. First, it is inherently a peacetime function. Second, it is more concerned with the identification of patterns of behavior and the reasons for them than it is with the evaluation of specific actions such as would be essential to monitoring agreed limits.

The experience to date with Stockholm inspections is perhaps most relevant here.[3] Although those inspections were primarily designed to verify compliance with the agreed confidence and security building measures, (CSBMs) the reports on them suggest that their greatest value to the allies so far has been to increase the understanding of normality as it concerns Warsaw Pact training activities. The report by the U.S. inspectors on the sixth of the ten inspections conducted by mid-1988 states that not only was the inspection useful for verification but that it also made "a significant contribution to openness and the confidence-building process." The State Department's twenty-third semiannual report on the implementation of the Helsinki Final Act gives a more specific indication of how this contribution is being made: "as additional observation experience has been obtained, there is some sense that the stilted nature of Eastern activities may reflect actual differences in the way the Warsaw Pact trains, with less force-on-force and free-play action than in NATO exercises." Improvements in understanding of this kind could not be expected to continue indefinitely. But, once achieved, the repeated confirmation by observation that actual practice corresponded to previously established patterns—or departed from them in benign ways—could serve the purpose of sustaining confidence.

These conclusions may have particular force at a time at which there is discussion, at least, of a restructuring of Soviet and Warsaw Pact forces toward a more defensive posture. The ultimate practical significance, if any, of the measures recently announced by the Soviets and others that may follow remains to be seen. If anything practical comes of them, on-site observation could have a useful role to play in confirming the change. Moreover, presumably the Soviets would be anxious to have the West notice the change and should therefore not be averse to allowing it to be observed, within some reasonable limits.

Just what types—or additional frequency—of on-site observation would be desirable for this purpose beyond those already permitted or required by the Stockholm agreement is hard to say. On the face of it, the type of observation possible by liaison officers or military attachés with reasonable freedom of movement and access would probably be more valuable than intermittent observations by special teams. But whatever the most appropriate technique, the general point is that negotiating some observation measures may deserve high priority in order to build confidence in the significance of unilateral measures to restructure their forces that both sides may take over time.

Here too there is a concern about deception. Various schemes can be imagined for creating a pattern of normality that differs little from what would be expected for an abnormality—that is, preparation for an actual attack—at least in terms of the activities that would be observed in the Warsaw Pact forces in Central Europe. Such deception might be harder to carry out on a worldwide basis—for example, in terms of the surging of nuclear-powered ballistic-missile-carrying submarines (SSBNs) or other likely prewar measures—without triggering concern.

In that situation, the question would be whether on-site observation could be manipulated in such a way as to reassure, or at least confuse and so partially paralyze, the Western allies (the malign intention-ambiguous perception case in the schema suggested earlier). But that is, once again, to say little more than that once the peacetime function of these measures—as a pane of glass separating peacetime from crisis—had ended, they might actually do more harm than good. The challenge is to locate the pane of glass so that it gets shattered as early and unambiguously as possible in a preattack sequence and thus serves as a deterrent in itself.

Having discussed those types of on-site observation of nonnuclear forces that rely on the generation of information for the observing side, a word should be said about measures that operate in a different manner. Two such measures are the idea of inspections designed to disrupt the timing of a Warsaw Pact surprise attack, proposed by James Blaker, and the idea of permanently observed storage sites for equipment.[4] The latter is actually a hybrid measure in that it operates partly by the provision of information that the situation is normal and partly in the pane of glass mode that could serve as a deterrent.

From the vantage point of my general thesis here—that it is hard to expect any on-site observation measures to operate effectively in a deepening crisis—the idea that an inspection scheme can be used to disrupt key elements of preparations for a surprise attack in the two or three days before the attack is due to be launched seems heroic. An agreement that would permit inspections to be claimed at that stage of a crisis might, admittedly, yield the benefit of forcing the Soviets to deny an inspection and so to some extent tip their hand. Were such a denial to come out of the blue, it would certainly tend to confirm suspicions of malign intent. More likely, however, the signal would be more ambiguous, since in all probability the game of seeking and delaying or denying observations would have started earlier in the crisis and by the late stages it would no longer be clear whether such actions were responses to earlier actions by the other side or genuine efforts to cover up attack preparations. Thus, the value of the information that the denial of an observation would represent would not necessarily be unambiguous. And, in any case, as Blaker himself points out, existing intelligence-gathering techniques should be giving clear warning of Soviet intentions in the two or three days before an attack.

The idea of permanently supervised storage of equipment is interesting in the way in which, unlike other combinations of constraints and on-site observations, it bridges the peacetime role of on-site observations and their potential value in crises. The measure potentially offers unambiguous indications of mobilization—and perhaps premobilization training—activities that could be undertaken only at the political cost of breaking the pane of glass separating peacetime from serious military preparations.

The question is whether either side would agree to a measure that put an effective fence around equipment essential to the execution of key military missions. Thus as long as the Warsaw Pact requires the capability to execute a short-warning attack, it is hard to understand why it would agree to a measure of this kind. This is, of course, no reason why the allies should not propose such a measure. And here again, if the Soviets are serious about restructuring their forces in a more defensive direction, this is the kind of measure that might help build allied confidence that they were in fact implementing the change. Lastly, it is worth pointing out the potential synergy between equipment tagging and measures of this kind.[5]

Some preliminary conclusions can be suggested on the basis of the discussion thus far. First, it is important not to lose sight of the goals of whatever agreements are being discussed and to relate proposals for on-site observation to those goals. If the primary goal is to make surprise attack more difficult, if not impossible—a goal that Gorbachev has enunciated, for whatever reason, as well as Western spokesman—then the entire nonnuclear arms limitation regime should be calculated to achieve that goal, and any on-site observation measures should support it. The same is true for the other possible goals of a regime.

A second conclusion is that, especially in view of the quantities involved, on-site observation measures are unlikely to be able to play a major role in the verification of quantitative limits established in a nonnuclear forces arms agreement. There may, however, be a limited role for them in the establishment of a baseline for verification by generating information important to ongoing monitoring by national technical means and by providing a capability for random spot checks associated with certain types of quantitative limits. However, a carefully conceived and thorough exchange of data might be more valuable, and politically more acceptable, than the use of extensive on-site observation for the purpose of establishing a baseline and of subsequent monitoring of compliance.

Third, the best use of on-site observation of nonnuclear forces seems to be in the creation and maintenance of a good understanding of the normal pattern of activities of Warsaw Pact forces, especially during a period in which they may be undergoing significant structural change. For this purpose, measures that provide essentially continuous observation—such as liaison officers, expanded attaché systems, and possibly some permanent observation of equipment storage sites and other facilities or zones—may offer advantages over short-notice inspections on demand or on challenge.

Fourth, beyond this function of essentially building confidence, on-site observation may not have much to offer in the quest to deal directly with the problem of surprise attack. By the time such observations would most likely be available to help, other means of surveillance would almost certainly show even stronger evidence of Soviet–Warsaw Pact intentions, and there is little likelihood that inspections could be used to disrupt or delay attack preparations.

If on-site observations could be designed to give better information about the long lead, and probably more political, indicators of an attack, a different conclusion might be warranted. The idea of using permanently supervised storage of equipment that would be needed for premobilization training, even in connection with a short-warning attack, is one such approach that deserves further study. But in general, the kind of observations most often discussed (inspection of military units and activities) do not seem especially well calculated to assist in this regard.

Fifth, it is hard to propose measures that are explicitly designed to reduce the potential for Soviet political coercion of the Eastern European countries. To some degree, general confidence-building measures of the Stockholm variety will serve this purpose, although the alert exception to notifiable activities, which it is hard to imagine either side agreeing to drop, will always provide a way out for the Soviets. And it is possible to imagine a situation in which the presence of observers from allied countries and even from the targets of the coercion at activities in compliance with the agreement would actually amplify rather than diminish the political impact of Soviet military activities. One might hope, however, that if confidence were to grow and the sense of insecurity in Europe to diminish, it may be possible to arrive gradually at an agreed reduction in the total number of military activities and so make the use of routine activities for coercive purposes more difficult.

On-Site Observation in the Real World

It remains to comment on some practical and operational aspects of on-site observation measures as they would actually operate.

Alliance Factors

The complications presented by the fact that any nonnuclear forces arms agreements would affect all the members of the Atlantic Alliance have already been mentioned, but they deserve some elaboration. While it is obviously open to one or more of the allies to act alone in connection with any such agreements (such as in response to a perceived Warsaw Pact violation), such action would be more impressive if it came from the alliance as a whole. This lays on any on-site observation scheme the burden that it should not tend to increase the divisions within the alliance on the proper way to act in any given situation.

There are two ways in which such a scheme could increase alliance divisions:

1. It could affect the timing of an allied action. There is a good chance that, given the opportunity to use on-site observation to confirm a suspected Warsaw Pact breach of an agreement, some allies would wish to do so before reaching judgment. The consequent delay might or might not be serious. But the prospect of such a delay tends to confirm the view that the operation of on-site observation measures in a crisis, when time could be at a premium, could be problematical.

2. It could generate information that tended to increase the ambiguity of a situation that information from other sources made appear relatively, and correctly, unambiguous. In this situation, those in the alliance who might be looking for a reason not to make a strong response could use the on-site observation information to bolster their case.

This second point would be of particular importance if, as can be argued plausibly, the information generated by on-site observation, when set alongside information from other sources, would, at least in certain circumstances, have an inherent bias toward increasing ambiguity in Western perceptions. This bias could derive from two sources. The first is the nature of the on-site observation process itself and the interest that the side being observed will almost certainly have in acting in ways that increase the ambiguity of the observations. This could as well happen as a result of a misguided instinct to protect quite benign phenomena from observation (as has already been seen in some of the early Stockholm inspections) as from a conscious attempt to conceal malign phenomena in a crisis. It is probably fair to say that in peacetime this problem is not especially serious. There is at least a good prospect that as the process of Stockholm-type inspections shakes down, the rules of the road will become better understood and applied, and the potential for heightening ambiguity will diminish. At the same time, the beneficial results of such inspections may be increasingly recognized. But in periods of crisis, such an optimistic conclusion may not be warranted. Indeed, it can be argued that as intelligence information about military activities steadily improves, the premium on deception in a serious crisis steadily grows. If so, there would be a greater number of circumstances in which information generated by on-site observations would tend to add to the ambiguity.

Second is the fact that the value of the on-site observations, and of the ability to make them in different situations, will be different for different members of the alliance. For the United States, with its full panoply of national technical means of observation and its long experience of evaluating the information they yield, the incremental value of an on-site observation may be rather different from that for another alliance member. While this situation may change as a result of greater intelligence sharing among the allies and of technological developments (for example, Western European access to satellite surveillance information from Système pour Observation de la Terre (SPOT) and future systems), the United States is likely to find itself in a distinctly privileged situation for some time to come.

Against these arguments must be set two ways in which on-site observation could, at least in theory, have a beneficial effect within the alliance. First, by providing information that would be publicly usable, without any concern for security, it could make the presentation of strong allied responses to Warsaw Pact moves easier. Second, it could have an immediacy that would help to convince reluctant allies that something bad was afoot. The Cuban missile crisis, in which the aerial photography of the missile sites played an invaluable role in persuading European governments of the correctness of the U.S. view, is a case in point. The question is whether in practice the information from on-site observations would be such as to have either of these effects.

The proper balance to strike between these two sets of arguments is a matter of opinion. The most serious risk of damaging effect seems to be in a crisis situation, when the time for response may be short and the concern of some allies to avoid provocation high. If the measures were generally agreed by the allies to operate primarily, if not exclusively, in peacetime, the risks would be smaller and the possibility of realizing the benefits greater.

Cost

It is not easy to say much about the cost of on-site observation measures in the absence of a clearly defined regime. Suffice it to say that cost considerations tend to reinforce the conclusion that on-site observation is unlikely to be a useful primary tool for monitoring quantitative limits on nonnuclear forces. The reason for this is once again the numbers of objects, including people, that would need to be observed. The burden on the intelligence apparatus of monitoring such a regime is likely to be quite large without adding the requirement for a huge additional observation machine, which would probably make only a marginal contribution to the vertification process. Beyond that, the likely cost, human and material, of any on-site observation measures should be looked at carefully in relation to the expected benefit and in the light of growing experience with the INF treaty and possible future monitoring schemes in the nuclear realm.

Reciprocity

Somewhat similar arguments arise in connection with the need for reciprocal application of any measures on the allied side. In both the MBFR and CSCE/CDE negotiations there was a long struggle to find a regime that the Federal Republic of Germany would accept as not requiring an undesirable level of oversight of German territory by the East. There would surely be a similar struggle if there were any suggestion of an on-site observation regime for nonnuclear forces comprehensive enough to enable it to make a significant contribution to the monitoring of quantitative limits or other stringent measures. In addition, the rather different sensitivities of the French will now have to be accommodated.

There is the additional point that any level of access demanded by the allies will have to be conceded in reverse. Again it is hard to draw any precise conclusions without specifying in some detail the regime envisaged. But it is a reasonable assumption that the allies would not find it easy to allow the degree of access needed to provide high assurance of compliance with a complicated regime of quantitative equipment and manpower limits.

Finally, there seems to have been relatively little study of the potential value of military attachés with expanded access and in larger numbers or of the idea of liaison officers with military units. The experience of the Military Liaison Mission in Germany is obviously relevant in connection with the first of these ideas. The value of using liaison officers would presumably be directly proportional to the degree of freedom of movement and action that the officers would have. Both concepts deserve greater study, especially in relation to logistical factors, such as communications and transportation, which could prove to be their Achilles heels by initiating the timely flow of information additional to that already available from other sources.

Challenge and Response

The history of arms control offers many examples, some discouraging, of how agreements can become the object of elaborate games among the parties. Often these revolve around questions of compliance. On-site observation measures should fit into this pattern since challenge inspection measures lend themselves particularly well to mutual testing of the limits of tolerance of the other side. Some of this may already have occurred with the Stockholm inspections in relation to the provisions for sensitive points and restricted areas. Other schemes have also been suggested, such as packing the list of notified activities to make military preparations that might be needed for coercive or hostile purposes seem routine.

If an arms limitation regime is to create greater stability and less risk, games of this kind will have to be prevented to avoid undermining the confidence that the regime could help build. Two possibilities suggest themselves:

1. Some sort of dispute-settlement system that might involve neutral and nonaligned countries as well as NATO and Warsaw Pact members. Such a scheme, which might specify special on-site inspections, could help build political consensus behind well founded allegations of noncompliance.

2. Some kind of tit-for-tat response scheme designed to promote cooperative behavior and reinforce the regime.[6] Although the theory of this approach might not be controversial, the practical application of it on an alliance basis would no doubt be difficult. There would almost inevitably be disagreements among the allies about the scope of Warsaw Pact infringement of the letter of the agreements and about the nature of appropriate allied responses.

The importance of using some such measures to preserve the rules of the road necessary for the satisfactory implementation of an agreement should not be overlooked.

The games would become especially delicate in a building crisis. Both sides no doubt would wish to use the on-site observation measures to embarrass the other while freeing themselves from any inconvenient restraint the measures might impose. In terms of existing or future CDE inspection measures, there would be the additional complications introduced by the neutral and nonaligned countries, which, particularly if they were involved in the crisis (as, for example, Yugoslavia could well be), could introduce a wholly new dimension to the game. Consideration of on-site observation measures in crisis scenarios suggests that there would be multiple opportunities for one side to try to put the onus on the other for undermining the regime, in effect, absolving itself from continuing to honor it.

By the same token, scenarios involving domestic political crises in Eastern European countries suggest ways in which on-site observation measures could be exploited by one or other faction in the dispute to try to draw outside countries (willingly or unwillingly) into the situation in potentially provocative ways. These are some of the perverse effects of such measures that need to be explored more thoroughly.

Crisis Escalation and Deescalation

The problem of avoiding the potentially damaging effect of on-site observation measures in a crisis has led some people to suggest that there should be a mechanism for suspending their application once a crisis has started to build. It has even been suggested that the very act of suspending the measures could have a salutary effect, serving as a warning of the seriousness with which one side views an emerging situation. Conversely, there is the argument that the act of suspension could in itself heighten tension and would most likely be seen as provocative by at least some of the NATO allies in almost any situation, to the point that it might never be made.

There is no wholly satisfactory resolution of this problem. In all likelihood, both sides would willingly let the measures lapse at a certain point while trying to pin the blame on the other side. The most that can be hoped is that if a crisis develops, the sharing of intelligence among the allies will be sufficiently good that the potential value of on-site observations will seem trivial to all of them and therefore not a hindrance to decision making. But that would not automatically dispose of the political arguments for using them as a delaying tactic.

The value of on-site observation in helping build confidence in the deescalation of a crisis is a relatively unexplored subject. But the same features that make such measures attractive for peacetime confidence building also apply to deescalation situations. Both sides could be presumed to have an interest in building confidence in such a situation, since by definition the crisis would have passed its peak. Admittedly a similar problem of timing as was noted in connection with a decision to suspend measures in a crisis would arise in reaching the decision that deescalation had started. Nevertheless, there would almost certainly be a time at which both sides had reached the conclusion that the other wanted to deescalate. At that point, the introduction (or reintroduction) of some on-site observation measures could be useful.

The Role of Time

One of the paradoxes of arms agreements is that they attempt to apply a static and precise approach to the creation of greater security in a highly dynamic world and in a field—military affairs—in which precision is hard to achieve and uncertainty is rife. This could hardly be more true than of the nonnuclear balance in Central Europe. Not only are the purely military relationships involved changing continually but the political relationships are also in flux. Indeed, it is a fundamental tenet of Western policy that the political arrangements established after World War II are unacceptable to the West in the long run.

The evolution of greater security in Europe at lower levels of armaments will be more an organic political process than the product of a series of discrete acts such as nuclear arms agreements. If there are certain military changes that need to be made on the Western side to accommodate an imperative of reducing U.S. forces, for example, it is probably preferable to make them unilaterally rather than to force them into the straitjacket of an arms negotiation in which they may become involved with new problems, not least verification.

One might conclude that a desirable characteristic of any nonnuclear arms agreements in Central Europe should be their ability to accommodate change over time. This is especially true at a time at which there is a prospect of significant change in the orientation of Soviet forces, as a result of Gorbachev's recent initiatives, and of an evolution in the political relationships within the Warsaw Pact and between its members and NATO. On-site observation measures offer one means for making benign change of this kind more visible and thus more readily accepted. As always, there is the problem of spoofing, but the attempt to spoof is not without risk to the spoofer. And, again as always, the military significance of cheating needs to be evaluated alongside the potential benefit of a proposed agreement.

Can of Worms or Box of String?

It is hard to draw definitive conclusions from such a broad discussion. Nevertheless, if only to provoke debate, it is important to try to sketch a bottom line.

The first point to note is that, after being early in the field as compared with other areas of arms negotiations, on-site observation of nonnuclear forces arms agreements is now in the shadow of experience and theology.

This is potentially a dangerous situation. It is important to consider non-nuclear force arms negotiations in their own terms and in the light of the very different challenges they present, notably because of the numbers and complexities of the forces involved and of the political relationships on which they impinge.

Second, on-site observation measures have a role in this process, but they are inherently fragile and should not have too great a burden placed upon them. In the present political and intellectual climate, in which nearly 100 percent certainty of prompt verification of even small and strategically insignificant violations of agreements is important, it would be wrong to expect on-site observation measures to make up for the inadequacy of other techniques for monitoring nonnuclear forces. Given the logistical, political, and other problems associated with a tight on-site observation regime, it would be preferable by far to confine their role to what they can do with some assurance: help build confidence and serve as a pane of glass that stands in the way of an aggressor. Just as no one expects a window to prevent burglary, so no one should expect on-site observations to prevent a surprise attack or an act of military repression or even to provide much advance warning of its coming.

Third, the objectives stated for on-site observation measures, and for nonnuclear forces arms agreements in general, should be commensurate with reasonable expectations of what they can achieve and compatible with the view that improving security in Europe is most likely to be the product of complex political processes over a long period of time, not of major doses of negotiated limitation and reduction. The most viable objectives may be among the most modest, and the most ambitious—such as preventing or reducing the risk of surprise attack—may be beyond reach.

It need not be an admission of failure to accept this fact. Indeed, as I have repeatedly suggested, the prospect of a serious move toward the restructuring of Warsaw Pact forces creates an opportunity for the introduction of on-site observation measures in advance of, or separate from, quantitative limits on force levels. By making more transparent whatever changes the Soviets and their allies decide to make and by providing a means for NATO to reassure—or disarm—those on the Warsaw Pact side who argue that NATO has offensive intent, well-conceived on-site observation measures could facilitate the eventual negotiation of more stringent quantitative limits. . The possibility of making the negotiation of such measures a high priority for NATO in the new talks on conventional forces in Europe deserves greater attention than it has so far received from NATO governments.

Imposing too ambitious a set of demands on on-site observation in connection with nonnuclear forces arms agreements in Europe could very well turn the measures into a can of worms. I believe that it would be preferable to treat them more as the British gentleman once treated certain pieces of string—by putting them into a box marked "too short to sell, too long to throw away." In the same way, on-site observation measures are too weak to provide major support for quantitative limitations on nonnuclear forces or to deal with the surprise attack problem but too strong to be discarded altogether as instruments to promote greater security in Europe and, by extension, elsewhere.

Notes

1. See James Blaker, "Transparency, Inspections and Surprise Attack," in *Common Security in Europe, vol. 2: Cooperative Security* (Adderbury, Oxfordshire: Foundation for International Security, May 1987).
2. For a fuller and more detailed statement of the general view put forward here, see Robert D. Blackwill, "Conceptual Problems of Conventional Arms Control," *International Security* 12 no. 4 (Spring 1988).
3. These comments are based on review of the results of Stockholm inspections up until the summer of 1988.
4. Blaker, "Transparency." Blaker's claim is that as a result of such an inspection, compounded by subsequent NATO military action, a "delay of up to 28 hours in the arrival of the lead elements of a second echelon army seems reasonable" and that the combat potential of first-echelon divisions could also be significantly degraded.
5. Similar arguments apply to proposals for border zones free of particular types of weapons, though such proposals can pose additional operational problems in terms of their application to NATO.
6. For a discussion of the theory of this idea and its application to nuclear arms agreements, see Christopher J. Makins, "The Superpower's Dilemma," *Survival* (July–August 1985).

8
Verification of a Chemical Weapons Ban: The On-Site Inspection Burden

John Barrett

T he Soviet Union's acceptance in August 1987 of the principle of stringent anytime, anywhere challenge inspections, first proposed in the draft chemical weapons treaty tabled by the United States at the multilateral Geneva Conference on Disarmament in 1984 constituted a significant step toward a chemical weapons convention. Yet even as the Soviet Union moved to the U.S. position on verification, there have been signs of some uneasiness in the West concerning the intrusiveness of on-site inspection, especially short-notice, challenge inspections. Chemical industries in Western countries have begun to look closely at the impact of such inspections on day-to-day operations and to assess the risk of loss of confidential commercial information. National security establishments have started to highlight possible compromise of sensitive national security data. For the United States, constitutional protection for private businesses could clash with the kind of powers of search to be wielded by inspectors from the chemical weapons convention inspectorate in carrying out challenge on-site inspections.

Increased reliance on more systematic on-site inspection based on exchanges of data and information would be a possible alternative to extensive emphasis on challenge inspections. Routine advance notice inspections (for example, to confirm data on chemical weapons–related activities), as well as continuous monitoring with instruments (of civilian chemical facilities, for instance) could be both more technologically feasible and politically acceptable. In effect, greater emphasis might be placed on verification of countries' declarations—as with safeguards under the Nuclear Non-Proliferation Treaty—rather than on detection of illegal activities.

But will increased reliance on systematic monitoring of declared activities be considered adequate verification?[1] There already is a growing debate in the West about the adequacy of on-site inspection, even with extensive challenge inspections, to monitor compliance with a complete and total ban

This chapter was completed before the author joined the Canadian Department of External Affairs. It represents his personal views and not necessarily those of the Canadian government.

of chemical weapons. What are the limits of on-site inspection in verification of a chemical weapons ban? What measures could be taken to compensate for those limits, from increasing the costs of noncompliance to strengthening security guarantees and assistance to new adherents? How would such measures affect the risks of adherence to a complete ban, from the perspectives of Western and Third World countries?

The first step toward assessment of these issues is an understanding of the general features of the projected Chemical Weapons Convention, along with a detailed description of its on-site inspection provisions. This is based on the current rolling text, (the draft treaty, parts of which are agreed to, and parts of which are under negotiation or remain incomplete) as set out in Conference on Disarmament document CD/881 (February 3, 1989).

Basic Undertakings of the Draft Chemical Weapons Convention

The overall goal of the Chemical Weapons Convention now being negotiated is complete and total chemical weapons disarmament. As stated in Article I of the rolling text, each party to the convention undertakes not to "develop, produce, otherwise acquire, stockpile or retain chemical weapons, or transfer, directly or indirectly, chemical weapons to anyone." Parties also agree not to "assist, encourage or induce, in any way, anyone to engage in activities prohibited to Parties under this Convention" or to use chemical weapons. Each party further undertakes to destroy its chemical weapons, as well as the chemical weapons production facilities in its possession or under its "[jurisdiction or] control."[2]

Consistent with these basic obligations regarding chemical weapons activities, Article II of the convention (as elaborated by Article VI) divides the chemicals that might be used in a weapons capacity into three main categories, or schedules. Schedule[1] comprises supertoxic lethal chemicals, such as nerve agents and mustard gas. These have no purpose other than to be used in a chemical weapons capacity. Except for limited quantities for research, medical, or protective purposes, the production, stockpiling, and possession of these chemicals are prohibited. Schedule [2] chemicals are largely those that do have a legitimate commercial application yet can still serve as so-called key precursors to the banned chemical weapons agents listed in Schedule [1]. Schedule [3] lists chemicals that have a chemical weapons potential but are used on a large scale for legitimate peaceful purposes; examples are phosgene, chlorine, and hydrogen cyanide.

Article II also defines purposes not prohibited by the convention: "(a) industrial, agricultural, research, medical or other peaceful purposes; and military purposes not connected with the use of chemical weapons; (b) protective purposes, namely those purposes directly related to protection against chemical weapons."

Other articles of the convention obligate parties to undertake a series of actions to implement the basic ban on chemical weapons activities. Article III requires declarations concerning the existence or possession of chemical weapons and/or the facilities to produce them on its national territory; Article IV contains the basic obligations and undertakings regarding chemical weapons possession and the process by which such weapons will be destroyed; Article V sets out requirements for closure of chemical weapons production facilities, as well as steps for the destruction of the factories that produce chemical weapons; and Article VI regulates chemical production activities, including civilian chemical industry processes, that are not prohibited by the convention. In addition, under Article VII, the Organization for the Prohibition of Chemical Weapons is created, with a consultative committee or general conference, an executive council, a technical secretariat, and an international inspectorate.

Because of the limits of national technical means, the Chemical Weapons Convention relies heavily on an international on-site presence for monitoring compliance with its obligations. In part, this entails continuous monitoring of sites and facilities with specialized on-site instruments, such as automatic data gathering and sampling devices, tamperproof seals, and cameras. It also involves international on-site inspections conducted on both a routine (or systematic) and ad hoc (or challenge) basis.

Verification Provisions I: Continuous Monitoring and Systematic International Inspections

Continuous monitoring and systematic inspections, carried out by an international inspectorate within the technical secretariat created by the convention, are to be used to monitor a broad range of treaty-limited activities, from declarations of chemical weapons stocks to permitted activities with certain chemical weapons precursors.[3]

Verification of Declarations of Chemical Weapons

According to the convention, each state party possessing chemical weapons must specify "the [precise location,] aggregate quantity and detailed inventory of any chemical weapons under its jurisdiction or control" (Article IV, para. 22) and submit the declaration within thirty days after the convention enters into force for it. After submission of declarations concerning chemical weapons' possession, their location, and quantities, access is to be provided promptly to the international inspectorate to all declared chemical weapons storage sites and depots to "verify the quantity and identity of chemicals, types and number of munitions, devices and other equipment" (Annex IV, section II, para. 4a). Agreed seals, markers, and other inventory control procedures would be used to ensure that an accurate inventory of chemical weapons at each storage facility can be established and maintained to preclude the possibility of stocks being removed surreptitiously.

International Systematic Monitoring of Storage Facilities

International systematic monitoring is provided to ensure that no undetected removal of chemical weapons takes place from declared storage facilities (Annex IV, section II, para. 5a). Such monitoring is to be initiated "as soon as possible after the declaration of chemical weapons is submitted and shall continue until all chemical weapons have been removed from the storage facility" (Annex IV, section II, paras. 5b, 5c). The actual details of such monitoring will result from a follow-up agreement on subsidiary arrangements between the host state and the convention's technical secretariat. It will rely on both continuous monitoring with instruments and systematic verification by international on-site inspections.

With regard to periodic on-site inspections of storage facilities, guidelines are now taking shape, though the frequency of systematic inspections has yet to be determined. Routine inspections of storage facilities would need to be announced forty-eight hours prior to the planned arrival of the inspection team at the facility. During the visit, parties must provide "unimpeded access to all parts of the storage facilities including any munitions, devices, bulk containers, or other containers therein" (Annex IV, section II, para. 7c). The items to be inspected will be chosen by the inspectors. If any ambiguities arise from the inspection that cannot be resolved, the inspectors are to inform the technical secretariat (Annex IV, section II, para. 7e). In addition, immediate on-site inspection is permitted if instrument monitoring data transmitted from each storage facility to the international verification headquarters indicate an irregularity (Annex IV, section II, para. 5e(iv)).

International Verification of the Removal of Chemical Weapons for Destruction

For moving chemical weapons from the storage facility to the destruction facility, the convention requires that a party notify the technical secretariat of the exact timing of the removal and provide a detailed inventory of the stocks to be moved. The convention requires that international inspectors be present to verify that the chemical weapons in the inventory are loaded on the transport vehicles and delivered to the destruction facility (Annex IV, section II, para. 6b). Agreed seals would be employed, as appropriate, to assist in detecting any diversion of chemical weapons agents.

International Verification of the Destruction of Chemical Weapons

Systematic international on-site inspection is provided to monitor the destruction of chemical weapons. It would entail "the continuous presence of inspectors and continuous monitoring with on-site instruments" (Article IV, para. 6). The convention sets out principles and methods dealing with various aspects of the destruction process. These are designed to facilitate monitoring by the international inspectorate of the identity and quantity of chemical weapons stocks to be destroyed and then their actual destruction (Annex IV, section V, para. 1). For example, access by inspectors to the chemical weapons destruction facility must precede by thirty days the actual destruction (Annex IV, section V, para. 6) and must continue (along with access to the storage facility) "during the entire active phase of destruction" (Annex IV, section V, para. 7a).

International Verification of Declarations of Chemical Weapons Production Facilities and Cessation of Their Activities

Parties to the convention are required within thirty days of entry into force to submit declarations to the technical secretariat covering location, products, and other details for any chemical weapons production facilities and outlining the general actions planned to close, and then destroy, those facilities (Article V, para. 4). Immediately after the declaration, initial on-site inspections will be carried out "to confirm that all activity has ceased except that required for closure; to confirm through on-site inspections the accuracy of the declarations made in accordance with Article V" (Annex V, Section V, para. 1a). These inspections shall employ, as appropriate, agreed seals, markers, or other inventory control procedures to facilitate an accurate inventory (Annex V, section V, para. 1a(iii)).

To permit follow-up systematic monitoring of nonproduction or diversion of declared items, further detailed procedures and arrangements for the installation, operation, and maintenance of seals and monitoring devices are to be put in place within [6] months in the form of subsidiary arrangements between the parties to the convention and the international authority. Absent agreement on a subsidiary arrangement, a continuous on-site inspection presence could be maintained (Annex V, section V, paras. 4a–c). Instrument monitoring is to be backed up by periodic on-site inspections by the international inspectorate of closed production facilities.

In that regard, the convention calls for notification of an impending routine or systematic inspection or visit forty-eight hours prior to the planned arrival (Annex V, section V, para. 7a). At the facility, the inspectors "may request clarification of any ambiguities arising from inspection" (Annex V, section V, para. 7e). They shall "have unimpeded access to all parts of the production facilities," be able to choose the items on "the declared inventory to be inspected," "bring with them and use such agreed instruments as may be necessary for the completion of their tasks," and "shall communicate freely with the Technical Secretariat" (Annex V, section V, para. 7c).

International Verification of Destruction of Chemical Weapons Facilities

International on-site inspection is to be used to monitor destruction of chemical weapons productions facilities. Detailed plans for destruction and verification are to be worked out in consultations between and technical secretariat and a party to the convention and agreed between the convention's executive council and that party (Annex V, section V, para. 5d). As part of such plans, on-site inspectors are to be present to witness the destruction of the production facility (Annex V, section V, para. 5h). Once the destruction is certified complete by the technical secretariat, international systematic monitoring of the chemical weapons production facility would cease, and the monitoring devices and equipment would be removed (Annex V, section V, para. 5k).

Verification of Single Small-Scale Production Facility

Parties retain the right to develop, produce, and use toxic chemicals and their precursors for purposes not prohibited by the Chemical Weapons Convention. Subject to certain conditions, this includes production and use of Schedule [1], Schedule [2], and Schedule [3] chemicals.

Parties would be permitted to retain a single small-scale production facility with a capacity to produce no more than 1 metric tonne of Schedule [1] supertoxic chemicals per year for research, medical, or protective purposes (Annex VI, [1] para. 1). On-site inspection, as well as continuous monitoring with on-site instruments, would monitor that the aggregate amount of permitted chemicals at this single small-scale production facility did not exceed 1 metric tonne. It remains to be determined, however, whether on-site inspection would be systematic or permanent (Annex VI [1], II).

Monitoring of Key Precursor Chemicals in Civilian Industry

Production, processing, and use also is permitted of some legitimate civilian chemicals (listed on Schedule [2]) that are key precursors for chemical weapons. For these key precursors, the convention calls for annual declarations of aggregate national data on their production, processing, and consumption for facilities that produce an as yet to be agreed threshold quantity. In addition, routine systematic on-site inspections and on-site monitoring with instruments are to be permitted for facilities above specified thresholds to confirm nonproduction of supertoxic chemicals as well as that the chemicals produced are not diverted or used for purposes prohibited by the Chemical Weapons Convention. (The purpose of requiring declaration and monitoring only for production levels above a threshold is to minimize intrusiveness.)

Although each declared facility is subject to on-site inspection, the actual conduct and timing of inspections for a particular facility "shall be based on the risk to the objectives of the Convention posed by the relevant chemical, the characteristics of the facility and the nature of the activities carried out there" (Annex VI, [2] para. 5(iv)). Some civilian chemical industry facilities may not be inspected in practice. These on-site inspection provisions also reflect more specific concerns about intrusiveness and the need not to impair peaceful chemical activities. For example, efforts are to be made to "avoid undue interference," "to protect confidential information" and to require the "minimum amount of information and data necessary" (Article VI, para. 9).

Monitoring of Chemicals Produced in Large Commercial Quantities with Possible Chemical Weapons Purposes

Monitoring of Schedule [3] toxic chemicals produced in large commercial quantities is a troublesome area for verification. These potentially dual-purpose agents—including phosgene, cyanogen chloride, hydrogen cyanide, and chloropicrin—may be produced in quantities large enough to raise fears of possible diversion to chemical weapons purposes.

Verification provisions for these permitted activities have yet to be fully developed but include two main elements at this stage. As with verification of other undertakings, the convention provides for declarations regarding production and use of such chemicals above specified threshold quantities. The declarations would include chemical name and structural formula; total amount produced, consumed, imported, and exported in the previous calendar year; and final product or end use (Annex VI [2], para 1). These data are to be monitored by the technical secretariat to detect any discrepancies or anomalies. (Some delegations believe that provision needs to be added for routine on-site inspection spot checks of data supplied.)

Routine or Systematic International Inspection: Summary

Table 8–1 summarizes the range of chemical weapons verification tasks and the application of different systematic or routine inspection techniques to them.

Verification Provision II: Challenge Inspections

Anytime, anywhere challenge inspections were one of the key elements of the draft chemical weapons treaty submitted by the United States to the

Table 8–1
Routine On-Site Inspection: Articles III–VI

Subject	Verification Task	Verification Method[a]
Verification of destruction of stockpiles and factories (Articles III, IV, V)		
Chemical weapons (Articles III and IV)	Validating declarations	A
	Confirming destruction of declared stocks	B + C
Chemical weapons storage sites (Article IV)	Ensuring no undetected removal	A + B or C
Chemical weapons factories (Articles III and IV)	Validating declarations	A
	Monitoring closing of declared facilities	A
	Verifying no resumption of production or removal of declared items at closed facilities	A + B or C
	Confirming elimination of declared facilities	A/C
Verification of Nonproduction (Article VI)		
Single small-scale production facility (Schedule [1] chemicals)	Validating declarations, including capacity	A
	Monitoring permitted production	A + B
Civilian industry (Schedule [2] chemicals)	Monitoring quantities of Schedule [2] chemicals produced, for consistency with permitted purposes and for verification of nondiversion	A + B + D
	Verifying that declared facilities of this type do not produce any Schedule [1] chemicals	A + B + D
Civilian industry (Schedule [3] chemicals)	Monitoring quantities produced, for consistency with needs and verification of nondiversion	D

Source: Derived (with modifications) from M.M. Kaplan and J.P. Perry Robinson, "Verification of Chemical Disarmament," Background Paper XXXVII-C-14, 37th Pugwash Conference on Science and World Affairs, CD/CW/WP.167, April 27, 1987.

[a]A, systematic verification by on-site inspection;
B, continuous monitoring by on-site instruments;
C, continuous presence of international inspectors;
D, monitoring of reported data

Conference on Disarmament in 1984. While routine or systematic inspections are directed at the monitoring of declared sites and/or facilities, the aim of anywhere, anytime challenge inspections without a right of refusal is to uncover clandestine activities in the chemical field. Specifically, the goal of challenge inspections is to detect in a timely fashion (and thus deter) any undeclared chemical weapons stocks or production facilities, any undeclared production of prohibited chemicals, or any diversion of key precursor or other toxic chemicals from civilian chemical industry to weapons purposes.

Possible provisions for challenge inspection in a chemical weapons convention are set out in part I of a paper entitled "On-Site Inspection on Challenge," in Appendix II of CD/881. This part of the verification mechanism of the Chemical Weapons Convention, however, is less developed than provisions for routine or systematic on-site inspection. Many aspects remain quite controversial, and agreement on these procedures has yet to be reached.

Each party to the convention would have "the right at any time to request an on-site inspection of any site under the jurisdiction or control of a State Party, anywhere, in order to clarify doubts about compliance with the provisions of the Convention" (para. 1). The draft language places the obligation on the requested state "to demonstrate its compliance with the Convention" (para. 2).

Any request for such a challenge inspection is to be submitted to the head of the technical secretariat. To avoid mischief making, the current language requires that requests "shall as precisely as possible specify the site to be inspected and the matters on which reassurance is required, including the circumstances and nature of the suspect non-compliance, as well as indicate the relevant provision(s) of the convention, about which doubts of compliance have arisen." (para. 4) How soon a team of inspectors would be expected to arrive at the site to be inspected is still to be determined, but a time span of twenty-four to forty-eight hours from request to arrival has been discussed (para. 6). Once at the site, the inspectors "shall conduct the inspection in the least intrusive manner possible to accomplish their task" (para. 11).

The idea of challenge inspections without a right of refusal has been controversial. Several important Third World countries, such as China and India, have indicated opposition. Many Western countries, while supporting the United States publicly, have also been skeptical. Other countries have suggested a limited right of refusal with an offer of alternative arrangements to resolve compliance questions.

The Soviet Union has suggested the following alternative arrangements: provision of pertinent information by the challenged party, visual inspection of the suspected facility without entering it, partial access to the facility in question, and collection and analysis of air and water samples around the facility for traces of relevant chemicals. Partly as a response, the draft paper also states: "In the exceptional case the requested State proposes arrangements to demonstrate compliance, alternative to a full and comprehensive access, it shall make every effort through consultations with the requesting State to reach agreement on the modalities for establishing the facts and thereby clarifying the doubts" (para. 12).

The Federal Republic of Germany has put forward a proposal for "ad hoc checks" in the verification of nonproduction as a means of reducing the requirement for challenge on-site inspections.[4] Its suggestion is that

> the international authority should be empowered . . . to carry out on its own initiative *Ad hoc* checks at short notice in production facilities of the chemical industry. These checks should serve solely to ascertain whether, at the time of the check, substances listed in the Annexes to Article VI and not reported for the facility in question were being produced there.

This would lessen reliance on challenge inspections and establish routine or systematic monitoring as the central on-site verification method. Its purpose would be to assist in allaying political concerns over the excessive or inappropriate use of challenge inspections.

The International Inspectorate: Management Challenges and Cost

Establishment and effective operation of the international inspectorate is essential to verification of the Chemical Weapons Convention. The inspectorate will be required to inspect and monitor declared chemical weapons stockpiles and storage depots, destruction facilities, production facilities, and relevant segments of the civilian chemical industry. This will imply a broad range of activities, including:[5]

- Data collection, reporting, checking, and analysis;
- General examinations of facilities or operations;
- Interviewing (for example, facility operators);
- Developing and transmitting questionnaires (for example, on facilities);
- Performing material (energy) balances;
- Advising (for example, on plans for destruction);
- Planning and designing;
- Counting declared items;
- Weighing items;
- Obtaining and analyzing samples;

- Installing, calibrating, checking, testing, servicing, and removing instruments;
- recording readings and monitoring camera or instrument signals;
- Supervising state or facility personnel;
- Carrying out inspections;

Each of these activities requires different skills and will draw on different professional and technical qualifications. Engineers, analytical chemists, toxicologists, and industrial hygienists, for example, plus a technical support staff of interpreters, data specialists, and laboratory technicians, will be needed.[6]

Although it is possible to identify many of these activities and requirements in advance of a convention, the actual required size of the inspectorate is more difficult to estimate. This will depend on the number of chemical weapons–possessing states that declare their stockpiles, as well as on the number and identity of chemicals used in civilian industry placed on the control lists (and the agreed production and consumption thresholds). That information will determine the number of chemical production facilities subject to systematic on-site inspection and monitoring. Other factors determining the inspectorate's size will be the size and complexity of the facility or area requiring inspection, proximity of areas requiring inspection, duration of operations, frequency of inspection, the type of inspection or verification, percentage of time spent traveling and report writing, training requirements, requirements for challenge inspections, and cost considerations.

Accurate estimates of the costs of running the inspectorate are elusive. Those costs will depend on the number of inspectors employed, types of inspectors employed, size of the technical support staff, amounts and types of inspectorate instrumentation and equipment required for verification purposes, form of data management utilized, size of the administrative support, locations of inspectorate main offices, travel requirements, and challenge inspection costs.[7] Moreover, the number of inspectors and size of technical support staff will be highest in the period immediately following the convention's entry into force, with decreases expected only as destruction operations are completed over the projected ten-year period.

It will be important to the viability and success of the Chemical Weapons Convention to have the organization, administration, and preparation of the inspectorate well in hand before the convention enters into force. Verification of the declarations concerning chemical weapons stockpiles and production facilities is to begin within thirty days. Confidence that the convention's verification provisions can be credibly implemented once it enters into force is important to gain needed adherence.

In that regard, further efforts to garner experience and build confidence in the international inspection system in advance of the convention through trial inspections appear desirable. Such trial inspections might be carried out initially on a national basis. In a second stage, the results would be pooled and evaluated in the light of the relevant provisions of the Chemical Weapons Convention. In the third stage, trial inspections could be undertaken with multilateral participation. Trial inspections could identify means to lessen the degree of intrusiveness required for on-site inspections. They would likely yield useful results concerning problems of confidentiality associated with extensive on-site, continuous monitoring with instruments.

In addition, there probably are lessons from the experience of the Safeguards Division of the International Atomic Energy Agency in regard to staffing requirements, budget, training, and the many other activities of international on-site inspection. These can be usefully applied in helping to meet the eventual requirements of the technical secretariat and the international inspectorate.[8] It also will be important to move cautiously in extrapolating from the International Atomic Energy Agency experience because of the differences between chemical weapons verification and monitoring peaceful nuclear activities.[9]

The On-Site Inspection Debate: Adequacy and Intrusiveness

The two issues of the adequacy and intrusiveness of on-site inspection, especially challenge inspections, have become the focus of discussions of verification for chemical weapons disarmament. Conclusions concerning the adequacy of the on-site inspection provisions to verify compliance with a complete and total ban—and how high a price to pay in terms of intrusiveness—are still to be reached. Answers will depend partly on future success in developing verification technology. The organization and operation of the international inspectorate, as well as the detailed agreements reached between countries and the technical secretariat, also will make a difference. Nonetheless, the main areas of potential agreement, as well as the lines of debate, have become clear.

Adequacy of Verification

There is fairly broad agreement that the routine, systematic on-site inspections in the current rolling text of the Chemical Weapons Convention would likely be adequate to monitor declared stocks and facilities and to verify the destruction of declared stockpiles and chemical weapons facilities. For example, routine on-site inspections, backed up by technical monitoring with instruments, would have a high likelihood of detecting attempts to divert declared stocks or make use of closed facilities. Particularly for many countries lacking advanced intelligence capabilities, moreover, these extensive provisions for routine, continuous on-site monitoring and inspection would offer considerable transparency about neighboring countries' chemical activities. This would help to build confidence among them.

Monitoring of national chemical industries to ensure the nonproduction of schedule 1 supertoxic chemicals, as well as the nondiversion of schedule 2 key precursors from legitimate, permitted purposes to weapons making, would be a considerably more demanding task. The likelihood that a party could illegally produce Schedule [1] chemical agents at such a facility or divert Schedule [2] key precursors to manufacture supertoxics elsewhere without being detected is a matter of considerable (and unresolved) debate. More reliable and robust monitoring instruments, prompt and unfettered access to the site for inspectors, and advanced portable sampling technology for accurate detection of trace residues of banned chemicals would increase the likelihood of detection.

Data reporting and materials accounting for schedule 3 toxic chemicals is another troublesome verification area. Even with advanced computer-based materials accounting, keeping track of large quantities of dual-use chemicals will be difficult. At the same time, it is widely thought that this approach is acceptable because of these chemicals' lesser military significance.

The most difficult verification task clearly is detection of nondeclared chemical weapons stockpiles and production facilities and nondeclared production and/or diversion of Schedule [1], [2], and [3] chemicals. For its proponents, this is the purpose of challenge inspection of suspect sites, anytime, anywhere. But whether such inspections could provide adequate assurance is itself challenged by critics of the Chemical Weapons Convention.

Critics and supporters disagree over whether international inspectors would even be permitted access to a suspect site or facility or whether inspection would be refused or blocked in some other way. Assuming access to a site, they also disagree over whether evidence of cheating could be cleaned up or otherwise destroyed, and how soon. Differences are evident as well concerning the likely effectiveness of the international inspectorate in terms of organization, equipment, and the technical expertise of its personnel. Considerable research remains to be done to resolve these technical questions.

Further, because challenge inspection relies on the cooperation of the requested state, its effectiveness would decline in a situation of crisis or even war. In cases of alleged chemical weapons use, for example, on-site inspection would take place either "on invitation, probably by the party which is victim of the attack, or as a challenge inspection at locations under the control of the alleged violator."[10] But would there be a real possibility for challenge inspection in such circumstances, for example, during the Gulf

War between Iran and Iraq, particularly where chemical weapons incidents took place on Iraqi territory?[11]

Similarly, challenge on-site inspection might play only a limited role in reducing concerns about breakout by the rapid weaponization of covertly developed chemical weapons agents by a potential adversary. In a situation of deepening crisis or war, cooperative measures such as systematic and challenge inspections will have likely been already suspended. Consequently officials' estimates of the likelihood of breakout—or of breakout potential—under a Chemical Weapons Convention would depend most on the quality of national intelligence gathering and analysis. Here, however, there could be a significant disparity between the intelligence capabilities of smaller Third World countries in regions of conflict and the two superpowers.

These considerations suggest that in the final stages of negotiating the verification provisions of the Chemical Weapons Convention, more emphasis could usefully be placed on routine or systematic monitoring (rather than challenge inspections) as the central on-site verification method. This would still leave open, nonetheless, questions about the intrusiveness of on-site inspection, particularly throughout the civilian chemical industry.

Intrusiveness

Concerning the risk that the confidentiality of commercial information would be jeopardized or an excessive burden placed on the inspected civilian factory, a number of steps could be taken to avoid or significantly reduce both problems. These include limits on data to be removed from the site, procedures within the technical secretariat to maintain confidentiality, and careful selection of inspectors.

The problem should not be overstated. Verification of nonproduction "is not to control what is happening but to verify that something, i.e. chemical weapons production, is not happening."[12] The search is for well-known chemical warfare agents and related compounds. Consequently the techniques used to confirm their absence may, with sufficient advance knowledge of the chemical plant's design, limit the degree of intrusiveness required. In turn, other data-reporting requirements for Schedule [3] (widely used) chemicals with possible chemical weapons uses would not necessarily be more onerous than those already in place in some industrialized countries for environmental and safety reasons or for local and central government records.

Compliance, Noncompliance, and Adherence

Verification, compliance, and responses to noncompliance in chemical weapons arms control, as in other arms control areas, are closely linked. In the absence of effective responses, the benefits of even a very strong on-site inspection system would be reduced significantly. Conversely, the prospect of response can help to deter potential evaders and affect the calculations of their neighbors concerning the risks of adherence to the Chemical Weapons Convention.

Enforcing Compliance

References to compliance concerns are found in several parts of the rolling text of the Chemical Weapons Convention, especially in Article VIII, "The Organization," and Article IX, "Consultations, Co-Operation and Fact-Finding." The executive council of the chemical weapons organization has competence to consider compliance concerns and to bring such matters to the attention of the parties. For its part, the technical secretariat would serve as the bridge between the international inspectorate and the executive council. As defined in the rolling text, the technical secretariat's duties include:

> [to] inform the Executive Council of any problems which have arisen with regard to the execution of its functions, and of [doubts, ambiguities or uncertainties about compliance with the convention] which have come to its notice in the performance of its verification activities and/or which it has been unable to resolve or clarify through its consultations with the State Party concerned. (Article VIII, section D, para. 2d)

There still is considerable disagreement and much work to be done, however, on the question of what the executive council should be empowered to do either to penalize the violator or assist threatened countries if a violation is established as a consequence of the inspectors' report. Suggested measures that might be taken in the event of noncompliance vary in intensity. A request might be made to the violator to remedy the situation. That country's rights and privileges could be suspended or other sanctions imposed. A special meeting of the consultative committee/general conference could be held. Or assistance might be provided to parties against which chemical weapons have been used or which believe themselves threatened with chemical weapons use as a consequence of the violations.

Assuming that the eventual language of the Chemical Weapons Convention does not resolve the problem of what specific steps the organization may take in the event of noncompliance, the menu of responses outside a future convention is basically limited to three choices. The first is to continue expressing moral outrage at such incidents. World opinion would condemn any state using chemical weapons or seeking to acquire them. This approach, however, has been devalued by the failure of many countries to condemn Iraq for its repeated use of chemical weapons in the Gulf region.

The second approach would be to institute sanctions and stiff economic and diplomatic penalties for such deliberate flaunting of international norms and agreements outlawing chemical weapons use and following a Convention, acquisition. But in the case of Libya, a number of Western countries have shown themselves to be incapable of exercising even the requisite control over their own chemical firms' dealings with a "problem country." Can it be expected that they would be prepared to introduce tough international sanctions on those countries bent on acquiring the relevant equipment, technology, and materials for chemical weapons manufacture?

The third approach in response to noncompliance would be the traditional one of deterrence and the threat of retaliation in kind. The Soviet Union and the United States may decide separately that while they have no intention of initiating the use of chemical weapons against each other or each other's allies, some kind of chemical stockpile is required to deter any third parties from making chemical weapons threats against them. If this conclusion is reached, a mutual lowering of stockpiles between East and West could be anticipated but not global chemical weapons disarmament.

The Adherence Connection

Effective handling of the interrelated issues of enforcement of compliance and assistance to threatened parties—either within the convention or on its margins—will have an important bearing on the decisions of countries to adhere to a complete chemical weapons ban. This is likely to be especially so for Third World countries.

Until recently, the chief protagonists in the Conference on Disarmament's Ad Hoc Committee on Chemical Weapons have been the United States and the Soviet Union, both of which have admitted to possessing large stockpiles of chemical weapons. The main negotiating tussles have tended to reflect East-West security considerations. North Atlantic Treaty Organization (NATO) countries are concerned over the extent of the Soviet chemical weapons capability and the potential for clandestine production after a convention is signed. The Soviets want to restrain the new round of chemical weapons production recently begun by the United States after a twenty-year moratorium. However, a growing pragmatism in the Soviet Union, especially in military and arms control affairs, has produced a noticeable convergence of positions between East and West regarding the Chemical Weapons Convention. In short, it is not farfetched to think that with sufficient political determination, a treaty banning chemical weapons could be reached in principle between NATO and the Warsaw Pact.

This optimism is less warranted if a North-South, rather than an East-West, perspective is adopted. The Conference on Chemical Weapons Use, held in Paris in January 1989, illustrated that neither the Soviet Union, the

United States, nor the allies of the two superpowers have any program of action to bring countries of chemical weapons concern in the developing world—Libya, Syria, Egypt, Israel, Iraq, Iran, Korea (North and South), and others—into the Chemical Weapons Convention. Indeed, the fact that Iraq emerged politically and economically unscathed after its use of chemical weapons in the Gulf War has without doubt emboldened the military in many developing countries to retain the chemical weapons option. At the same time, Iraq's successful violation of the Geneva Protocol also has undoubtedly led still other countries to ask what assistance would be made available to them if they renounced chemical weapons only to discover that their neighbor had not. For both chemical weapons haves and chemical weapons have-nots, a system of adequate verification and on-site inspection is likely to be less important in getting acceptance of the idea of chemical weapons disarmament than their assessments of existing means to enforce compliance or provide assistance.

In particular, countries confronting neighbors that might be seeking chemical weapons will likely focus heavily on this assistance aspect of the convention (Article X). Along with technological and economic help in developing their civilian chemical industries, these countries will look for what positive security assurances the other treaty signatories are prepared to give, particularly in regional conflicts where the convention is being, or is about to be, violated. For them, undertaking challenge on-site inspections to confirm allegations of chemical weapons use or manufacture would not be regarded as a sufficient promise of assistance. In addition, they will want to know whether measures ranging from censure and economic sanctions to possible collective military action would be taken in response to noncompliance on behalf of the state requesting assistance.

The Defenses Conundrum

The draft Chemical Weapons Convention as currently conceived, places no limits on chemical weapons defenses, nor has there been any serious discussion at the Conference on Disarmament or elsewhere of such limits. Instead it has been widely accepted that parties to the convention would still be permitted to develop protective clothing and techniques, to train and exercise for defense against a chemical weapons attack, and to undertake similar defensive activities. Continued defensive activities, however, could pose several sorts of problems for the chemical weapons disarmament objectives of the convention.

Under some conditions, defensive chemical weapons operations and measures could be a guise for developing a covert offensive capability. Defensive measures would make it easier to weaponize covertly produced stocks of chemical weapons agents and prepare for their use. More broadly, to the extent that weaponization was relatively easy to achieve, concern about breakout hidden by defensive activities would increase. At the least, permitted defensive activities would make it harder for the national intelligence capabilities of neighboring countries and others to assess and monitor the status of any chemical weapons activities in these countries.

Moreover, the vigorous pursuit of defensive safeguards to hedge against breakout or noncompliance—allowable under the convention's terms—might itself prove unstable. It could foster fears in other countries that such defensive preparations were a means of training troops or conducting maneuvers for purposes of offensive chemical weapons actions. This could be particularly so if there were widespread concerns that a militarily significant amount of Schedule [1] supertoxic chemicals could be clandestinely produced or hidden effectively and then matched in quick succession to dual-capable delivery systems.

Given these potential repercussions of defensive measures, therefore, it may be useful after the convention has come into force to explore the possibility of further negotiated, phased restrictions on chemical weapons defensive equipment to allay concerns over elaborate defensive preparations. With defensive restrictions, any large-scale breakout from the treaty regime and use of chemical weapons on the battlefield would be detected sooner, with more time for countermeasures or outside assistance. It would be considerably less useful militarily for the attacking forces. Such limits also would increase the likelihood of detecting through national intelligence capabilities weaponization of illegally retained or produced chemical weapons stocks. As such, they could provide a partial alternative to reliance on challenge on-site inspections in the period following destruction of declared chemical weapons stocks.

Conclusion

Systematic international on-site inspection is interwoven throughout the verification provisions within the rolling text of the draft Chemical Weapons Convention. Quite likely, some forms of challenge and ad hoc inspections will also be included within any eventual convention. In both cases, the goal of these extensive verification arrangements is to help convince countries that their national security concerns would be better met by chemical weapons disarmament than by acquisition of chemical weapons.

For countries with strong national intelligence-gathering capabilities, these verification provisions would provide an important supplement. It also would help provide publicly usable information about compliance or noncompliance. For countries with far less national intelligence capabilities—the majority of potential parties to a Chemical Weapons Convention—the provisions for routine, systematic international inspections would be the key to increase the transparency of neighboring countries' chemical activities. Along with provisions for assistance in the event of a chemical weapons threat, this greater transparency will eventually prove the deciding factor in building the confidence needed to opt for prevention of chemical weapons use through stringently verified chemical weapons disarmament rather than deterrence of chemical weapons use through the threat to retaliate.

Notes

1. For a discussion of adequacy versus feasibility of verification, see M.M. Kaplan and J.P.P. Robinson, "Verification of Chemical Disarmament," Background Paper XXXVII-C14, 37th Pugwash Conference on Science and World Affairs, Gmunden am Traunsee, Austria, September 1–6, 1987.
2. The question of jurisdiction or control appears in many parts of the convention and is still under discussion.
3. The detailed verification and monitoring provisions of the chemical weapons convention are contained in several annexes to Articles IV, V, and VI. Appropriate citations are included in the text to specific parts of these annexes.
4. "Verification of Non-Production: The Case for Ad Hoc Checks," U.N. Document CD/CW/WP. 183, January 25, 1988, submitted by the Federal Republic of Germany to the Conference on Disarmament.
5. See "Factors Involved in Determining Verification Inspectorate Personnel and Resource Requirements," U.N. Document CD/823, March 31, 1988, paper submitted by Canada to the Conference on Disarmament.
6. See Ronald G. Sutherland, "The International Machinery Required to Monitor a Chemical Weapons Convention," *Pugwash Newsletter* 25, no. 3 (January 1988): 128–135.
7. "Factors Involved in Determining Verification Inspectorate Personnel and Resource Requirements," U.N. Document CD/823, March 31, 1988.
8. See chapter 3 in this book. Also see James F. Keeley, *International Atomic Energy Agency Safeguards: Observations on Lessons for Verifying a Chemical Weapons Convention* (Ottawa: Department of External Affairs, September 1988).
9. See the discussion in J.P. Perry Robinson, "The Present Situation in the Negotiations for a Chemical Weapons Convention," *Pugwash Newsletter* 25, no. 3 (January 1988): 124–125.
10. Rolf Ekeus, "The Negotiations in the Conference on Disarmament on a Ban on Chemical Weapons," in *The Holmenkollen Report on the Chemical Weapons Convention* (Oslo: Norwegian Ministry of Foreign Affairs, 1987), p. 27.
11. Also see Walter Krutzsch, "Verification on Challenge in the Event of an Alleged Use of Chemical Weapons," in *Holmenkollen Report*, pp. 99–100.

12. See Barend Ter Haar, Henk Boter, and Alber Verweij, "Verification of Non-Production of Chemical Weapons: An Adequate System Is Feasible," *NATO's Sixteen Nations*, (August 1987): 51.

III
Political and Legal Imperatives

9
Public and Congressional Attitudes Toward On-Site Inspection

Janne E. Nolan

T he broad bipartisan support for the Treaty on the Elimination of Intermediate-Range and Shorter Missiles (INF), particularly as contrasted to the generally negative view of the previously most recently negotiated agreement, SALT (Strategic Arms Limitation Talks) II, is often attributed to its achievements and innovations in intrusive on-site inspection measures. The exacting verification standards contained in the agreement have been acclaimed by a majority in the Congress and broad elements of the media and public. Together with the treaty's elimination of two entire classes of weapons, the verification provisions are widely praised as signs of unprecedented progress in the conduct of arms control and a political tour de force for the Reagan administration.

The far greater complexities of a prospective START (Strategic Arms Reduction Talks) agreement notwithstanding, the success of the INF treaty has encouraged optimism among many that comprehensive strategic reductions might be achievable. The INF treaty is credited with providing the basis for the agreement signed at the December 1987 summit outlining START verification provisions, including continuous on-site monitoring of designated production and support facilities, short-notice on-site inspections of declared locations, and challenge inspections at sites where covert, illegal actions are suspected of occurring. The achievement of even tentative accords on such ambitious verification measures vastly exceeded the expectations of both congressional arms control proponents and critics.

The appearance of broad political consensus on behalf of on-site inspection (OSI) is misleading, however. Current support for the INF agreement in no way implies the dawning of a new age of consensus in the Congress or among the public in favor of strategic arms control or about verification. To the contrary, the evolving INF debate has forced a far greater appreciation in the Congress of the complexities associated with defining the objectives and desired scope of all future verification measures and on-site inspection in particular. The on-site inspection measures in the INF treaty have engendered new congressional controversies and political realignments as it is discovered that on-site inspection is not the panacea for high-confidence verification that many had assumed. After years of championing on-site inspection as the only barometer of effective verification, many in the Congress, particularly conservatives, have now turned their attention to its danger and limitations.

This chapter provides a historical context for the current political debate on on-site inspection, tracing congressional and public attitudes during the 1950s, 1960s, and 1970s, and analyzing the changes that have emerged since the signing of the INF Treaty. The key challenge is to identify prospects for, and constraints on, an effective executive-legislative strategy for developing consensus on the role of on-site inspection for future arms control efforts.

Key Congressional and Public Concerns: Overview

Congressional and public attitudes on on-site inspection are still embryonic. Although the number of members and staff with technical expertise grew in response to INF, verification in general and on-site inspection in particular are far too arcane for informed congressional adjudication. It is axiomatic that highly complex issues fare badly in the adversarial process of democracy and that political alignments on such subjects are based only rarely on detailed analysis.

Before the INF treaty, moreover, few members found it interesting or advantageous politically to pay attention to the technicalities of potential on-site inspection schemes. Despite the rich history of such discussions in such international forums as the International Atomic Energy Agency and the Committee on Disarmament in Europe, as part of nuclear testing limitation efforts, including the unratified Peaceful Nuclear Explosions (PNE) and Threshold Test Ban (TTB) Treaties, in the chemical weapons area, or as part of mutual and balanced force reductions, most of these negotiations have attracted scant congressional attention. For the most part, on-site inspection was little more than a rhetorical rallying point in partisan disputes about the desirability and negotiability of various nuclear arms limitation measures. Those generally supportive of arms control tended to be least concerned about on-site inspection requirements, whereas those who were opposed tended to advocate high levels of intrusion—arguably as much to preempt agreements as to ensure their verifiability.

The modest amounts of funds allocated to on-site inspection technology and research, moreover, meant that even the authorization and appropriations processes offered little incentive or opportunity for policy attention. With the exception of a few individuals with a strong interest in arms control, some members of committees with jurisdiction for verification funding (Armed Services, Intelligence, and Defense Appropriations) or those who represented districts or states with installations in which such activities are conducted, on-site inspection was a salient issue only as part of a larger debate about Soviet compliance. The degree of controversy in the current debate reflects not only the lack of operational experience with on-site inspection but also the fundamentally new political challenges posed by unexpected Soviet flexibility in this area.

For a majority in the Congress and the public, attitudes toward on-site inspection are a dependent variable. They derive from more general attitudes toward arms control and U.S.-Soviet relations, and in some cases simply from partisan loyalty. Despite the appearance of careful examination of such issues as portal monitoring, the inspection protocol, and the meaning of force majeure in recent INF committee hearings, moreover, only a small minority have expressed interest in the details of the agreement. In truth, even some senators who offered verification amendments to the treaty would not likely explain their motives to be purely technical in nature.

But congressional intrusion into the content of verification arrangements is not likely to recede in the near future. The current political environment has prompted new levels of congressional micromanagement. In what may be a record for such actions, the Senate Armed Services Committee submitted a list of 150 questions to the administration on INF verification as part of its ratification deliberations.[1] The three committees with jurisdiction for the treaty conducted over sixty open hearings, thirty closed hearings, and countless numbers of private briefings for members and staff, with a substantial portion devoted to verification.[2] Many members who do not serve on these committees, moreover, were active participants in the floor debate.

In short, INF has accorded on-site inspection a pronounced political profile, widely seen as the sine qua non of any durable arms limitation agreement. Paradoxically, the ratification debate has also accelerated congressional recognition of the risks and limitations of on-site inspection, generating a second-order category of political disputes about how to contain the unintended consequences of Soviet intrusion or to protect against new and more subtle forms of Soviet deception. The general congressional view of on-site inspection has shifted from a perception of an a priori benefit for U.S. security, were it ever to prove negotiable, to the realization that on-site inspection measures are not ends but means, which may pose unanticipated operational and political difficulties.

The current controversies over INF verification would likely seem quite modest compared to congressional scrutiny of any START agreement, moreover. It is generally agreed that ratification of the INF treaty not only does not guarantee a favorable environment for a START treaty but, to the contrary, has served to whet the congressional appetite for more pointed examination of subsequent arms limitation proposals. This is especially the case for those who believe the administration is moving with undue haste to conclude an agreement on central strategic systems. The Senate Intelligence Committee's caveated support for INF states categorically that monitoring compliance will be vastly more complicated in a START environment.[3] The key political challenge identified recently by Senator Bill Bradley (D–New Jersey), how to define "how much verification is enough," will not be easy now that it is recognized that even very exacting on-site inspection does not provide anything approximating the degree of technical certainty necessary to insulate arms limitation agreements from politics.[4]

The Historical Context

The concept of on-site inspections began its political history as part of a series of quixotic and politically elusive efforts for broad international agreements to control atomic energy and weapons. Initial optimism in the 1940s and 1950s about the possibility of comprehensive international agreements gave way to more pragmatic and modest proposals in the 1960s and 1970s when it was clear that the Soviet Union would not agree to intrusive monitoring. All early efforts to establish comprehensive international controls over nuclear weapons, including the Baruch Plan, Eisenhower's "open skies," and the Kennedy efforts for a Comprehensive Test Bank (CTB), had stumbled over this issue. Since it was always the Soviets who demurred, the scope of possible U.S. domestic reaction to intrusive measures was never actually tested.

During the Truman administration, the United States and Great Britain invited the Soviet Union to join in cosponsoring a resolution in the United Nations General Assembly to establish the U.N. Commission on Atomic Energy (UNAEC). Supported by all three countries, the resolution passed unanimously in January 1946. A special committee, chaired by Under Secretary of State Dean Acheson and assisted by a panel of consultants led by David Lilienthal, subsequently devised a plan for the international control of atomic weapons and energy. Their effort called for the creation of an international board with full control over nuclear weapons research and development.

Presented by Truman adviser Bernard Baruch to the UNAEC in modified form late that year, the proposal, now known as the Baruch Plan, urged the cessation of production of all atomic bombs, the destruction of the U.S. atomic arsenal (retaining nine atomic bombs until the regime was in place, apparently the number of operational weapons at the time), and full authority for atomic matters vested in an international agency. The Soviets saw the proposal for an international management and inspection regime as a means for Western governments to stymie communist military developments, however. As such, Soviet rejection of the Baruch Plan represented the first formal failure of an international on-site inspection regime.

A decade later, President Eisenhower presented a new approach to arms control and verification in his open skies proposal revealed at the 1955 U.S.-Soviet summit. Calling for reciprocal aerial inspection of the United States and Soviet Union and for the exchange of blueprints on the two sides' military establishments, the proposal aimed to establish a regime that would lessen the probability of surprise attack. Insisting that complete disarmament was a precondition, the Soviets again refused.

There was virtually no debate in the Congress about either the Baruch or open skies plans, but twenty-eight years after Eisenhower's proposal, Senator William Proxmire (D–Wisconsin) hailed the latter as the antecedent to contemporary on-site inspection efforts. He spoke on the Senate floor on July 13, 1983:

> 28 years ago, President Eisenhower proposed and the Soviets rejected the suggestion that the United States and the Soviet Union exchange blueprints of their military establishments and provide each other facilities for aerial photography and reconnaissance. . . . President Reagan should revive the Eisenhower proposition but bring it up to date by providing that each country could at will—day or night—send investigators into the other country to check nuclear installations without prior notice.[5]

Senator Proxmire's entreaty in 1983 was received by most of his Senate colleagues in the same spirit as open skies: not much more than a rhetorical expression of overconfidence in the prospects for Soviet agreement to intrusion, a reflection of his exaggeratedly sanguine view of the Soviet Union.[6]

The year 1955 also marked the beginning of congressional attention to cooperative international efforts to control nuclear energy. Appointed by the Joint Committee on Atomic Energy, the new Panel on the Impact of Peaceful Uses of Atomic Energy urged more stringent controls to prevent diversion of atomic power to military uses, laying the groundwork for an international enforcement body, later formalized under the International Atomic Energy Agency.

Efforts by Eisenhower and Kennedy to achieve a comprehensive test ban were more directly impeded by Soviet rejection of on-site inspections. As the CTB negotiations reached a head in 1962, various compromises about the number of necessary inspections were considered, but ultimately the two sides could not agree. Although the talks failed, the CTB effort marked the first instance in which the Soviet Union indicated even in principle that it would permit on-site inspections.

The domestic politics surrounding the CTB, and subsequently the Limited Test Ban, underscore the traditional sensitivity of the issue among political conservatives. Republican House members were sharply critical of the Kennedy administration for offering compromises on the number of on-site inspections required to verify a comprehensive ban on nuclear testing and set up the Republican Conference Committee on Nuclear Testing, chaired by the senior Republican on the Atomic Energy Committee, Congressman Craig Hosmer (R–California), which spearheaded the congressional opposition.

Joining in the debate, Senate conservatives were equally virulent. Senator Thomas Dodd (D–Connecticut) charged on February 21, 1963, that the United States "had a record of consistent and continuing retreat from the basic principles of inspection, particularly on-site inspection." Senator John Tower (R–Texas) fueled the opposition to the Limited Test Ban Treaty by offering an amendment during the ratification debate that would have prohibited the treaty from going into effect until it included on-site inspections to detect violations. Although defeated by an overwhelming majority, the text of the amendment and ensuing debate sound startlingly similar to more contemporary congressional controversies.[7]

By the time of SALT negotiations, beginning in 1969, advances in technology permitting more robust national technical means of verification, and the now largely unquestioned assumption that on-site inspection was not negotiable, led to the widely held assumption that the United States should not pursue arms limitations that required intrusive measures. It was agreed almost as an article of faith that the limits of national technical means set the outer boundaries of potential arms control agreements, albeit with some modest "associated measures" to ensure that national technical means were not subject to interference. While this limited the scope of possible limitations on Soviet systems, it also provided a political pretext for avoiding limitations on technologies the US wanted to pursue.

Tentative discussions about banning multiple independently retargetable reentry vehicles (MIRV) in the 1970s, for example, were readily dismissible because of the requirement for what was widely believed to be an impossibly exacting verification regime. No one could argue credibly that the United States or the Soviet Union would permit the other side to examine missiles physically in order to count the number of deployed warheads, the only way to verify MIRV limits.

As Senator Edmund Muskie (D–Maine) put it in floor debate on April 9, 1970, once MIRV deployment went forward, "the door is completely shut on the possibility of banning MIRVs. For once MIRVs are placed on missiles, the only means of verification is on-site inspection and a can-opener. Neither the Russians nor ourselves are ready for this kind of intrusive inspection."[8] For MIRV critics, the nonverifiability of MIRVs was a key reason they should be banned. As long as on-site inspection was agreed to be a political illusion, however, MIRV critics had to cede the terms of the debate to the administration, which used the nonverifiability of MIRV bans as an unassailable pretext for why the United States could not pursue such proposals.

Verification was not a major congressional concern when the Anti-Ballistic Missile (ABM) Treaty and SALT I Interim Agreement were submitted to the Congress in 1972, although controversies did arise sporadically during ratification and, more seriously, once the agreements were in force. The main task for the administration was to assure critics that U.S. national technical means were fully adequate to detect Soviet violations and to monitor Soviet advances, including the possible Soviet development of ABM systems and deployment of mobile missiles.

Illustratively, during the Senate Armed Services Committee hearings in 1972 about ABM and SALT I, Senators Henry Jackson (D–Washington) and Howard Cannon (D–Nevada) raised questions about the need for on-site inspection. Presaging today's controversies over possible limitations on defensive technologies, Senator Jackson was particularly concerned about how the United States could monitor development of banned ABM systems without on-site observation. In a colloquy with chief of the air force, General John D. Ryan and head of the Safeguard program, army Brigadier General Walter P. Leber, Jackson asked:

Senator Jackson: "I am saying you are prohibited from developing an [ABM] system that is sea-based, air-based, space-based, or mobile based. . . . I have said we have national means to monitor testing. But tell me, how do we monitor development work in a laboratory?

Ryan: Senator, as you know, there is no way we could.

Leber: [But] . . . development is a very major undertaking; it is not something that you can complete in a laboratory . . . early in the development they start testing components of radars, putting them in the air. Those are things that you can observe and detect.[9]

In the same set of hearings, Senator Cannon asked Defense Secretary Melvin Laird if existing national technical means were adequate for monitoring mobile intercontinental ballistic missiles (ICBMs) and distinguishing between intermediate-range ballistic missiles (IRBMs) and ICBMs. Laird responded:

I believe that we have effective verification means to verify all points that are in this agreement. When you get into the area such as improvements, mobile systems and certain parts of the follow-on talks, the question of verification is going to be a much more difficult question to address.[10]

The Nixon administration succeeded in defusing compliance concerns, and no significant treaty amendments affecting verification were adopted. The ambiguities of the two treaties did lead to considerable compliance controversies in the press and in the Congress during the mid-1970s, however, and set the stage for more protracted disputes during the Carter administration. The relative quiescence of the Congress during this period is largely attributable to the fact that a hard-line Republican president is far less vulnerable to political attacks from conservatives—the mainstay of the verification constituency. The less ambitious scope of SALT I, moreover, largely absent qualitative limits that would test national technical means capabilities, also helped to dampen congressional verification disputes.

The Carter Administration

During the Carter administration, most of the substantive progress in on-site inspection occurred in the CTB negotiations, although these developments were largely ignored in the Congress. The negotiations elicited tangible signs of Soviet willingness to agree to challenge inspections and to permit the installation of unmanned seismic stations on Soviet territory. A report containing the draft proposals was submitted to the Committee on Disarmament in July 1980. Championed by only a small coalition of congressional liberals, however, the CTB deliberations were vastly overshadowed by a preoccupation with SALT II.

In addition, the Carter administration's brief flirtation with a multiple protective shelter (MPS) basing mode for the MX focused Congress's attention on cooperative measures to monitor the configuration and number of deployed mobile missiles, but again this was transitory. The debate ended abruptly when the Reagan administration cancelled plans for MPS in 1981.

Congressional and public disputes over verification were galvanized to an unprecedented extent by SALT II. The perception of Jimmy Carter as a weak president bent on excessive accommodation with the Soviet Union coincided with growing Soviet global adventurism and perceptions of wilful efforts to test the limits of agreements. Although cautiously supportive, both the Senate Intelligence and Foreign Relations Committees noted the political problems posed by the Soviets pressing the ambiguities in treaties and urged in their respective reports on SALT II that even violations that were not "militarily significant" be "quickly and forcefully" pursued, no matter how minor.

The inclusion of qualitative limits in SALT II also complicated the task of reassuring the Senate about verifiability, and questions were raised about the meaning of vague assurances, such as "low incentives to cheat" on particular provisions. The Senate Foreign Relations Committee noted a number of monitoring uncertainties posed by SALT II provisions, including mobile ICBM deployments, MIRV breakout potential, deployment of cruise missiles, and problems posed by a potential increase in the range of the Backfire bomber.

Almost in passing, the Senate Foreign Relations Committee report urged more on-site inspection provisions for future agreements.[11] But it was largely assumed by the majority of the committee that more stringent cooperative measures were neither necessary nor feasible for SALT II. The Senate Intelligence Committee report noted the problems posed by qualitative limitations but concluded that SALT II strengthened "the ability of the US to monitor those components of Soviet strategic weapons . . . subject to the Treaty limitations" and that "most counting provisions can be monitored with high confidence." There is no reference to intrusive on-site inspection in the report.[12]

Similarly, Congressman Les Aspin (D–Wisconsin) stated in 1979 that national technical means were fully adequate to monitor SALT II: "the national technical means of surveillance . . . are multiple, redundant, and complementary . . . . They are in fact far more reliable than most human intelligence gathering which may yield second-hand, dated information or even false, planted information." At the same time, Aspin noted that technological advances, including cruise missiles and rapid reload of missiles, would stretch verification capabilities in SALT III: "These systems under a SALT III agreement may well require a substantial lowering of the present standards of confidence for detecting violations."[13]

As the debate evolved, however, the impression that the Carter administration had agreed to vaguely worded provisions that exceeded the capability of national technical means monitoring gained ground in the Congress. The view that one could trade off some verification certainty in favor of imposing desirable constraints on the Soviets could not sustain a consensus.

The loss of listening posts in Iran after the fall of the Pahlavi regime helped fuel opposition to the Treaty on grounds of its nonverifiabillity, a controversy led by Senator John Glenn (D–Ohio). Glenn and other members of the Foreign Relations Committee received lengthy reassurances from the intelligence community that the posts would be replaced—partly with new facilities in China—and monitoring capabilities fully restored. Nonetheless, Glenn continued to refer to Iran as the reason for his opposition to the treaty, a shift from his previous position. Like his predecessors who opposed MIRV limits, Glenn apparently used the verification issue as a political maneuver to distance himself from a politically unpopular treaty.

The failure to submit the SALT II treaty to the Senate for ratification arguably had more to do with the decline of the Carter administration's domestic support and the deterioration of U.S.-Soviet relations than with its actual content. But the politically divisive atmosphere that accompanied the signing of SALT II laid the groundwork for unparalleled politicization of the verification issue, identified as the most obvious Achilles heel of the treaty by SALT opponents.

The Political Legacy

The legacy of the Congress's interest in on-site inspection in the pre-Reagan years has three main components. First were growing questions about the largely unchallenged assumption that the capabilities of national technical means set the outer boundaries of arms control. Despite the protracted discussions of on-site inspection schemes as part of negotiations for chemical weapons, testing limits, and even mutual and balanced force reductions, these had received scant congressional attention. But the verification disputes in SALT II underscored the clear trade-off between high-confidence verification and the breadth and ambition of limitations.

Second is the extent to which perceptions of verification derived from the broader political environment. More easily defused during the Nixon administration, concerns about U.S. willingness and ability to enforce Soviet arms control compliance came to the fore when the president was perceived as weak, as was the case under Presidents Ford and Carter. It is only now being rediscovered that monitoring uncertainties in SALT II are in many cases not dissimilar to those being contemplated for START and that dynamic compromise between absolute certainty in verification and desirable strategic policy is an inescapable element of arms control.

Third was the emerging demand that the Congress should have full access to information about verification and Soviet compliance, a view upheld in Senate committee amendments to SALT II. Reflecting the Congress's distrust of the executive under the Carter administration, the amendments were designed to grant broad procedural powers to ensure congressional oversight of all future treaties, an infrastructure of political authority that virtually guaranteed that the future role of the Congress would be far more assertive.

The Reagan Years and Beyond

The election of Ronald Reagan in 1980 and the coincident ascendance of the conservative wing of the Republican party was accompanied by a pointed elevation of the importance of on-site inspection in arms control. Decrying the SALT II treaty as "fatally flawed," the Reagan administration put forward unprecedentedly stringent verification standards as preconditions for any arms control agreement. If the Soviets were sincere, it was implied, they would not hesitate to open their borders to U.S. inspection; they refused to accept on-site inspection only because they fully intended to cheat. As it was, all previous administrations had been so mesmerized by the alleged benefits of arms control that they had failed consistently to enforce agreements or to challenge the Soviets when they had violated agreements.

Congressional battle lines were drawn around the heated issue of Soviet arms control violations, and verification standards became a litmus test of partisan loyalty and toughness toward the Soviet Union. Beginning in 1983, the Congress required the administration to issue an annual report on Soviet treaty violations. This conservative initiative was designed to force the administration to take explicit positions on compliance issues, ensuring a firm foundation for opposing future agreements until these matters had been settled. The unclassified version helped publicize the charges, prompting more widespread public and congressional debate. The steady politicization of the issue included the unprecedented appearance of senior officials from the Central Intelligence Agency at open hearings of the Senate Armed Services and Appropriations committees, prompting charges that the intelligence community was being exposed unduly to partisan politics.

The conventional wisdom that the Soviets would never accept U.S. access to sensitive military sites had gone largely unquestioned for three decades. As recently as 1983, almost 80 percent of respondents to a Gallup poll said they believed the Soviets would never agree to on-site inspection.[14] Similarly, in 1982, Senator Steve Symms (R–Idaho) read a statement into the *Congressional Record* identifying Soviet resistance to on-site inspection as the "underlying problem" impeding arms control, a view shared by many in the administration as well as the Congress.[15]

As a general principle, it was widely assumed among legislators and publics that, however elusive, on-site inspection would be in the national interest, increasing the ability to monitor and enforce compliance to arms limitations and thus providing the basis for more comprehensive agreements. One could even caricature the traditional political perception as a belief that if a little on-site inspection is good, more is always better. Public opinion polls conducted in the late 1970s and early to mid-1980s mirrored this view. Over 60 percent of respondents to a poll conducted by the Public Agenda Foundation in 1984 said they believed on-site inspection was needed to make sure the Soviets were not cheating, and over 75 percent said the United States should not sign any agreements that did not include on-site inspection.[16]

The sudden discovery by the Congress in 1986 of some of collateral risks of on-site inspection for domestic security belies the protracted debate that has gone on among experts in such areas as chemical weapons bans and limitations on nuclear testing. Challenge inspections have long been part of the formal U.S. chemical weapons proposals in Geneva, and cooperative measures for monitoring testing limitations have been discussed as part of a PNE and CTB regime for decades. These proposals received little congressional attention, however.

Public Activism

The relatively low priority accorded to arms control negotiations by the Reagan administration in the early 1980s, coupled with the Soviet walkout from the INF negotiations in 1983, encouraged new levels of congressional and public activism on behalf of arms control. Somewhat paradoxically, it was the nuclear freeze movement in the early 1980s that prompted new levels of congressional attention to on-site inspection. Under the Carter administration, the lackluster support for SALT II among liberals was based on the perception of its excessive modesty—a "ratification of the arms race," as some described it—which in turn derived from its exclusive reliance on national technical means to set the parameters of possible restraints. Coupled with the virulent public reaction to the anti–arms control posture of the new administration, a grass-roots movement on behalf of more sweeping arms restraint won some support in the Congress beginning in 1982.

From its inception, the nuclear freeze movement went to great lengths to defend itself against charges of nonverifiability. As a result, the freeze prompted broader political and expert attention to the challenge of intrusive measures. A freeze resolution introduced in the House of Representatives on August 5, 1982 by Foreign Affairs Committee chairman Clement Zablocki (D–Wisconsin), for instance, called for "providing for cooperative measures of verification, including on-site inspection, to complement national technical means of verification and to ensure compliance."[17] Analysts provided proposals for verifying a freeze and tried to lend credence to its verifiability.

Regardless, the freeze resolutions lacked technical credibility and were politically short-lived. The minority views in a House Foreign Affairs Committee report in 1982 reflected the general feeling among the majority in the Congress that intrusive on-site inspection measures to monitor "a prohibition on warhead yields, improved throw-weight, or even new missiles," as would be required by a freeze, "would be necessary but unachievable."[18] Nevertheless, the congressional freeze debate, in combination with the administration's exigent requirements for verification, helped to bring on-site inspection to more broad-based, popular attention.

Beginning around 1983, liberal legislators repeatedly offered amendments urging the administration to undertake more vigorous efforts to restrain nuclear testing. Resolutions urging ratification of the PNE and TTB treaties, resumption of negotiations on a CTB, or eventually for a moratorium on tests with yields exceeding 1 kiloton, are a mainstay of arms control supporters in both the House and the Senate. Although binding legislation is supported by a fairly modest minority in the Senate, these resolutions have gained majority votes in the House every year since 1985.

Debate on these measures has served as one important source of congressional exposure to on-site inspection concepts. The divisions in the scientific community about the Soviet compliance record and the verifiability of any of these testing limits have tended simply to be duplicated within the Congress and competing arguments repeated ad hominem. Outside groups fueled disagreements among their respective advocates in the Congress, and no prospect of consensus seemed possible.

Administration efforts to achieve cooperative measures for seismic monitoring may change the tenor of the debate in the future. This includes an agreement reached in 1986 and formalized at the 1987 summit that provides for the United States and Soviet Union to detonate nuclear devices at each other's test sites, allowing calibration of the seismic instruments used to monitor underground tests. The Joint Verification Experiment is aimed at addressing uncertainties surrounding the verification of the PNE and TTB Treaties and may help dispel partisanship on this issue.

In 1985, the perception among some critics that the Reagan administration was advancing compliance charges without commensurate efforts to resolve disputes prompted a new kind of congressional-public assertiveness in verification, in the form of independent on-site inspections. The Natural Resources Defense Council (NRDC), for example, a privately funded environmental advocacy group, established an unprecedented program of exchanges between American and Soviet seismologists to conduct experiments to test seismic capabilities. Similarly, a group of congressional members and staff visited the Soviet Union in August 1987 to inspect the large phased-array radar in Krasnoyarsk. An offshoot of the NRDC efforts, the Krasnoyarsk visit was heralded by one participant as a step "which should go some distance towards dispelling the lingering doubts about the USSR's willingness to adopt a significantly more forthcoming approach to the verification of arms control agreements."[19]

To the contrary, efforts such as these have not enjoyed broad political support or helped dispel suspicion among critics that the Soviets have done little other than to become more adept at public relations. Partly this has been due to the composition of the delegations, which have not been bipartisan. More important, it reveals the inherent limits of unofficial site visits. If anything, these citizen-diplomat efforts have intensified conservatives' fears that on-site inspections are a new weapon in the Soviet's arsenal of propaganda and deception.

Congressional Funding for On-Site Inspection

One of the paradoxes of the compliance controversies of the 1980s is the relatively low priority accorded to relevant funding for verification technologies. The unclassified budget line items for verification activities are in the Department of Energy and Defense Advanced Research Program Agency (DARPA) budget submissions. Together, these amounted to an annual average of $70 million between fiscal years 1985 and 1988. Since these funds are also used to support activities unrelated to on-site inspection, including the operation of sensors and data processing for the Global Positioning System, satellite monitoring of the Non-Proliferation and Limited Test Ban Treaties, and other associated measures, the actual amount dedicated to research and development of new on-site inspection concepts is modest.

In fact, efforts to accelerate research in these areas have not been championed by the most ardent advocates of high-confidence verification. Occasional efforts to amend the defense authorization or appropriations bills to add funds for verification have tended to be sponsored by political moderates and, until the conclusion of INF, fared badly. Two examples illustrate the phenomenon.

In 1985, Senators Edward Kennedy (D–Massachusetts), Jeff Bingaman (D–New Mexico), and Gary Hart (D-Colorado) offered an amendment to the fiscal year 1986 defense authorization bill to give an additional $10 million to DARPA and the nuclear laboratories to pursue promising research in seismic monitoring. Underscoring the critical need to develop new avenues to ensure verification, the request was a tiny fraction of an overall authorization bill that exceeded $280 billion.

Although seemingly meritorious, the amendment incited partisan suspicion because of its sponsors. The add-on was approved after protracted debate in the Armed Services Committee and passed on the Senate floor only as a result of complicated behind-the-scenes negotiations with Republican members. By the time it emerged from the appropriations process, the amendment had been reduced to $3.5 million, the bulk of which was eventually awarded to Los Alamos to avert cutbacks in its CORRTEX program (CORRTEX is a system for on-site yield estimation of nuclear test explosions).

In fiscal year 1987 Senator William Cohen (R–Maine) attempted to add funds to the authorization Bill to augment activities relating to the monitoring of a chemical weapons ban. Noting the current lack of preparedness in the United States to verify its own draft chemical weapons treaty, Cohen urged additional funding for a program for mobile instrumentation developed by the Army Chemical Research and Development Center at Aberdeen Testing Grounds. Although approved by the authorizing committees, the request for $6 million in reprogrammed funds was resisted by the administration and axed by the Appropriations Committee, which deemed it "unnecessary."

Similarly, a House intelligence report in November 1987 noted the general lack of support for and interest in promising seismic technologies:

> US intelligence has been slow to adopt new state-of-the-art technologies and analytical techniques in seismology and slow to hire the necessary skilled analyst personnel . . . . True state of the art monitoring technologies that are "on the shelf" and those currently under examination by DARPA, DOE (Department of Energy) and the National Laboratories will require a sig-

nificant increase in the level of effort required to achieve their timely physical deployment, and to assure adequate data processing and analysis capabilities.[20]

Support for intrusive verification for future arms control agreements has yet to be tested fully on fiscal grounds, but this is a looming controversy of potentially major proportions in a constrained fiscal environment. The demand for funds to implement the INF agreement, to say nothing of a possible START or conventional forces reduction treaty, is already a source of congressional friction. The administration's estimate that it would cost $180 million to $200 million in 1988 alone to fund the requirements of missile dismantlement and establishment of monitoring sites caused consternation among members of the Armed Services and Foreign Relations committee. Although some estimates, including that of the Congressional Budget Office, suggest substantial savings accrued from lower force levels over time, the initial years still would require substantial add-ons and reprogramming.[21] Simply by undoing the public perception that arms control "saves money," on-site inspection may undercut one source of public support for future agreements.

More important, the INF debate was seized upon by the intelligence community and its supporters on the Intelligence Committee as an opportunity to highlight the perceived deficiencies in U.S. intelligence capabilities. Lurking behind the cautious prose allowing the verifiability of INF in the Intelligence Committee report is an urgent plea for funds. As the unclassified version put it, "The Committee accordingly recommends that the Congress authorize and appropriate funds required to initiate a long-term program to modernize and improve upon current plans for intelligence collection. It specifically recommends investing more in programs that would be most helpful in verifying a START treaty, in preventing technological surprise and in supporting US policy and operations in crises."[22]

Underscoring the new demands placed upon intelligence by on-site inspection and portal monitoring, particularly counterintelligence problems posed in a START regime, the committee also has established the principle that U.S. intelligence capabilities must not be dictated by arms control. Capabilities must be beefed up "to provide timely warning of possible threats that are not prohibited by the Treaty," they argue, with or without START— to include violations of limits and sublimits (as opposed to bans) of systems, unanticipated improvements in Soviet strategic forces, and possible Soviet technological breakthroughs.[23] In other words, arms control or not, there is a compelling strategic imperative, brought to light by INF, for major increases in the intelligence budget.

Senator Jesse Helms (R–North Carolina) joined the fiscal debate in late 1988 with vivid denunciation of the waste of taxpayers' money involved in the INF regime. Challenging the Congressional Budget Office estimates, Helms provided an alternative cumulative cost estimate for the thirteen-year duration of the treaty of $263.3 billion—contrasted to the $2.6 billion suggested by the administration.[24] Presaging a debate that is likely to be joined by other conservative critics of arms control in the event a START treaty is presented for ratification, Helms argued that the Defense Department had deliberately concealed costs "to prevent the American public from knowing how much they are paying to destroy their property."[25]

The establishment of new jurisdictional structures for treaty implementation may also prove grounds for interagency competition and congressional disputes, especially if it involves diversion of funds from existing programs. To date, it is not clear how the On-Site Inspection Agency will carry out its mission or be funded, but it is safe to predict that any fiscal competition with installations that have powerful congressional representatives, such as the nuclear laboratories, is likely to be met with resistance.

Major Outstanding Issues

The extremely high standards imposed on arms control verification by the nation's most conservative postwar president raised dramatically public and congressional expectations about the need for highly intrusive verification measures. Although the Senate's approval of the INF Treaty was overwhelming, its provisions were subject to intense scrutiny by numerous congressional and outside skeptics, notably some former administration officials.[26] The level of contentiousness underscored the political reality that the INF verification regime has come to be perceived as an inadequate standard for any subsequent efforts for limitations on strategic forces. Given the far more challenging verification problems posed by START, the political appetite for extremely high-confidence verification may not be easy to satisfy.

If it persists, the highly charged political environment for verification may test the ability of legislators to reach agreement on such difficult questions as how to define effective verification, how to plan for new fiscal resources to meet on-site inspection requirements, how to assess the military significance of violations, and how to enforce treaty compliance once a violation is detected. Several broad issues divide congressional opinion.

Desirable Levels of Intrusion

Having sold verification as an end in itself, the administration obscured for years the difficulties posed by on-site inspection and the fundamental trade-offs between fail-safe verification and flexibility in arms restraints. The administration also underestimated the domestic complexities associated with on-site inspection, which forced it to revise its original package of proposals for intrusive measures when the Soviets indicated interest. The appearance of U.S. capitulation created a built-in political liability, which INF critics duly exploited. Many of the same critics can be expected to scrutinize any START or conventional force reduction verification package with equal vigor.

Illustratively, the "walk-back" from the original verification package for INF prompted former assistant secretary of defense Richard Perle to observe that the restriction of challenge inspections to designated areas is worse than useless: "The last place the Soviets would choose to hide missiles is in the relatively few areas that we would be permitted to inspect . . . . Something like 99.999 percent of Soviet territory would be off-limits to US inspectors."[27] A group of hard-line conservatives agreed with Perle's assessment, including Senators Helms, Symms, James McClure (R–Idaho), and Larry Pressler (R–South Dakota), along with former senator Dan Quayle before he was elected vice-president. As Helms noted during committee hearings, "In the closing weeks of deliberations, almost 100 unresolved items were concluded. The United States gave up what had been considered fundamentally important issues during this period . . . including the right to check suspect sites."[28]

The difficulties of balancing the need for intrusion against concerns about counterintelligence will become far more conspicuous in a START environment or, equally, in efforts to limit conventional forces. The prospect of Soviet inspectors in the United States is already proving to be a logistical and political challenge, from mundane issues concerning visas and housing to more serious questions about access to sensitive military sites. The criticism by the Joint Chiefs of the first package of U.S. INF verification proposals in 1986 revealed one kind of domestic controversy prompted by excessively ambitious on-site inspection schemes, the kind of interagency wrangling that is likely to become more frequent as broader schemes are considered. *Collateral intelligence* quickly became a buzzword on Capitol Hill after the INF ratification debate, threatening to replace compliance as a partisan issue.

What Is a Military or Politically Significant Infraction?

Having challenged the acceptability of ambiguity in verification for seven years, the Reagan administration found itself struggling to develop political consensus for less than perfect assurances of compliance. The recognition that no agreement is ever technically or politically unassailable forced administration spokesmen to revive the pre-1980 vocabulary of arms control. Many have noted the irony of administration witnesses resorting to language about confidence in verification capabilities reminiscent of the SALT II ratification process. As the Senate Foreign Relations Committee Report noted:

The Committee notes the similarity between the Reagan Administration's verification standard for the INF Treaty and the verification standard the Carter Administration sought to apply to SALT II . . . . Ambassador Nitze testified that "effective verification" means "If the other side moves beyond the limits of the Treaty in any significant way, we should be able to detect such violation in time to respond effectively and thereby deny the other side the benefit of the violation." As Senator Biden pointed out, this statement is "not dissimilar" to what Harold Brown said eight years ago with regard to the SALT II Treaty.[29]

This does not amount to congressional consensus about how to define "significant," however. The INF deliberations revealed that supporters of the treaty emphasize military significance of breaches—calculable losses to Western security—whereas opponents stress the importance of even marginal infractions—signs of Soviet intent or theoretical capacity to cheat. Even if there were agreement on what might be militarily troublesome, the political challenge of defining violations or perceived violations will still be daunting if the Congress continues its current level of partisan scrutiny.

Can On-Site Inspection Ever Substitute for National Technical Means?

There is a fundamental and unresolved conflict in the political perception of the benefits of on-site inspection whose antecedents go back to SALT I. The question is whether on-site inspection can increase confidence to the point of permitting more ambitious arms control limitations, not just complementing but in some cases superseding the requirement for verification by national technical means, or if it always will be so fraught with technical and political difficulties that it is at best a modest confidence-building measure, which provides limited support to national technical means functions.

The hard-line "liberal" view in the current environment is that the degree of cooperation implied by intrusive measures suggested prospects for broader accommodation between the superpowers. The cooperation involved in monitoring activities in and of itself provides an operational avenue for confidence building, they argue, much like risk reduction centers or improved communications links. As the Senate Foreign Relations Committee report assets, "The INF Treaty's on-site inspections could promote a desirable opening up of Soviet society which could ease superpower tensions."[30]

By contrast, many conservative and moderate members have turned their attention to the possible dangers posed by the INF on-site inspection regime. As summarized in the dissenting views of the Republican minority members of the House Select Committee on Intelligence in November 1987:

Badly conceived on-site inspection provisions may be worse than nothing because they encourage a false sense of security. There is a danger that we will spend large sums of money on systems to monitor weapons destruction, production, or deployment at declared sites, simply shifting the incentive for cheating to other unmonitorable locations and using money that could have been spent better on other forms of collection . . . . Monitoring only destruction of acknowledged assets can also be dangerously misleading if we do not know how many were produced in the first place and if we cannot guarantee that production has ceased . . . . Even challenge inspections can be foiled if there is a short lag-time before investigators are allowed at the site. Virtually no one seriously believes the USSR in practice would allow an inspection that might confirm a Soviet violation, although the USSR might allow observation if there was an opportunity to remove such evidence first, thereby encouraging Western self-doubt or complacency.[31]

In a sense, the debate seemed to have come full circle. Where on-site inspection was once the only way to ensure that the Soviets would not dupe the trusting West, it could now serve as the very method by which to do so.

The majority view is likely to fall somewhere in the middle, recognizing that on-site inspection functions can provide a backup to national technical means and provide operational experience in cooperative measures. As noted by majority members of the House Intelligence Committee in the same report:

On-site inspections are generally regarded as a way to supplement National Technical Means in order to permit highly specific and restrictive arms control provisions. Testimony revealed, however, that policy planners must be cautious in relying on on-site inspection as a solution to verification problems. Challenge inspections in particular are inherently susceptible to being impeded by the challenged party using its physical control of the area to be investigated.[32]

Monitoring Certainty versus Strategic Flexibility

Another issue remaining for political resolution is the desirable balance between high-confidence verification and flexibility in strategic plans—a fundamental issue that originated with the first efforts at strategic arms control. The Senate Intelligence Committee report on the INF treaty, for instance, emphasizes as one of its main themes that the benefits of high-confidence verification should not be oversold, noting a "tension between monitoring requirements and overall strategic needs" in such decisions as the ban on ground-launched cruise missiles and the exclusion of anywhere, anytime inspection measures, which pose Soviet counterintelligence concerns.[33]

By contrast, the Senate Foreign Relations Committee questioned the wisdom of not banning submarine-launched cruise missiles (SLCMs), saying a majority "found it difficult to understand why protecting US conventional cruise missile capabilities and options is more important than insuring the overall verifiability of the emerging START treaty."[34] With the Senate Armed Services Committee generally in agreement with the Intelligence Committee, there is a clear split with the Senate Foreign Relations Committee on both the approach to verification and to SLCMs specifically. This problem will prove even more difficult in defining the U.S. approach to such contentious issues as a ban or limitation of mobile missiles under a START regime.

Can We Create Credible Enforcement Mechanisms?

Both the Senate Armed Services and Intelligence Committees stressed the need to enforce compliance for both militarily significant and other types of infractions and to increase the range of U.S. options for responding to infringements. As the Intelligence Committee report put it, "seeking Soviet compliance by diplomatic means, denouncing the violation publicly, threatening to withdraw from the treaty, or ultimately countering the violation with new military programs of our own."[35] Similarly, the Armed Services Committee report stated that the committee "accepts the assessment . . . that the Treaty was effectively verifiable, which was described as high confidence that a militarily significant violation would be detected. At the same time, the Committee would object strongly if this proper focus on militarily significant violations were interpreted as a lack of concern over violations that failed to meet this criteria." It urged "an effective compliance policy as a high priority" and supported a broader compliance reporting requirement to include a range of compliance activities.[36]

Given the current political climate, it is not at all clear that consensus can be reached about appropriate enforcement mechanisms. The new Special Verification Committee provided for in INF—to complement the Standing Consultative Commission—is also a matter of some dispute.

Recommendations for an Executive-Congressional Strategy for On-Site Inspection

The legacy of the on-site inspection debate in the 1980s suggests some general areas for improvement in the political strategy for arms control and verification:

1. The need for active consultation with congressional leaders on all aspects of treaty verification. There has been a clear pattern of success in those instances when the Senate leadership—particularly the Arms Control Observer Group—has been included in sensitive deliberations. By contrast, all efforts to circumvent congressional authority proved demonstr-

ably self-defeating. The Congress may be weak in its ability to absorb technical details, but it is consistent in the protection of one sacrosanct principle: prerogative.

2. Intensive consultations with responsible congressional leaders on the verification requirements of any prospective START agreement are vital. There is time for new administration officials to carry out a series of private conversations before completing the verification package for START, along with a national program to expand intelligence capabilities, to ensure a workable two-thirds majority in the Senate for the prospective agreement. It is evident that a minority will never be satisfied; a coalition of liberals and moderates should not be too difficult to put together, given flexibility on the administration's part.

3. Too often in the past, consultations with the Congress have been interpreted in the executive branch to mean cursory briefings, intended solely to inform a dependent partner. During the Reagan administration, the Congress demonstrated convincingly its determination and ability to play a decisive role in arms control. Given the already heated nature of the debate on START, well in advance of the treaty's conclusion, it is clear that what is needed now is true collaboration.

4. Over the longer term, three types of actions are necessary to ensure the effective verification of arms control agreements. First, greater thought must be given to verification requirements, including the intensity and desirability of on-site inspection, prior to the tabling of new draft agreements or negotiating positions. The U.S. draft chemical weapons agreement is a persuasive case in point. Virtually no consideration was given to how such an agreement actually might be verified prior to its tabling because no one took the possibility of such an agreement seriously. As was demonstrated with the zero-option, however, and now again with the draft chemical weapons agreement, such predictions are hazardous at best. This leaves the United States with the unhappy choice of hammering out intrusive verification procedures, many of which it would prefer not to see implemented, or to attempt to back-pedal away from supposedly principled arms control advocacy—with unsettling political effects on allied governments, as well as friendly publics. It is far better to evaluate verification requirements ahead of time and to table agreements for which the necessary means of verification would be acceptable and are technically in hand.

Second, investments should be made to develop cooperative technical schemes for verifying arms control arrangements. Some of this work might be done in cooperation with the Soviet Union; most should be done in U.S. laboratories. Schemes involving the use of sophisticated remote sensors and other devices can reduce requirements for on-site inspections, thus ensuring confidence in the ability to verify compliance with agreements without creating opportunities for Soviet deception or intelligence gathering. Many such ideas already exist in laboratories and think tanks around the country; high-level political attention is necessary, however, along with adequate funding, to ensure their implementation.

Third, Congress and the executive must work out a long-term funding strategy for verification that fully accommodates intelligence requirements for the future and balances priorities among participating agencies. In a fiscal environment in which deficit reduction is overshadowing all other priorities, advance planning for verification funding, based on bipartisan support, is the only way to mitigate the likelihood of excessive cuts or erratic appropriations for vital monitoring and enforcement functions.

Notes

1. U.S. Congress, Senate Armed Services Committee, "Questions on the Meaning of the INF Treaty," March, 1988 internal memo.
2. See, for instance, Senate Armed Services Committee, *NATO Defense and the INF Treaty*, Report and Hearings, vols. 1–4, 100th Cong. 1988; Senate Foreign Relations Committee, *The INF Treaty*, Report and Hearings, vols. 1–5, 100th Cong. 1988; and Senate Select Committee on Intelligence, *The INF Treaty: Monitoring and Verification Capabilities*, unclassified report.
3. Senate Intelligence Committee, *INF Treaty*, p. 14.
4. Senator Bill Bradley, "Beyond the Question of INF Verifiability," *New York Times*, April 11, 1988.
5. *Congressional Record*, July 13, 1983.
6. Ibid.
7. Ibid., February 21, September 23, 1963.
8. Quoted in *Congressional Quarterly Almanac* (1970), p. 303.
9. U.S. Congress, Senate Armed Services Committee, *The Military Implications of the Treaty on the Limitation of Anti-Ballistic Missile Systems and the Interim Agreement on Limitation of Strategic Office Arms* 92nd Cong. 2nd Sess. (Summer 1972).
10. Ibid.
11. U.S. Congress, Senate Foreign Relations Committee, Executive Report, *The SALT II Treaty*, 96th Cong. 1st Sess. 1979, pp. 48–49.
12. Senate Select Committee on Intelligence, *Principal Findings on the Capabilities of the United States to Monitor the SALT II Treaty*, 96th Cong. 1st Sess. 1979.
13. Les Aspin, "The Verification of the SALT II Agreement," *Scientific American* (September 1979).
14. Gallup Organization, May 13, 1983.
15. *Congressional Record*, April 14, 1982, p. S3440.

16. Public Agenda Foundation polls, May 21, 1984.
17. U.S. House of Representatives, H.J. Res. 521, August 5, 1982.
18. U.S. House of Representatives, House Foreign Affairs Committee, *Report Calling For a Mutual and Verifiable Freeze on and Reductions in Nuclear Weapons and For Approval of the SALT II Agreement*, minority views, 97th Cong. 2nd Sess., 1982.
19. Memorandum from Christopher E. Paine to Senator Edward M. Kennedy, September 9, 1987.
20. U.S. House of Representatives, Permanent Select Committee on Intelligence, *Intelligence Support to Arms Control*, 100th Cong., 1st Sess., 1987, p. 24.
21. Congressional Budget Office, *Cost Estimate for Treaty Document 100-11, The Treaty between the United States of America and the Union of Soviet Socialist Republics*, March 10, 1988.
22. Senate Intelligence Committee report, p. 16.
23. Ibid.
24. Senate Foreign Relations Committee, *SALT II Treaty*, cit., p. 334.
25. Ibid.
26. See, for instance, the detailed analysis prepared by Richard Perle, and Frank Gaffney, "Article by Article Review of the INF Treaty," *AEI Occasional Papers*, American Enterprise Institute, February 3, 1988.
27. Quoted in *Congressional Quarterly*, December 5, 1987, p. 2971.
28. Quoted in ibid., January 30, 1988; p. 197.
29. Senate Foreign Relations Committee, *SALT II Treaty*, p. 43.
30. Ibid., p. 50.
31. Permanent Select Committee on Intelligence, House of Representatives, *Intelligence Support to Arms Control*, op. cit.
32. Ibid.
33. Senate Intelligence Committee, *INF Treaty*.
34. Senate Foreign Relations Committee, *SALT II Treaty*.
35. Senate Intelligence Committee, *INF Treaty*.
36. Senate Armed Services Committee, *Military Implications*.

10
The Evolution of Soviet Attitudes Toward On-Site Inspection

William C. Potter
with
Leonid V. Belyaev and *Mark Lay*

A cceptance of intrusive forms of inspection has long served as the touchstone by which U.S. officials judged the seriousness of Soviet arms control and disarmament proposals. Until recently, Soviet initiatives generally have failed that test, at least in Western eyes. And yet one can identify a number of cases in the pre-Gorbachev era in which Soviet proposals embraced varying degrees of on-site inspection. Some were incorporated in arms control accords. How did these earlier Soviet proposals for intrusive inspection differ from those associated with the new political thinking? To what extent have the basic principles underlying Soviet policy toward on-site inspection actually changed? If there are fundamental changes, what are the sources of the policy innovation, and what are likely to be their long-term consequences? In order to address these questions, this chapter elaborates a framework for assessing different components of Soviet policy toward on-site inspection and then applies the framework in a comparative fashion to Soviet verification policy in representative arms control and disarmament forums from the beginning of the post–World War II era to the present.

A Framework for Assessing Soviet Verification Policy

One can identify a number of recurrent themes or principles in Soviet thinking about verification in the post–World War II period. Examination of the

The author wishes to express his thanks to Leonid V. Belyaev and Mark Lay for their excellent research assistance. He is grateful to Lewis Dunn, Warren Heckrotte, Elaine Holoboff, Andrzej Karkoszka, and James Schear for their thoughtful comments on an earlier draft of this chapter. He wishes to acknowledge the cooperation of the Institute of World Economy and International Relations, which hosted his visit to the Soviet Union, January–February 1989, and facilitated interviews with Soviet arms control negotiators and civilian and military strategists. Subsequent interviews were conducted in Moscow in March 1989.

application of these principles (or lack thereof) in past negotiations and agreements provides one means to chart the continuity and change in Soviet policy toward verification. In order to gauge better the evolution of Soviet thinking with respect to on-site inspection in particular, the inventory of basic themes[1] is supplemented by a checklist of verification behavior that corresponds to varying degrees of intrusive inspection.[2] The composite checklist is provided in table 10–1.

Recurrent Themes

Verification Should Be Narrowly Defined

Soviet negotiators traditionally have sought to define verification narrowly and to distinguish legitimate verification procedures from routine intelligence gathering.[3] This tendency has led some observers to characterize the Soviet approach to verification as one of strict constructionism.[4] Somewhat oddly, given this orientation, is the customary Soviet usage of the word *kontrol'* for verification of arms control accords, despite the Russian word's broad connotation implying monitoring as well as verification. *Proverka*, literally "checking up," has a narrower connotation than *kontrol'* but is less often used in the context of arms control.[5]

Table 10–1
Indicators of Soviet Thinking about Verification

Recurrent themes
1. Verification should be narrowly defined.
2. Verification procedures should not compromise the national sovereignty of the Soviet Union.
3. Verification measures are appropriate only for disarmament purposes.
4. Verification means must be proportional to the disarmament obligations undertaken.
5. Agreements on the scope of an accord must precede detailed discussion of verification measures.
6. Verification should not be based on the principle of distrust.
7. International forms of verification should be limited.
8. It is impossible to conceal a militarily significant arms control violation.
9. Verification is mainly a political, not a technical, matter.

Measures of intrusive inspection
1. Verification involves physical presence of inspectors on Soviet territory.
2. Inspectors remain on Soviet territory for extended periods of time.
3. Inspections are scheduled in advance.
4. The locale to be inspected is designated in advance.
5. Inspection is by demand.
6. International agency has the authority to determine noncompliance.

Verification Procedures Should Not Compromise the
National Sovereignty of the Soviet Union

In March 1981, the Soviet ambassador to the Conference on Disarmament in Geneva, Viktor Israelyan, set forth seven basic principles underlying the Soviet approach to verification. Although many of these principles no longer characterize Soviet thinking about verification, they provide a useful standard against which to chart continuity and change in Soviet perspectives.

Heading the list was the principle that the conduct of verification should in no way prejudice the sovereign rights of states or permit interference in their internal affairs.[6] This principle is also identified as central to Soviet verification policy in what are probably the two other most detailed public statements of Soviet thinking about verification prior to Gorbachev: an article by R. Zheleznov in *International Affairs* in 1982 and a book by Roland Timerbayev, *Kontrol' za Ogranicheniyem Vooruzheniy i Razoruzheniyem* (Verification of arms limitation and disarmament) in 1983.[7]

According to Timerbayev, a senior Soviet diplomat, "no verification system is valid unless it is based upon [the principles of] noninterference in the internal affairs of states and sovereign equality of states."[8] Timerbayev emphasized as "an absolute condition of verification" that it "not damage the security of the participating states."[9] More than once, Timerbayev maintains, the United States has proposed verification schemes whose implementation would have constituted interference in the internal affairs of states.[10] Put somewhat differently in a more recent commentary by a Soviet general:

> The USSR is categorically opposed to "inspections" like the notorious "Baruch Plan," the "open skies" concept and others that were put forward by the USA in the past and had the nature of the intelligence-gathering operations. The Soviet Union will not agree to such "verification."[11]

Verification Measures Are Appropriate Only for
Disarmament Purposes

Until recently, a recurrent theme in Soviet commentary was that verification should be about disarmament measures, not armaments. This point is made explicitly by both Timerbayev and Zheleznov and is one of the basic principles cited by Israelyan.[12] A clear statement of the principle was also made much earlier by Deputy Foreign Minister Valerian Zorin during the negotiations of the 1961 McCloy-Zorin Agreed Statement of Principles relating to general and complete disarmament.

According to Zheleznov, verification "can only be a component of a disarmament agreement and serve as an instrument helping to fulfill the agreement." Divorced from disarmament, it becomes pointless.[13] Similarly, Timerbayev argues that prior "attempts to separate verification from disarmament have totally discredited themselves."[14] He cites the League of Nations, which gathered military data over a period of years, as a typical example."[15] He also makes the point that "Western concepts of verification, which are based on interference in the internal affairs of sovereign states and attempts to establish control over existing armaments (and not disarmament) . . . [are] the equivalent of legalizing reconnaissance activities."[16] The 1946 Baruch Plan and the 1955 "open skies" proposals by President Eisenhower are cited as examples.[17] In 1961 Zorin also rejected the U.S. efforts by McCloy to add as part of their agreed statement the sentence: "Such verification should ensure that not only agreed limitations or reductions take place but also that retained armed forces and armaments do not exceed agreed levels at any stage."[18] "Such control," Zorin argued, "[would in fact mean] control over armaments . . . [and] would turn into an international system of legalized espionage."[19]

Verification Must Be Proportional to the Disarmament Obligations Undertaken

One of the most frequently recurring themes in Soviet commentary on verification is that the scope and forms of verification should be geared to the character and scope of the disarmament measures undertaken.[20] In the words of Timerbayev,

> There must be organic interaction between verification and disarmament. The verification means, forms and methods and the rights, the authority and the functions of the corresponding verification agency must be precisely commensurate with the nature and the scope of arms limitation measures being worked out and implemented.[21]

This emphasis on proportionality is in contrast to what Soviet commentators perceive to be an American tendency to pursue verification as an end in itself and to insist on relatively extensive monitoring requirements for arms control measures that themselves are quite modest in scope. This contrast in approaches, Soviet commentators note, makes implementation of the principle of proportionality difficult although not impossible to achieve. The 1974 Threshold Test Ban Treaty and the 1976 Treaty on Underground Nuclear Explosions for Peaceful Purposes are cited as examples of negotiating successes.[22]

Without repudiating the insistence that verification measures not compromise national sovereignty or violate the principle of proportionality, Soviet commentators have increasingly acknowledged the legitimate role played by satellite reconnaissance in monitoring compliance with arms control accords since the early 1970s. This view represents a major change from the early 1960s, when aerial reconnaissance was equated with espionage and violation of Soviet airspace.[23] Informal Soviet acceptance of satellite reconnaissance for purposes of verification, however, and Soviet recognition of the ability of satellite monitoring in support of other foreign policy objectives (such as crisis management) have not led to formal recognition of the legality of monitoring by satellites.[24]

Agreement on the Scope of an Accord Must Precede Detailed Discussion of Verification Measures

A corollary of the principle of proportionality is that of prior agreement in principle. This theme, also cited by Israelyan and Timerbayev, addresses the Soviet preference for agreeing on the substance of arms limitations before considering verification arrangements.[25] Otherwise, Soviet commentators caution, verification methods may be designed for purposes other than control over disarmament—for example, collection of military intelligence.[26] This was the Soviet assessment of U.S. intent with the 1955 "open skies" proposal.

Verification Should Not Be Based on the Principle of Distrust

Soviet writing about verification traditionally has emphasized the importance of trust. "Any international agreement," Timerbayev asserts, "must be based on a certain degree of mutual trust among the parties to the agreement." Otherwise "it is impossible and inconceivable to initiate appropriate talks, to see them through to a successful conclusion and then to maintain the viability of the agreements concluded and effectively implement them."[27]

The traditional Soviet attitude toward trust in arms control differs markedly from the U.S. perspective that verification should be a substitute for trust.[28] Soviet commentators do, however, acknowledge that "in many cases . . . trust alone is not enough to provide confidence that an agreement is being fulfilled absolutely by all the parties."[29] Nevertheless, trust is seen as emanating from a mutual interest in limiting arms. Recently the concept of glasnost has been cited as a means of increasing confidence and building trust.[30]

International Forms of Verification Should Be Limited

One of the seven basic verification principles identified by Israelyan in 1981 concerns Soviet aversion to international, multilateral forms of verification. This theme, however, no longer characterizes Soviet commentary on verification and in fact has been replaced by a positive view of the potential role for international verification bodies, especially multilateral accords.[31]

It Is Impossible to Conceal a Militarily Significant Arms Control Violation

The last of the basic principles of verification noted by Israelyan suggests that the current level of technology makes it impossible to conceal militarily significant arms control violations.[32] Stated somewhat differently by Timerbayev, a secret violation "would have to be a small violation and consequently involve little reward."[33] As Allan Krass notes, the Soviet perspective resembles the double-bind principle articulated by former secretary of defense Harold Brown and may explain why Soviet requirements for reassurance in the area of verification generally have been less demanding than those of the United States.[34]

Verification Is Mainly a Political, Not a Technical, Matter

Soviet commentators on verification grant that technological advances have facilitated the negotiation of verification provisions in arms control agreements. Nevertheless, they assert that verification is mainly a political, not a technical, matter.[35] In the words of Zheleznov, "political factors underlie the whole problem."[36] Politics, however, may also provide an answer to the problem. "Detente contributed toward greater confidence in relations between states thus creating additional possibilities for the evolution of concrete verification problems."[37]

Measures of Intrusive Inspection

In order to assess the evolution of Soviet thinking about on-site inspection, it is useful to supplement the preceding inventory of basic themes with a list of measures that reflect more directly relative support for, or opposition to, alternative means of intrusive inspection. Many of the measures discussed below are also identified by Alan Sherr in his "Typology of Verification Regimes,"[38] and most of these require little explanation.

Verification Involves Physical Presence of Inspectors on Soviet Territory

This item is designed to distinguish intrusive inspections conducted with unmanned tamperproof installations (for example, "black boxes" used to record seismic activity) from manned inspections. It also differentiates between intrusive inspections in which the Soviet homeland is not involved (for example, the 1959 Antarctic Treaty and the post–World War II military liaison missions in East and West Germany) and those that require the presence of inspectors on the *rodina* (motherland).

Inspectors Remain On-Site for Extended Periods of Time

This measure distinguishes short-term inspection visits from extended or permanent inspection installations.

Inspections Are Scheduled in Advance

This measure reflects the distinction between scheduled inspections and those of an ad hoc nature, such as challenge inspections.

The Locale to Be Inspected Is Designated in Advance

This measure distinguishes between inspections in which the site (or sites) is (are) designated in advance and those in which the inspecting party is free to choose the site for inspection.

Inspection Is by Demand

This measure distinguishes between inspections in which the inspecting party may demand the right of inspection and those in which requests are nonbinding.

International Agency Has the Authority to Determine Noncompliance

This measure identifies the nature of the inspecting party (national or international) and its authority to determine whether noncompliance has occurred.

Continuity and Change in Soviet Verification Policy

A systematic comparison and analysis of the applicability of the themes and measures noted to the actual record of Soviet negotiating behavior is beyond the scope of this study. Instead a summary of Soviet verification policy with respect to these criteria, as evidenced in a variety of arms control and disarmament forums since World War II, is presented in Table 10–2. The table also indicates my judgment about the relative U.S.-Soviet strategic balance,

Table 10–2
Continuity and Change in Soviet Verification Policy

Forum	Themes Applicable	On-Site Inspection Measures
Baruch Plan (1946)	3,4,5,8	a,b,i
May 10, 1955, Proposal	2–6,9	a,b,g,i
Open skies (1955)	1–9	
Antarctic Treaty (1959)	2–5,8,9	b,d,f,g
McCloy-Zorin Agreement (1961)	2–9	a,d,f,g,i
Partial Test Ban (1963)	1–9	[2]
Outer Space Treaty (1967)	2–5	c,f,[3]h
Tlatelolco (1967)	3,4,5,8	d,f,g,[4]h
NPT (1968)	3,4,5,8	d,[5]e,h,i
Seabed Treaty (1971)	2–6	i
Biological Weapons (1972)	1–6	i
SALT I (1972)	1–9	
TTBT (1974)	1–5,7,8	
PNET (1976)	1–5,7,8	a,c,e,g
SALT II (1979)	1–9	
CTB negotiations (1977–1980)	1–5,7,8	a,d,f,h
IAEA inspections (1985)	3,9	a,d,e,h,i
Stockholm CSCE (1986)	4	a,d,f,[7]g
INF (1987)	3,4,8	a,b,d,e,g
Chemical negotiations (1987–)	3,4	a,b,d,f,g,i
START/Space (1987–)	3,4,8	a,b,d,e,g
MBFR/Vienna (1987–)	3,4	a,b,d,f,h

KEY

Themes	On-Site Inspection Measures
1. Narrow definition of verification.	a. Inspectors on Soviet territory.
2. No infringement of sovereignty.	b. Long-term presence of inspectors permitted.
3. Verification only over disarmament.	c. Time of inspection is set by host.
4. Proportionality.	d. Time of inspection is set by inspector.
5. Prior agreement in principle.	e. Locale is designated (preselected).
6. Emphasize trust.	f. Locale is not preselected.
7. Oppose international inspection.	g. Inspection is by demand.
8. Significant concealment impossible.	h. Inspection is by request.
9. Verification predominantly political.	i. International body can determine noncompliance.

Sources: *Documents on Disarmament, 1945–1959* (Washington, D.C.: GPO, 1960); *Arms Control and Disarmament Agreements, 1959–1972* (Washington, D.C.: GPO, 1972); Arms Control and Disarmament Division, Canadian Department of External Affairs, *Compendium of Verbatim Statements on Verification*, vols. 2–3 (Ottawa, Canada, 1985); Timerbayev, *Kontrol' Za Ogranicheniyem Vooruzheniy i Razoruzheniyem;* Heckrotte, "Verification of Test Ban Treaties," 63–80; Krass, "The Soviet View of Verification," pp. 37–62; Sherr, *Other Side of Arms Control;* John H. Barton and Lawrence D. Weiler, eds., *International Arms Control* (Stanford: Stanford University Press, 1976); Lincoln Bloomfield et al., *Khrushchev and the Arms Race* (Cambridge: MIT Press, 1966); Alexander Dallin et al., *The Soviet Union, Arms Control, and Disarmament* (New York: Columbia University School of International Affairs, 1964); and *Arms Control Reporter.*

Strategic Balance	Arms Control Priority	Perceived Need for On-Site Inspection[1]
US adv.	low	no
US adv.	low	yes
US adv.	low	no
US adv.	low	?
US adv.	low	yes
US adv.	moderate-high	no
parity	low	?
parity	moderate	yes
parity	moderate-high	yes
parity	low	?
parity	low	no
parity	moderate-high	no
parity	moderate	no
parity	low	yes[6]
parity	moderate	no
parity	moderate	yes[6]
parity	low	yes
parity	moderate-high	yes
parity	high	yes
parity	moderate	yes
parity	high	yes
parity	high	yes

[1]This column reflects my judgment of the perceived need on the part of the Soviet leadership for on-site inspection.

[2]Does not incorporate any on-site inspection measures. During the course of the test ban negotiations, however, Khrushchev agreed to three on-site inspections but contended they were unnecessary. See Bloomfield et al., *Khrushchev and the Arms Race*, pp. 240–241.

[3]Under the terms of the treaty all stations, installations, equipment, and spacecraft on the moon and other heavenly bodies are open to inspection by other parties to the treaty on a reasonable basis. Advance notification is required. See Timerbayev, *Kontrol' za Ogranicheniyem Vooruzheniy i Razoruzheniyem*, pp. 34–38.

[4]The Treaty of Tlatelolco (Nuclear Free Zone in Latin America) envisages both IAEA safeguards and special inspections in which the host state has no right of refusal. See David Fischer and Paul Szasz, *Safeguarding the Atom* (London: Taylor & Francis, 1985), p. 69, and Timerbayev, *Kontrol' za Ogranicheniyem Vooruzheniy i Razoruzheniyem*, pp. 38–40.

[5]Although the IAEA routinely gives advance notification, the model NPT Safeguards Agreement of 1971 (INFCIRC/153) permits the IAEA to carry out unannounced inspections. See Fischer and Szasz, *Safeguarding the Atom*, pp. 30–31.

[6]One may argue that the Soviets would have been quite content to have had no on-site inspections in the PNET or a CTB. Nevertheless, they accepted the logic of them in these cases, even if it was political necessity rather than the logic of the matter that led to their decision. I am thankful to Warren Heckrotte for this distinction.

[7]The inspecting party designates a specific area within the predetermined "zone of application for confidence and security-building measures." The host state, however, may deny inspectors access to certain "restricted locations, installations, and defense sites."

the degree of Soviet interest in arms control, and the perceived need on the part of the Soviet leadership for on-site inspection at the time of and in relation to the corresponding negotiations.

Any effort to compress a large body of complex data into neat tabular form runs the risk of imposing patterns when there are none. This danger is increased when there is considerable variation among the attributes being measured *within* a given case (for example, changes in the relevance of Is-raelyan's basic principles and the posture toward on-site inspection during negotiations on a chemical weapons ban). Nevertheless, with these caveats in mind, a number of propositions are suggested by the table.

Perhaps the most striking feature of table 10–2 is the extent of fluctuation in Soviet verification policy revealed over time, both with respect to basic principles and to on-site inspection. One discerns, for example, numerous precedents for Soviet acceptance of intrusive inspection long before the emergence of Gorbachev's "new thinking" about security policy. This apparent fluctuation in policy and the presence of precedents for on-site inspection may be partially a function of the table's failure to distinguish between serious Soviet initiatives and those that were primarily propagandistic in nature. The erratic tendencies remain, however, when one controls for this possibility by excluding accords that were not actually adopted (as with the first three entries in the table).

The most enduring and constantly applied of the nine themes is that pertaining to proportionality. Indeed, the theme is reflected in all but the unilateral decision in 1985 to allow International Atomic Energy Agency (IAEA) inspection of select Soviet nuclear power facilities.

One may argue that theme 3 (verification only over disarmament) also is applicable to all but the 1986 Stockholm Accord on confidence-building measures.[39] However, although the Soviets continued until recently to say that verification should be over disarmament and not arms,[40] their support of national technical means of verification in such forums as SALT (Strategic Arms Limitation Talks I and II) and the Strategic Arms Reduction Talks (START) implicitly acknowledges the legitimacy of the use of verification to monitor armaments (residual forces).[41] Gorbachev explicitly noted this role for verification in his April 1987 speech in Prague:

> The appropriate verification measures, including on-site inspections, must encompass the missiles and launchers remaining after the reduction, including those on combat duty and at other facilities, testing grounds, manufacturing works, training centers, etc.[42]

A significant pattern that emerges regarding Soviet attitudes toward intrusive inspection is a willingness since the late 1950s to become party to international accords with provisions for on-site inspections. Although these accords vary markedly in the activities proscribed and the measures permitted, until the Treaty on Peaceful Nuclear Explosions in 1976 all shared the characteristic that the Soviet homeland was not subject to inspection.[43] This exclusion also applies to the infrequently noted but significant inspection agreement involving military liaison missions in East and West Germany, although this is not strictly an arms control accords.

Another trend emerging after 1976 and becoming most pronounced in the Gorbachev period is the acceptance of nearly the entire range of on-site inspection measures, including in some instances inspection on demand. At the same time that more intrusive measures have found their way into Soviet negotiating postures across a broad spectrum of arms control forums, Soviet commentators, including Israelyan, have ceased to emphasize a number of previously heralded basic principles. Some, like those pertaining to national sovereignty, prior agreement in principle, trust, and the possibility of significant concealment, are not given much attention.[44]

Instead, Soviet commentators—at times including Gorbachev—are inclined to emphasize their readiness to accept the toughest standards of verification ("triple verification" if need be) in order to achieve arms control progress.[45] Stringent verification measures, which include intrusive forms of inspection, are seen as a means of alleviating suspicion. As Alan Sherr has pointed out, the present Soviet leadership seems to understand that "verification must precede trust rather than vice versa."[46] By the same token, the traditional dictum of "prior agreement in principle" has tended to give way to a readiness to discuss verification and substance simultaneously.[47] This shift has been apparent at least since the Reagan and Gorbachev November 1985 summit in Geneva and is reflected in all of the ongoing arms control negotiations.

While the Soviets under Gorbachev have chosen simply to mute the importance of some traditional verification themes, one of Israelyan's basic principles—the limitation of international forms of verification—has been totally revised. This shift in thinking actually preceded Gorbachev and was first clearly signaled in 1982 in a statement by Yuri Andropov in the 1982 Zheleznov article and again in the 1983 book by Timerbayev.[48] The latter two sources, both written by Timerbayev, cite the vast verification experience accumulated by the IAEA and suggest the relevance of this international approach to verification to other arms control areas.[49]

Significantly, praise of the IAEA verification model coincided with the June 1982 announcement by Andrei Gromyko at the Second U.N. Special Session on Disarmament that the Soviet Union might be willing to place part of its peaceful nuclear installations under IAEA control.[50] Such an agreement was subsequently concluded with the IAEA and entered into effect in 1985. More recently, the Soviet Union has endorsed the concept of third-party verification activities such as the 1986 six-nation proposal.[51] Although most

Soviet verification analysts regard international verification measures, including on-site inspection, to be most relevant to multilateral arms control accords (for example, a comprehensive test ban or chemical weapons ban), one can also find proposals for their use in bilateral superpower agreements.[52]

Table 10–2 highlights the major discontinuities in Soviet thinking about verification policy and about on-site inspection in particular. Less apparent from the table is the distinction between *change* in Soviet policy (deviation from prior policy) and policy *innovation* (change that is nonincremental, is sustained over time, and has systemic significance).[53]

Based on a survey of Soviet verification policy in nearly two dozen arms control forums over three and a half decades, one can argue that while there are numerous instances of policy change or fluctuation, there are only two clear instances of policy innovation: in the mid-1960s, when the Soviet Union accepted the legitimacy of satellite reconnaissance for purposes of verification, and in the mid-1980s, when Soviet negotiators began to support stringent verification measures, including on-site inspection. This second sustained shift in Soviet verification policy, which is relevant for this study, is distinguished by its theoretical underpinnings, the general consistency with which it has been applied, and the degree to which Soviet commentators themselves acknowledge that an innovation has occurred.

Although there were harbingers of the new policy as early as 1982 and one can point in retrospect to select indicators of the policy innovation under both Andropov and Chernenko, it remained for Gorbachev and his advisers to provide a practical and theoretical basis for the new commitment to stringent verification methods. Glasnost and the new political thinking, with its emphasis on reasonable sufficiency, served those functions.

At a more theoretical level, the new thinking on security policy starts from the premise that U.S. and Soviet security interests are intertwined and that Soviet security interests are better served by political than military-technical means.[54] Under conditions in which "security can only be ensured by political means," it is argued, "the role of verification objectively grows as does Soviet support for the most stringent forms of inspection."[55] As the press background document for the Moscow Summit puts it:

> The main thing for the USSR now is not methods, but ensuring complete confidence that treaties . . . are scrupulously fulfilled . . . . Today, when the Soviet Union is told about the need for double verification, it responds with readiness for triple verification based on national technical means, international procedures and obligatory on-site inspections.[56]

Recognition of growing international interdependence and mutual security is also cited as a rationale for the pursuit of glasnost in international relations globally, including the establishment of reliable means of verification.[57] This point is well argued by Alexander Savelyev and Vladimir Frangulov in the most recent detailed Soviet treatise on verification:

> At the present-day level of nuclear confrontation, the security of every state has to be built with due regard for the interests of the security of the other side. In those conditions, the old criteria for military secrecy quite often become counterproductive, giving rise to suspicions about the other state's intentions to obtain unilateral advantages. Besides, greater openness in these questions reduces the possibility of overestimating the military plans and capabilities of the opposing side.[58]

It is of course, one thing to propose a new policy and quite another thing to implement it. Although one can point to certain counterexamples, one of the most significant aspects of the Gorbachev innovation in verification policy is the extent to which the new thinking actually has been reflected in a broad range of Soviet negotiating proposals. They include the acceptance of challenge ad hoc on-site inspections by demand in the case of the 1986 Stockholm Confidence and Security Building Measures Accord; ad hoc on-site inspection on demand as well as long-term, continuous on-site inspection in the 1987 INF treaty; ad hoc on-site inspection by demand in the ongoing negotiations to ban chemical weapons; and intrusive forms of inspection at least as stringent as those in the INF treaty for ongoing negotiations on strategic and space weapons. The Soviet Union also has moved closer to the U.S. position on on-site inspection in discussions about revising the unratified Threshold Test Ban Treaty and has accepted continuously manned seismic monitoring stations in an agreement with the private Natural Resources Defense Council (NRDC).[59] Even in the Vienna negotiations on conventional forces, (where progress has been slower than in most other arms control forums), the Soviet position on verification has evolved in the direction of ad hoc on-site inspection.

Prior shifts in Soviet national security policy were not heralded as such by Soviet commentators who preferred to accentuate continuity over change. Gorbachev, on the other hand, has chosen to highlight that which is new in Soviet policy. Not surprisingly, this approach applies to verification. Many commentators have called attention to a major revision in Soviet attitudes and behavior. No less a spokesman for Soviet verification policy than Ambassador Roland Timerbayev acknowledged in 1987 that the Soviet government had recently adopted a new approach to verification that "materialized in practice" at the 1986 Stockholm Conference.[60] In the words of Oleg Grinevsky, former head of the Soviet delegation to the Stockholm Conference and currently the head of the Soviet delegation to the Negotiations on Conventional Forces in Europe:

Over the past three years we in the Soviet Union have substantially revised our approaches to . . . verification . . . . The Soviet Union, more than any country, wishes to have reliable guarantees of its security and must be confident that disarmament arrangements are earnestly complied with by everyone . . . . We favor the most strict and efficient verification involving both national technical means and international procedures, including mandatory on-site inspections.[61]

The press background for the 1988 Moscow Summit makes a similar point but is even more forthcoming in acknowledging that the Soviet Union has lately given up some of its misguided stereotypes and outmoded behavior, including a prior tendency to react negatively "to all sorts of inspection and on-site verification."[62]

Sources of Change in Soviet Attitudes toward On-Site Inspection

In addressing the sources of the observed change in Soviet attitudes toward on-site inspection, it is useful to return to table 10–2. It is apparent from the "Arms Control Priority" column that there is a high correspondence between the priority assigned to arms control by the Soviet leadership and the Soviet posture toward on-site inspection. When arms control has a high priority, whether for economic reasons or otherwise, Moscow generally has been prepared to pay the price of intrusive inspections in order to obtain an agreement.

The emergence of U.S. weapon systems that are difficult to verify by national technical means also appears to have contributed to Soviet readiness to adopt cooperative measures, including on-site inspection. This attitude is most apparent with respect to mobile missile systems, especially sea-launched cruise missiles (SLCMs).[63] Indeed, Soviet concerns with verification problems associated with SLCMs have led to proposals with inspection provisions that the United States regards as too demanding.[64] Soviet scientists also have joined with American civilian arms control experts to explore novel inspection procedures designed to overcome the verification problems posed by new technologies.[65]

The Soviet Union also appears to have genuine verification concerns regarding the limitation of conventional forces. Although it is difficult to assess the extent to which these concerns drive Soviet policy on on-site inspection, one must take seriously Soviet arguments for a variety of intrusive inspection procedures, especially in the light of recent indications that the Soviet Union is prepared to negotiate substantial and asymmetrical reductions in conventional forces.[66] Typical of the new Soviet stance is Moscow's statement at the opening of the Negotiations on Conventional Forces in

Europe, which said the Soviet bloc would insist on "the most vigorous verification, including inspections without right of refusal."[67]

An important aspect of the new thinking that has reinforced Soviet re-
ceptiveness to intrusive inspection is the pursuit of strategic stability. Under
conditions of strategic parity, Soviet commentators maintain, "accurate information on the other side's strategic forces and military programs . . .
enhances strategic stability . . . since it helps to remove unnecessary concern
over the adversary's intentions."[68] This applies both to national technical
means and "the use of new and more radical forms of national, cooperative,
and international verification."[69] This perspective today is also echoed by
Israelyan, who is now less inclined to herald his seven basic principles and
emphasizes instead that "glasnost in international relations" is necessary in
order "to remove sources of suspicion and create an atmosphere of clarity
and predictability conducive to real disarmament."[70] Pursuit of glasnost in
international affairs, Israelyan acknowledges, requires standards of verification, including mutual inspection, that were "unheard of before."[71]

Related to the new political thinking and the concept of glasnost in
international affairs is a new attitude on the part of the Soviet Union with
respect to secrecy—a realization that secrecy has been detrimental to Soviet
interests and that intrusiveness no longer poses the threat that was once
presumed.[72] Having made that determination, the Soviet Union may have
decided to promote on-site inspection as much for the diverse set of political
benefits it is perceived to provide as for its newly appreciated technical requirements. These anticipated benefits probably include removing the burden of an outmoded policy, which often subjected the Soviet Union to
unnecessary embarrassment internationally,[73] and the opportunity to "stick
it to the Americans" who had so long touted on-site inspection as an arms
control panacea. At the same time, it is likely that Gorbachev also viewed
the revised Soviet position on verification as a necessary means to achieve
desired arms control accords. As such, Soviet verification policy served to
demonstrate how, in keeping with the new political thinking, Soviet security
could be increased by political means.

Finally, in considering the sources of change in Soviet verification policy,
it should be noted that Soviet analysts maintain that the "radical character
of the reductions" in the INF Treaty dictated more intrusive inspection.
"Further disarmament agreements," they contend, "will probably require
even more intrusive and comprehensive verification measures, embracing
NTM, military-technical procedures and counting rules, principles to assist
verification, data exchange, international and mutual on-site inspections."[74]
"Verificational deterrence" is the term coined by academician Vitaly Goldansky to describe this envisaged period of constantly lowering levels of
armaments, a period demanding "the most stringent mutual inspection."[75]

Future Developments

Just as it is a mistake to attribute the initiation of Soviet on-site inspection proposals to Gorbachev, so it is an error to assume that Soviet initiatives in this area will cease with his departure. More likely, Soviet policy toward verification will continue to be based on the Soviet leadership's perception of the balance of the verification costs and benefits. This calculation, in turn, will likely depend on the U.S.-Soviet strategic relationship, domestic economic demands, and the priority attached to additional arms control accords. Although repudiation of all or parts of the new political thinking would probably undermine the case for specific instances of on-site inspection, demands on the Soviet economy, further military-technical developments, and other Soviet foreign policy objectives might well lead to a new leadership's calculation of the continued utility of on-site inspection.

One of the defining characteristics of a policy innovation is its systemic impact. Domestically, one significant consequence of the proliferation of foreign inspectors on Soviet territory and the exchange of previously classified data is the increased access of Soviet civilian analysts to information pertaining to defense issues.[76] To be sure, increasingly routine Soviet support for intrusive verification measures did not in itself guarantee greater access by Soviet academics to previously classified information. It made it more difficult, however, for the military guardians of defense-related data to deny civilian analysts information readily available to Western governments. Although this consequence may well have been unanticipated and unintended, Gorbachev appears to have embraced its effect because it provides him with an expanded base of experts on which to call for defense-related advice.[77]

One should not conclude from the analysis that recent efforts to revamp Soviet thinking about on-site inspection have gone unopposed. One can find scattered references in the Soviet press, for example, that question the wisdom of allowing foreign inspectors on Soviet territory.[78] More numerous are articles in major Soviet publications like *Pravda* and *Krasnaya zvezda*, which express doubts about the terms of the INF treaty and the impact of its implementation on Soviet security.[79] The dissenting views would not have been published if they did not reflect the reservations of senior Soviet officials.

There does not, however, appear to be organized institutional opposition to the principle of on-site inspection. Opposition instead probably centers on the application of it to specific institutions whose representatives are wary of the impact of inspections on their organization's standard operating procedures.[80] This resistance is natural and has parallels in the United States among the nuclear laboratories and private defense contractors. Opposition to on-site inspection, however, is unlikely to be expressed very overtly because attitudes toward intrusive inspection have now become a litmus test in the Soviet Union for support of the new thinking about national security policy.[81]

Notes

1. Recurrent themes 2–8 correspond to the seven basic principles underlying Soviet verification policy articulated in March 1981 by Viktor Israelyan, Soviet ambassador to the Conference on Disarmament in Geneva. See Viktor Israelyan, "Statement to the Conference on Disarmament," Conference on Disarmament, Document No. CD/PV.119, Committee on Disarmament, Final Record of the 119th Meeting, Geneva, March 31, 1981. An excellent discussion of these principles is provided by Allan Krass, *Verification: How Much is Enough?* (Lexington, Mass.: Lexington Books, 1985), pp. 39–58.

2. Most of these intrusive inspection measures are identified by Alan Sherr in *The Other Side of Arms Control: Soviet Objectives in the Gorbachev Era* (Boston: Unwin & Hyman, 1988), pp. 262–272. See in particular his excellent "Typology of Verification Regimes," p. 263.

3. For an elaboration of the distinction among verification, intelligence, and espionage, see Allan S. Krass, "The Soviet View of Verification," in William C. Potter, ed., *Verification and Arms Control* (Lexington, Mass.: Lexington Books 1985), pp. 38–39.

4. See Abraham Chayes, "An Inquiry into the Workings of Arms Control Agreements," *Harvard Law Review* (March 1972): 937, and Krass, *Verification: How Much Is Enough?* pp. 38–39.

5. Recently Soviet commentators have begun to use the anglicized word *verifikatsiya*. On-site inspection is usually rendered as *inspektsiya na mestakh*.

6. Israelyan, "Statement to the Conference on Disarmament."

7. See R. Zheleznov, "Problema Kontrolya za Merami Ogranicheniya Vooruzheniy", *Mezhdunarodnaya Zhisn'* (1982): 77–87, and Roland M. Timerbayev, *Kontrol' za Ogranicheniyem Vooruzheniy i Razoruzheniyem* (Moscow: International Relations Publishing House, 1983), pp. 14–20. Zheleznov was a clever pen name for Timerbayev (the roots of both names mean "iron" in Russian and Tatar, respectively). Timerbayev is currently the Soviet ambassador to the IAEA and has a long background in arms control negotiations. For a perceptive review of the Timerbayev book, see Warren Heckrotte, "A Soviet View of Verification," *Bulletin of the Atomic Scientists* (October 1986): 12–16, as well as Alan Crawford et al., *Compendium of Arms Control Verification Proposals*, Operational Research and Analysis Establishment, Department of National Defense, Canada (July 1987), pp. 42–52. Timerbayev, in a response to Heckrotte's article, indicates that he wrote his book in 1981, although it was not published until 1983. See Roland M. Timerbayev, "A Soviet Official on Verification," *Bulletin of the Atomic Scientists* (January–February 1987): 8–10.

8. Timerbayev, *Kontrol' za Ogranicheniyem Vooruzheniy i Razoruzheniem*, p. 18. Gorbachev also restates the principle in *Perestroika i Novoye Myshleniye: Dlya Nashei Strany i dlya Vsego Mira* (Moscow: Izdatel'stvo Politicheskoi Literatury

1987), pp. 223–224, 243, where he talks about equality. Gorbachev mentions the willingness of the Soviet Union to go to the strictest means of verification, on the basis of equality, in his letter to the secretary-general of the United Nations of January 11, 1987, in *For a Nuclear-Free World*, (Moscow: Novosti Press Agency Publishing House, 1987).

9. Timerbayev, *Kontrol' za Ogranicheniyem Vooruzheniy i Razoruzheniem*, p. 20.

10. Ibid.

11. Major General Lebedev, "Washington's Speculations about Verification Issues," *Pravda*, May 3, 1984, cited by Krass "Soviet View," p. 45.

12. See Timerbayev, *Kontrol' za Ogranicheniyem Vooruzheniy i Razoruzheniem*, pp. 4, 15; Zheleznov, "Problema Kontrolya za Merami Ogranicheniya Vooruzheniy," pp. 75–76; and Israelyan, "Statement to the Conference on Disarmament," p. 16. Also see the replies to the secretary-general on U.N. resolution 40/152 O, "Verification in All Its Aspects," by the Soviet Union, the Belorussian SSR, and the Ukrainian SSR. All three statements restate this principle. Also, Gorbachev restated this principle in *The Challenge of Our Time: Disarmament and Social Progress: Highlights, 27th Communist Party Congress*, (New York: International Publishers, 1986), p. 77.

13. Zheleznov, "Problema Kontrolya za Merami Ogranicheniya Vooruzheniy," pp. 75–76. Also restated by Gorbachev in *Challenge of Our Time* a report to the 27th Party Congress, p. 77.

14. Timerbayev, *Kontrol' za Ogranicheniyem Vooruzheniy i Razoruzheniem*, p. 15.

15. Ibid, pp. 15–16.

16. Ibid, p. 4.

17. Ibid, p. 13.

18. Note, however, that the proposed Soviet all-embracing system of international security, voiced by Gorbachev at the 27th CPSU Congress (see Mikhail Gorbachev, "Politicheskiy Doklad Tsentral'nogo Komiteta KPSS 27 S"ezdu KPSS," (February 1986), essentially accepts the notion. Two of the fundamental principles of that systems state: (1) "A strictly controlled lowering of military capabilities of countries to limits of reasonable sufficiency" and (2) "elaboration of a set of measures aimed at building confidence between states and the creation of effective guarantees against attack from without."

19. Zorin, cited in Heckrotte, "A Soviet View of Verification," p. 13. See also Timerbayev, *Kontrol' za Ogranicheniyem Vooruzheniy i Razoruzheniem*, p. 18,

20. Cf. Israelyan, "Statement to the Conference on Disarmament," p. 17; Zheleznov, "Problema Kontrolya za Merami Ogranicheniya Vooruzheniy," p. 75; and Timerbayev, *Kontrol' za Ogranicheniyem Vooruzheniy i Razoruzheniem*, pp. 17–19. See also the replies of the Soviet Union, Belorussian SSR, and Ukrainian SSR to U.N. resolution 40/152 O, U.N. Document A/41/422, "Verification in All Its Aspects."

21. Timerbayev, *Kontrol' za Ogranicheniyem Vooruzheniy i Razoruzheniem*, p. 17.

22. See ibid., p. 19. For a similar assessment by an American negotiator of the test ban treaties, see Warren Heckrotte, "Verification of Test Ban Treaties," pp. 63–79.

23. A careful analysis of the evolution of Soviet views on satellite reconnaissance for

purposes of verification is provided by Stuart Cohen, "The Evolution of Soviet Views on Verification," in William C. Potter, ed., *Verification and SALT: The Challenge of Strategic Deception* (Boulder, Colo.: Westview Press, 1980), pp. 49–75. See also Krass *Verification: How Much Is Enough?* pp. 183–186; Krass, "Soviet View," pp. 46–51; and Sherr, *Other Side of Arms Control*, pp. 242–276.

24. Zheleznov, in "Problema Kontrolya za Merami Ogranicheniya Vooruzheniy" (p. 79), writes: "The use of observation satellites is within the norms of existing international law . . . . But not a single international legal document directly approves of the use of such satellites for monitoring and control."

25. See, for example, Timerbayev, *Kontrol' za Ogranicheniyem Vooruzheniy i Razoruzheniem*, pp. 13–14. A colorful illustration of the Soviet perspective on this issue is provided by S.K. Tsarapkin in Christer Jonsson, *Soviet Bargaining Behaivor: The Nuclear Test Ban Case*, (New York: Columbia University Press, 1979), p. 72.

26. Timerbayev, *Kontrol' za Ogranicheniyem Vooruzheniy i Razoruzheniem*, p. 14. See also the discussion in Krass, *Verification: How Much Is Enough?* pp. 115–119.

27. Timerbayev, *Kontrol' za Ogranicheniyem Vooruzheniy i Razoruzheniem*, p. 4.

28. See Krass, "Soviet View," pp. 55–56.

29. Timerbayev, *Kontrol' za Ogranicheniyem Vooruzheniy i Razoruzheniem*, p. 4.

30. See Viktor Israelyan, "Openess, Transparency, and Confidence Building," *Disarmament* (Summer 1988): 42.

31. See, for example, Zheleznov, "Problema Kontrolya za Merami Ogranicheniya Vooruzheniy," pp. 82–83; Timerbayev, *Kontrol' za Ogranicheniyem Vooruzheniy i Razoruzheniem*, p. 97; statement on verification by the Soviet Union in U.N. Document A/41/422, "Verification in All Its Aspects"; Vitaliy Goldansky, "Verificational Deterrence and Nuclear Explosions," *International Affairs* (June 1988): 32–33; and "USSR-USA Summit, May 29–June 2, 1988: Press Background," Novosti Press Agency (1988), p. 80. This change is discussed in more detail below.

32. Israelyan, "Statement to the Conference on Disarmament," p. 17.

33. Timerbayev, *Kontrol' za Ogranicheniyem Vooruzheniy i Razoruzheniem*, p. 24.

34. Krass, "Soviet View," p. 54. In testimony on the SALT II treaty, Brown referred to "a double bind which seems to deter the Soviet cheating. To go undetected, any Soviet cheating would have to be on so small a scale, that it would not be militarily significant. Cheating on such a level would hardly be worth the political risks involved. On the other hand, any cheating serious enough to affect the military balance would be detectable in sufficient time to take whatever action the situation required." Cited by Krass, *Verification: How Much Is Enough?* p. 54.

35. See Timerbayev, *Kontrol' za Ogranicheniyem Vooruzheniy i Razoruzheniyem*, p. 5, and Zheleznov, "Problema Kontrolya za Merami Ogranicheniya Vooruzheniy," pp. 78, 82. See also Colonel V. Chernishev, "Problemy Kontrolya: Trudnosti i Resheniya," *Krasnaya zvezda*, May 28, 1988.

36. Zheleznov, "Problema Kontrolya za Merami Ogranicheniya Vooruzheniy," p. 78.

37. Ibid.
38. Sherr, *Other Side of Arms Control*, p. 263.
39. Sherr maintains that because inspections under the Stockholm Accord concern armament, the principle of verification only over disarmament is not breached. This interpretation, however, is questionable. Ibid., p. 269.
40. Gorbachev himself reiterated this position at the 27th Party Congress but shortly afterward revised the Soviet stance.
41. I am grateful to Warren Heckrotte and James Schear for bringing this point to my attention.
42. "Mikhail Gorbachev's Speech in Prague," *News and Views from the USSR*, April 13, 1987, Soviet Embassy Information Department, Washington, D.C.
43. One might argue that the 1961 McCloy-Zorin Agreement is an exception to this statement. The accord, however, only set forth a statement of principles to guide disarmament negotiations and did not entail any restraints. Two earlier Soviet proposals, the counteroffer to the 1946 Baruch Plan, and the May 10, 1955, plan for the "Reduction of Armaments, the Prohibition of Atomic Weapons, and the Elimination of the Threat of a New War" also contained on-site inspection provisions. Neither of these proposals, however, led to an accord.
44. See Israelyan, "Openess, Transparency, and Confidence Building," pp. 41–44.
45. Numerous statements by Gorbachev: Mikhail Gorbachev, "Zayavlenie General'nogo Secretarya TsK KPSS ot 15 yanvarya 1986 goda," CPSU Central Committee (January 15, 1986); Gorbachev, *For a Nuclear-Free World*; and CPSU *Challenge of Our Time*. Precisely what is meant by "triple verification," however, has never been spelled out.
46. Sherr, *Other Side of Arms Control*, p. 261. This sentiment is echoed in Gorbachev's speech to the 27th Congress of the CPSU and the proposed all-embracing principles of security.
47. Ibid.
48. Referred to in an interview with a senior Soviet military strategist.
49. Zheleznov, "Problema Kontrolya za Merami Ogranicheniya Vooruzheniy," pp. 82–83, and Timerbayev, *Kontrol' za Ogranicheniyem Vooruzheniy i Razoruzheniyem*, pp. 81–97.
50. See Melvyn B. Nathanson, "Soviet Reactors Open for Internal Inspection," *Bulletin of the Atomic Scientists* (June–July 1985): 32–33.
51. See Gorbachev's "Reply to the Address of the Leaders of Argentina, Greece, India, Mexico, Sweden, and Tanzania," in Gorbachev, *For a Nuclear-Free World*, pp. 161–166. Also see Goldansky, "Verificational Deterrence and Nuclear Explosions," p. 33; Oleg A. Grinevsky, "The Verification of Arms Control, Disarmament Agreements, and Security," *Disarmament* (Summer 1988): 18; and Alexander Savelyev and Vladimir Frangulov, "Disarmament and Verification Measures," in *Disarmament and Security: 1987 IMEMO Yearbook*, (Boulder, Colo.: Westview Press, 1988), p. 299.
52. One recent proposal that envisages very intrusive inspection by an international body pertains to weapons in space. See Savelyev and Frangulov, "Disarmament and Verification Measures," p. 299, and *Pravda*, August 14, 1987.
53. For a discussion of these distinctions as they apply to foreign policy more gen-

erally, see William C. Potter, "Innovation in East European Foreign Policies," in James A. Kuhlman, ed., *The Foreign Policies of Eastern Europe* (Leiden: Sijthoff Publishing, 1978), pp. 253–302.

54. For an excellent analysis of the components of the new thinking, see Stephen M. Meyer, "The Sources and Prospects of Gorbachev's New Political Thinking on Security," *International Security* (Fall 1988): 124–163.

55. "USSR-USA Summit, May 29–June 2, 1988," p. 77.

56. Ibid, p. 78.

57. Israelyan, "Openess, Transparency, and Confidence Building," p. 41.

58. Savelyev and Frangulov, "Disarmament and Verification Measures," p. 191. See also Gorbachev, *Perestroika i Novoye Myshleniye: Dlya Nashei Strany i dlya Vsego Mira*, pp. 223–225.

59. A detailed analysis of Soviet-NRDC negotiations over verification arrangements is provided in Philip G. Schrag, *Listening for the Bomb: A Study in Nuclear Arms Control Verification Policy* (Boulder, Colo.: Westview Press, 1989).

60. Timerbayev, "A Soviet Official on Verification," p. 8.

61. Grinevsky, "Verification of Arms Control, Disarmament Agreements, and Security," p. 13.

62. "USSR-USA Summit, May 29–June 2, 1988," p. 78.

63. See Savelyev and Frangulov, "Disarmament and Verification Measures," pp. 301, 308.

64. The United States has consistently rejected Soviet verification proposals that entail inspection of submarines and surface ships.

65. Members of the Soviet Space Research Institute and the Committee of Soviet Scientists for Peace and Against the Nuclear Threat have been especially active in joint projects on verification topics. See, for example, Steven Fetter et al., "The Detection of Fissile Materials for Arms Control Verification" (July 1988), unpublished.

66. Soviet civilian and Foreign Ministry analysts are giving increased attention to verification demands associated with conventional force negotiations. One new analytical approach being explored by the Foreign Ministry is the use of simulations to anticipate verification difficulties likely to arise in negotiations over conventional forces (based on interviews with Soviet Foreign Ministry officials).

67. Michael Gordon, "In Key Areas, Arms Talks on Target," *International Herald Tribune*, March 3, 1989.

68. Savelyev and Frangulov, "Disarmament and Verification Measures," p. 310.

69. Ibid., p. 311.

70. Israelyan, "Openness, Transparency, and Confidence Building," p. 42.

71. Ibid. See also Andrei Kozyrev, "Confidence and the Balance of Interests," *International Affairs* (November 1988): p. 8.

72. I am grateful to Warren Heckrotte for noting this point.

73. Several former Soviet and East European arms control negotiators emphasized to me the important role unfavorable international reactions to Soviet positions on on-site inspection played in altering Soviet verification policy. Having been repeatedly embarrassed by untenable negotiating positions, a number of senior

Soviet diplomats sought, with only partial success, to persuade Gromyko in 1981 to modify Soviet verification policy (based on interviews).

74. Savelyev and Frangulov, "Disarmament and Verification Measures," p. 292.
75. See Goldansky, "Verificational Deterrence and Nuclear Explosions," pp. 27–35.
76. This point was confirmed in interviews with Soviet civilian arms control analysts.
77. See Meyer, "The Sources and Prospects," pp. 130–131, for a discussion of how Gorbachev has sought to alter the Soviet process of national security decision making.
78. See, for example, G. Dadyants, "Dialogue with a Reader: Why On-Site Inspection Is Necessary," *Sotsialisticheskaya Industriya* (February 1988): 3.
79. See, for example, I.S. Valmus's letter to the editors of *Krasnaya zvezda* and a reply by A. Goltz, *Krasnaya zvezda*, February 8, 1988. For a discussion of these dissenting views, see Robert l. Arnett, "Some Discussions of Gorbachev's Arms Control Policy" (paper presented at the Annual Meeting of the American Association for the Advancement of Slavic Studies, November 18–21, Honolulu, 1988), p. 2.
80. Based on interviews with Soviet officials conducted in London and Moscow, December 1988–March 1989.
81. Ibid.

11
The Law of On-Site Inspection: Arms Control Verification and the Fourth Amendment

David A. Koplow

P erhaps you've heard the story about the new lawyer, hanging out his shingle in the small rural village. Because he was the only attorney in the town—indeed, the only one in that entire part of the county—he was hopeful that he could soon attract a satisfactory clientele, and he held himself out to deal with the full range of local legal issues: wills, divorces, real estate conveyances, criminal defense, and so forth. Unfortunately for him, only a very few clients seemed to want to take advantage of his talents; people in that community simply did not feel very keenly the necessity for availing themselves of legal assistance. Try as he might to drum up business, he had little to show for it, and it seemed, over the course of several months, that the town and surrounding countryside did not present a sufficient demand for legal services to sustain him in practice there. One day, however, a second attorney moved into town and opened up his own competing practice there, offering to perform substantially the same range of work on behalf of the townspeople. Within weeks, with two lawyers now in town, there was suddenly more than enough legal business to support the both of them.

Arms control is now in approximately the same situation as that mythical small town. For a generation, the arms control process has proceeded with relatively little legal input. To be sure, each U.S. negotiating delegation has included a legal adviser, any many of the other delegates and staffers also have had prior legal training, but the content of the treaty documents, and the creation of the arms control institutions, always have been driven far more by considerations of high public policy and national strategy. Arms control may be the one area of American public life that has not yet become dominated by law and lawyers—an isolated community that, at least until now, has barely supported the endeavors of a small cadre of government attorneys. The idyllic life-style of that community, however, is about to be overwhelmed, in unprecedented ways, by the attention of a multitude of new legal concerns, issues, and practitioners.

It is not the purpose here either to lament or to laud this development.

There are certainly important advantages as well as important disadvantages to the new attention being paid to legal concerns in arms control, and it is entirely possible that the new, increasingly law-driven, regime of arms control will be even more productive and more protective of national and individual interests than the early efforts have already been.

Rather, the contention is that this incipient "lawyerization" of the arms control process is now inevitable, for better or worse. As arms control negotiators have become more successful and more ambitious and as the verification arrangements have become more stringent and more intrusive, the concerns of law and of legal institutions in arms control will be joined. On-site inspection in particular will be the vehicle for bringing lawyers fully into the national security fray.

The INF Treaty has already demonstrated the increasing role of domestic law in the arms control process, and it has foreshadowed the coming era in which the U.S. Constitution, almost as much as the considerations of military strategy, will exert a powerful impact in shaping arms accords. If the ongoing Strategic Arms Reduction Talks (START) proceed along their current projections, with substantial reductions in strategic arms eliciting unprecedented cooperative measures of on-site inspection for verification, then the limitations of the Constitution, principally those contained in the Fourth Amendment, will have to be examined with renewed care.

The Role of Treaties as U.S. Law

The Supremacy Clause

The point of departure for the assessment of treaties within U.S. jurisprudence is the supremacy clause of Article VI of the Constitution:

> This Constitution, and the Laws of the United States which shall be made in Pursuance thereof; and all Treaties made, or which shall be made, under the Authority of the United States, shall be the supreme Law of the Land; and the Judges in every State shall be bound thereby, anyThing in the Constitution or Laws of any State to the Contrary notwithstanding.

Although this language, and the case law interpreting it, are not entirely free from ambiguity, the modern view is clear: the clause establishes a hierarchy of laws, with the Constitution as the supreme source; with statutes and treaties next, possessing equal dignity; and with state and local ordinances entitled to the lowest deference.

This means, first, that all treaties are subservient to the Constitution and that treaties inconsistent with that document will be invalidated, just as an unconstitutional statute would be. Constitutional challenges to international agreements are exceptionally rare, and courts are likely to try to construe the two sources of law as being mutually accommodating, but the principle is clear that in cases of conflict, the Constitution (including the Bill of Rights and all the other amendments) must prevail.

Second, the equivalence of treaties and congressional enactments means that, wherever there is a conflict, the document that is later in time will prevail over the earlier authority. In this way, a newer treaty can supersede an earlier statute, replacing it as the law of the land, even without the participation of the House of Representatives. Subsequently, however, a newer statute (including one passed over the president's veto) could once again override the international agreement.

It is important to note in this context that the newer congressional action effectively overrules the older treaty—but does not repeal or invalidate it. Indeed, for purposes of international law (as opposed to the purposes of domestic U.S. jurisprudence), the international accord will retain its vitality. The other party or parties to the treaty will lawfully expect the United States to continue to abide by its international commitments, and the imposition of a contrary domestic statute is not a valid excuse for nonperformance.

The effect, therefore, of a subsequent statute's being inconsistent with a prior treaty would be to force the United States into breach of the treaty. The president, as chief executive, would be constitutionally bound to execute faithfully the law of the land, and that law would be the statute—even though performance of that duty would necessarily conflict with U.S. international commitments. (The analogy would be to a corporation, where the officers sign a contract obligating the corporation to take certain actions. If the board of directors disagrees, it can legitimately order the officers to fail to perform the valid contract, and the officers will have to obey, although the nonperformance will create liability to the other party to the contract.)

Finally, the base of the supremacy clause pyramid is composed of state and local law, which is always inferior to the federal actions. Regarding international relations in particular, there is strong Supreme Court language establishing the proposition that foreign affairs are inherently national affairs and that the individual states of the Union have a greatly reduced role. It is true that in some areas, the purposeful inaction of the national government could open a window for states to exercise jurisdiction, but this contingent competence is automatically revoked when the federal government acts in a fashion to preempt the field. Therefore, state laws, whether enacted before or after the arms control treaty has come into force, will not inhibit its effectiveness and need be of no special concern to federal enforcement officials.

Executive Agreements

In international law, a treaty is a treaty is a treaty, whether it is denominated as a treaty, agreement, convention, statute, protocol, memorandum of understanding, or by some other title. As long as the parties intend it to be a treaty, it will be dealt with as such. There are no important international distinctions among the various types of accords.

In domestic U.S. law, however, the Constitution establishes a major distinction between treaties and other categories of international agreements, usually referred to as executive agreements. A treaty is a document signed by the executive branch and submitted to the Senate, which has the opportunity to provide its advice and consent, by a two-thirds vote, prior to the time that the president can exchange instruments of ratification and bring the agreement into force.

An executive agreement, on the other hand, may be legitimated in several ways. First, some executive agreements (more properly known as legislative-executive agreements) are authorized by express congressional legislation. A prior statute may call for the president to negotiate a particular agreement or category of agreements; similarly, an agreement approved by majority votes in each House of Congress after the fact of negotiation may also provide the authority for an agreement that is not consented to by two-thirds of the Senate. A second category of executive agreement may be authorized by a previously ratified treaty, which may expressly contemplate subsequent implementing agreements, to be cast as executive agreements, not requiring another round of Senate approvals. Finally, some types of executive agreements are considered valid, without any congressional participation at all, as being undertaken pursuant to the president's inherent powers to conduct U.S. foreign affairs.

A special aspect of U.S. statutory law on this point is section 33 of the U.S. Arms Control and Disarmament Act:

> Provided, however, that no action shall be taken under this or any other law that will obligate the United States to disarm or to reduce or to limit the Armed Forces or armaments of the United States, except pursuant to the treaty-making power of the President under the Constitution or unless authorized by further affirmative legislation by the Congress of the United States.

This provision would have the effect of requiring that arms control agreements (at least those that reduced or limited the armaments of the United States) should not be implemented under the third scheme sketched above— that is, in reliance on the sole authority of the president as chief executive officer for foreign policy. Instead, arms reduction agreements should be undertaken only with congressional participation—either by a two-thirds vote of the Senate or with majority votes in each House.

Perhaps section 33 would be constitutionally vulnerable as congressional overreaching. It is possible that a court would still uphold, in a future controversy, an arms reduction executive agreement that did not enjoy any form of legislative approval if the court determined that the president did possess adequate constitutional authority for making the agreement based on the inherent powers of the presidency, notwithstanding the language of section 33. But as a practical matter, all contemporary arms reduction agreements have actually been implemented either as treaties (for example, the INF treaty and the Anti-Ballistic Missile Treaty) or as legislative-executive agreements envisioned by section 33 (as with the SALT I Interim Agreement on Strategic Offensive Arms). The only arms-related agreements that have been crafted on the sole authority of the president have been those that clearly did not reduce or limit arms, such as hot-line agreements.

Although treaties and executive agreements differ markedly in their origins, their effects as international and domestic law are identical: both are inferior to the Constitution, both are equivalent to ordinary statutes (so the most recent document in time will prevail for domestic purposes), and both will outrank a contrary state law. For most purposes, therefore, the documents are legally interchangeable, and the choice is one of politics (will the Senate consider an executive agreement to be an intolerable end run around its prerogative?) rather than of law.

Self-Executing Treaties

One of the minor conundrums of U.S. treaty law is the institution of a self-executing treaty. Briefly, the question presented is whether the particular treaty is designed to take effect immediately as law, or whether it is merely precatory, contemplating some further lawmaking steps in implementation.

Either sort of arrangement is tolerable in most instances, and either may be a plausible interpretation of a particular accord. Generally treaty interpreters will make recourse to the intentions of the drafters of the language and will search the treaty text for its "plain meaning" and the surrounding context for indexes of implicit understandings or purposes. If the language is relatively general and hortatory, probably the treaty was not intended to operate by itself to create immediate obligations of international and domestic law. If, on the other hand, the language bespeaks specificity and precision and if it otherwise appears that the parties were intending to create enforceable obligations with this document, then no further lawmaking steps will be required.

The U.S. Constitution imposes some additional hurdles on self-executing agreements. First, some types of legal outcomes cannot be reached by a self-executing treaty alone; implementing legislation is required. New authority to tax and spend, for example, or to declare new acts to be subject to criminal penalties probably could not be accomplished without both houses of Congress. Second, the doctrine of "justiciability" (and particularly the branches of it concerned with "standing to sue" and with "political questions") will probably inhibit an individual citizen's (or even a legislator's recourse to court to validate the provisions of at least some types of international agreements, starkly limiting the private enforcement of rights apparently granted by a self-executing treaty.

In the context of an arms control agreement, these constraints will probably not be of central concern. Whether or not the treaty is self-executing for purposes of domestic jurisprudence, it can impose international obligations, and it can subject its parties to possible sanctions for noncompliance. If either state fails to pass any necessary legislation as a precursor to the conduct of negotiated on-site inspection visits, for example, this failure cannot be excused simply on the basis of incompatible domestic laws or politics.

On-Site Inspection

Searchers and Searchees

Who Is Being Searched? For most purposes of arms control inspection inside the United States, the U.S. government is the only plausible target of inspection. Government ownership and operation of defense facilities and equipment, and government control of military activities, will ensure that the bulk of the on-site inspection regime will be targeted against installations that are solely federal.

As to these inspections, the Constitution is essentially irrelevant. The federal government possesses no Fourth Amendment rights, and the treaty could operate as a waiver of any conceivable claims that the government might have against foreign inspectors' oversight.

One step more complicated is the situation of a government contractor who operates a government-owned facility or maintains a private office or installation at which government-related work is performed. Many of these operate under contracts that may already contain language through which the contractor consents to various forms of government inspection, conceivably including arms control treaty on-site inspections. More definite provisions could be written into all future government contracts, and separate inspection contracts could be negotiated to cover places of special interest.

It is probably reasonable to anticipate that market forces alone will solve the prospective aspect of the problem as contractors adjust to the need to grant another new form of access as a condition of winning a government contract and as the U.S. government adjusts its pricing awards and allowances accordingly. A more difficult scenario is presented by the private firm that does not care to sustain an ongoing relationship with the government and accordingly does not have the incentive of prospective contracts operating as a spur to consent.

The most difficult scenario concerns entirely private activities, and these may be of increasing importance in the new era of arms control verification. Already OSIs are beginning to encroach upon this sphere. What happens when inspectors under a successor to the INF treaty enter a contractor's facility and want to look inside particular rooms or spaces (such as employee locker rooms or footlockers) that might be large enough to contain future treaty-limited items but are not fully under the control of the contractor company? What if inspectors express an interest in looking inside an employee's private automobile to determine whether the back of the van or the trunk of the car contains contraband?

Even more acute problems may be raised by other future accords. A chemical weapons treaty might contemplate inspections of private chemical factories, including factories that are not, and never have been, working pursuant to government contracts. A future START agreement might be premised upon a right to anytime, anyplace inspections, which could intrude on a private company's facilities—or a private person's backyard—in pursuit of possible evasion scenarios. An even more intrusive on-site inspection regime might seek the right to inquire into individuals' financial records, medical records, and other private matters on the chance that some information could be gleaned that would tip off an arms control violation.

In all of these scenarios, the concept of consent to the investigation may be stretched to, or beyond, its limits. Inspections of official government facilities, and of contractors intimately connected with the government, are easy cases. The harder challenges of the new regime of arms control on-site inspections will lie within the private sector.

Who Is Conducting the Search? The other half of the inspection operation—the identity of the inspectorate—poses fewer legal obstacles. Some multilateral on-site inspection schemes contemplate an international corps of designated inspection teams, comparable to those operated today by the International Atomic Energy Agency; most contemporary proposals for nuclear arms control inspection envision instead adversary inspection, with the United States inspecting the Soviet Union, and vice-versa.

In either scenario, the foreign inspectors could be legally empowered to function inside the territory of the United States with minimal obstruction, but they would have to assume those privileges subject to the same limitations that U.S. government officials would bear. That is, the Constitution probably does permit the delegation of certain low-level law enforcement functions, such as the conduct of arms control on-site inspections, to unusual groups, including Soviet or other arms control officials, who are not sworn to uphold and defend the Constitution as most ordinary enforcement officials are. If armed with this authority (pursuant to the treaty itself or, more likely, following a detailed implementing statute), inspectors could conduct a wide range of searches and could draw upon legal process for compulsion if access were denied. (In most on-site inspection scenarios, of course, personnel from the host state will accompany the foreign inspectors, assisting in their activities and observations and perhaps replicating their measurements. These host personnel would usually also be charged with primary responsibility for confronting domestic opposition and for providing the legal mechanisms through which lawful forced entry could occur. But the range of powers available to the inspectorate would be identical under either variation.)

At the same time, foreign inspectors under any scenario would stand legally in the same shoes as U.S. government inspectors and could be given no greater powers. Wherever the Fourth Amendment would limit U.S. government officials in performing an arms control inspection, identical restrictions would govern foreign inspectors who were operating under derivative authority. Thus, the analysis of the range of powers available to the U.S. government under the Constitution remains the relevant inquiry, regardless of the actual relationship between inspectors and host.

What to Guard Against

Targets of an arms control on-site inspection will have a wide variety of types of information to disclose or protect. Some of these data will be directly germane to the key issue at controversy: the determination of whether there has been any behavior incompatible with the obligations assumed under the treaty. Other kinds of information, however, also will be at risk, and the target of the investigation will seek to inhibit at least three types of losses. Even where the target of the inspection affirmatively wants to collaborate with the inspection function, there are nevertheless important associated costs to be considered and to be socially distributed.

The first category of unwarranted loss would be the compromise of properly classified national security information in the possession of the target. This is one of the principal dangers attendant to a program of any-time, anyplace inspections, and there is a substantial risk that legitimizing the regular presence of trained observers can thwart the best counterespionage efforts of the host state and company.

This danger could put a company into an untenable position: the treaty requires that the facility be open for foreign inspection, but the presence of alien on-site inspection teams would jeopardize the security of other ongoing projects of no legitimate interest under the treaty. The cost of relocating or reorganizing the physical facilities in order to minimize the danger of leakage, moreover, could be prohibitive.

There is no easy way out of this particular box, even at the level of legal principles. The company should allow the inspection to proceed as required by the treaty but should also take all reasonable protections to guard against any loss of classified information wider than would be necessary. The additional costs of compliance will have to be allocated in some equitable fashion. Partly these are to be borne by the company as just another price of compliance with new federal regulations. Partly, however, these are extraordinary costs associated with the public policy decision to proceed with a program of arms control, and not the product of the company's own faulty business choices. It may be appropriate for the government to indemnify the contractor for a portion of the costs of appropriate shielding or relocation.

The second category of lost information is proprietary data relevant to trade secrets or other unique production processes. In some instances, the mere presence of trained observers would be sufficient to reveal a hitherto secret aspect of a company's unique operations. In quite a few more cases, investigations of the depth contemplated in, for example, a chemical weapons convention on-site inspection would expose far more privileged business data.

Again, the principled resolution of this problem would be for the United States to mandate that the private firm allow the inspection to proceed and to attempt to contain the damage. If useful trade secrets were nonetheless lost, the company could seek a damages remedy from the government of the inspecting state, which improperly acquired and used the secrets, or from the U.S. government, which would look upon this transaction as yet another external cost of the arms control practice.

The final category of compromised information would be purely private information contained in personnel files, medical records, employment records, and the like. These would be of little or no value as national security information or trade secrets but would still violate the targets' expectations of privacy. In most plausible types of on-site inspection regimes, this type of collateral information is simply a nuisance to the inspectors, who will have to wade rather quickly past it in order to complete their appointed rounds, but many individuals may nevertheless experience the inquiry as an invasion of personal privacy.

Again, the solution is for the government to legislate an authorization for the investigation to proceed, as required by the treaty, and to establish a corollary claims mechanism through which aggrieved individuals can press for compensation.

All of this has so far assumed that the government does have the legal authority to order the inspection to proceed—that the Constitution permits the inquiry, and the only issue is the structure and extent of compensation for a corporation's loss of competitive edge or an individual's disrupted sense of quietude. In many applications, that perspective will certainly prevail— where the government has a right to inspect, the questions of damages and remedies will be relatively easy to contain. But the major inquiry of the issue, and the topic of the rest of this chapter, questions exactly this premise, and asks, "Under what circumstances may arms control inspectors enter private premises and make treaty-related observations over the objections of the proprietor?"

Approaching the Fourth Amendment

Before turning to a sequential evaluation of the possible inspection regimes, it is useful to pause for an overall impression of the courts' application of the Fourth Amendment. It is sometimes opined that in the exercise of their jurisdiction, the courts—however vigorous they are elsewhere—are likely to be especially wary of conflicting with important national security objectives and would be willing to treat arms control on-site inspections as sui generis, different in essential respects from the usual judicial fare.

There is an important element of truth to this sanguine prediction. Courts do regularly demonstrate unusual deference to the stresses of foreign policy and do allow the political branches of government a special leeway in dealings with foreign sovereigns. Matters of national survival, as reflected in a vital arms control agreement, would have to inspire unusual judicial self-restraint, and courts are likely to strain to sustain the exercise of foreign affairs power.

On the other hand, the evolution of the jurisprudence of the Fourth Amendment is in large measure the 200-year-old story of judicial resistance to a series of very similar executive branch protestations. The customary role of the executive, in fact, is to argue that a particular type of government inspection or interrogation is warranted because of the great social importance of the government's interest in suppressing crime, dealing with domestic violence or drugs, interdicting terrorists, and so forth. And the customary role of the courts has been to hear those claims and then to weigh them very carefully but skeptically against the equally profound social commitment to the Bill of Rights. We can be quite confident that the courts will be no more likely to cede the executive a carte blanche for dealing with arms control than they have for other critical areas of national life.

The possibility of an explicit national security exception to the usual requirements of the Fourth Amendment is equally problematic. The Supreme Court has never addressed the issue directly, and the few lower courts that have had the occasion to articulate rules have not been able to compile a coherent set of standards. One leading case determined that no such exception could be applied to situations of threatened internal subversion, where the alleged danger to national security emanated from a domestic U.S. organization, with no known contacts to foreign agents or governments. A later case also disallowed the executive's claims to operate outside the usual constraints of the Fourth Amendment, even when there was a type of "foreign connection" in which a domestic organization was reportedly planning criminal actions against Soviet diplomats inside the United States apparently to undermine U.S.-Soviet relations and provoke retaliation against American officers abroad. The court in the latter case appreciated the importance of the government's interest in protecting vital U.S. foreign policy goals but held that even this concern was insufficient rationale for suspending the customary protections of the Fourth Amendment.

In sum, U.S. courts are likely to be sympathetic to the special demands of arms control on-site inspections and will probably be willing to stretch the existing doctrines to accommodate the concerns of the treaty regime. But they are simultaneously very unlikely to approach the resolution of difficult cases uncritically. Prudent planners and negotiators should operate on the assumption that courts will continue their vigilance on behalf of individual constitutional rights.

Searches and Seizures in On-Site Inspections

The key legal standard governing governmental investigations is the Fourth Amendment to the Constitution, which provides that

> the right of the people to be secure in their persons, houses, papers, and effects, against unreasonable searches and seizures, shall not be violated, and no Warrants shall issue, but upon probable cause, supported by Oath or affirmation, and particularly describing the place to be searched, and the persons or things to be seized.

U.S. courts have created a variety of different conceptual categories for analyzing the legality of diverse government searches and seizures. The initial task for arms control advocates therefore may well be to attempt to fit the contemplated on-site inspections into one of the existing pigeon-holes, sheltered inside existing notions of legality.

Nonsearches

Some types of government inquiries, including certain procedures that look very much like searches in the ordinary language sense, are excluded from the ambit of the Fourth Amendment altogether.

The most obvious of these exceptions is consent. Everything is much easier when the primary target of the inspection is willing to permit the investigation, and this fortuity is likely to obtain in most arms control applications. Case law establishes that in most situations, even somewhat strained consent is sufficient to legitimate a search. The consent is not irretrievably tainted, for example, if it is procured by a certain amount of economic pressure, such as the fear that refusal to grant an advance consent would result in not being hired for a particular job. Contractors or individuals who provide certain limited types of blanket consent to reasonable searches probably could not later escape the reach of those consents by claiming undue economic pressure. On the other hand, courts would look much more critically at a very far-reaching type of blanket consent, such as one purporting to authorize, as a condition of employment, surprise inspections of an individual's residence during off-duty hours.

A related issue concerns the reach of a consent. Under most circumstances, the owner or manager of a facility is empowered to provide a valid permission for an official search of the entire premises and all major parts of it. However, where the facility also includes some small places that are physically segregated and identified as private reserves for individual employees, then the boss's consent may not run to those enclaves. A private locker, for example, or a locked desk drawer may be thought of as being sufficiently private, and sufficiently removed from the dominion and control of the facility, that the separate consent of the individual also is required. And, of course, the facility management will have even less claim to be able to provide valid consent to searches of privately owned property (such as an employee's automobile or briefcase) that is temporarily located inside the facility's grounds.

A second major category of nonsearch covers items and activities knowingly exposed to "plain view." In *Katz* v. *United States,* the leading Supreme Court Case on point, Justice Harlan focused attention on the Fourth Amendment's protection of a "justifiable expectation of privacy":

> What a person knowingly exposes to the public, even in his own home or office, is not a subject of Fourth Amendment protection. . . . But what he seeks to preserve as private, even in an area accessible to the public, may be constitutionally protected.

Thus, the inquiry is two-pronged: first, has the person manifested an actual subjective expectation that the activity in question has been withdrawn from public scrutiny and will not be observed by others, and second, is that expectation one that society is prepared to acknowledge as "reasonable"?

The evolution of the plain view doctrine has established that it is not a search when police or other law enforcement officers stand in public places (or in any other place they are legally authorized to be, by invitation or warrant) and utilize their ordinary human senses to see, hear, or smell activities conducted indiscreetly behind closed doors. Moreover, certain minor amplifications of ordinary senses, such as the use of flashlights, tape recorders, stepladders, and drug-sniffing dogs, are not usually considered to be searches within the ambit of the Fourth Amendment. When the police inquiry proceeds appreciably beyond ordinary human senses, however, the courts become more protective. Use of high-resolution, night-vision telescopes, for example, would likely be considered a search if the target of the investigation had taken sufficient precautions to guard against all customary forms of observation.

One salient branch of the plain view cases concerns aerial observation. Recent Supreme Court rulings have made clear that police or other law enforcement overflights are not searches, at least when the observations are made with equipment no more invasive than industry-standard cameras. In the 1986 case of *Dow Chemical Co.* v. *United States,* the Environmental Protection Agency (EPA) had overflown Dow's Midland, Michigan, plant in order to assess the extent of air pollution emitted by its power houses. Dow argued that this observation had compromised trade secrets by revealing the precise configuration of its buildings and pipes; that Dow had taken extraordinary measures to guard against ground-level inquiries (by constructing fences and implementing other security measures), thereby manifesting a subjective expectation of privacy; and that the EPA's actions constituted an impermissible governmental search. In sustaining the EPA action, the Court effectively held that if Dow truly wanted to remove its facility from plain view observation, it would have to construct a roof over the entire plant (or at least the part that it wished to protect). Failure to do so, the Court determined, constituted a willingness to expose the buildings and activities to government inspection outside the scope of the Fourth Amendment.

In assessing the implications that these nonsearch cases might have for arms control inspections, three observations seem timely. First, many, if not most, arms control on-site inspections will pose no substantial problems at all under the Fourth Amendment. Economic, political, and other forms of public pressure—as long as they do not exceed the undefinable bounds of reasonableness—are likely to ensure that consent is ordinarily granted. In most instances, the size of treaty-limited items will be sufficiently great that the danger is minimized that they could be squirreled away inside some recalcitrant employee's private desk drawer. Similarly, many of the activities of arms control inspectors will be validated under the plain view rubric; in particular, aerial overflights, including the use of precision aerial mapping cameras, would likely be allowed.

Second, the greater is the power of the observation methodology, the more likely it is to be considered a search. If the inspection personnel graduate from using ordinary eyesight and conventional 35 mm cameras and seek to apply state-of-the-art reconnaissance technology that is currently available only to the national security communities of the two superpowers, different rules might apply. Since ordinary people might not be expected to know about nighttime infrared satellite sensing, signals intelligence, and the like, they could not reasonably be expected to adopt measures to guard against this degree of inspection, and their failure to do so could not reasonably be considered a voluntary choice to expose the activities to plain view.

Third, the nonsearch cases demonstrate the willingness of the courts to inquire deeply into the precise facts of a particular case before fashioning a rule to guide future inspectors. Courts do not automatically extend a ruling from one area of practice to another but are more likely to operate incrementally, balancing the demands of law enforcement and civil rights on a case-by-case basis. It took the judicial system a long time, and a great many cases, for example, before recently concluding that there is no lingering expectation of privacy in household garbage, positioned outside in cans or bags for refuse collectors, so police may now examine it freely. Similarly, the rules regarding the use of electronic beepers (for easier tailing of suspects in public areas) or pen registers (for recording the numbers dialed from a particular telephone, without accessing the contents of the conversations) are complicated and still evolving.

In many instances, moreover, the current interpretation of the law will vary dramatically from circuit to circuit, or even from district to district, and it will be impossible to predict the outcome of a current case, let alone the future direction of judicial doctrine overall. Arms control inspectors, or their political supervisors, who seek concrete legal guidance and a definitive statement of their rights and limitations are likely to be frustrated by the ambiguity of the law in the area and by the difficulty of fashioning "bright line tests" between nonsearches and constitutionally problematic behaviors.

Pervasive Regulation

A second category of cases, triggering a second echelon of constitutional protections, concerns selected industries that are considered pervasively regulated. Within these particular trades, the Fourth Amendment applies, but certain inspection activities that would ordinarily be prohibited are now allowed due to the unusual nature of the industry and the history of close government attention. Distilleries, for example, are subject to warrantless government inspections, at any time of the day or night, and inspectors are provided with their own set of keys to the facilities in order to enforce compliance with revenue laws. The well-known special governmental attention to this industry, and the important social concerns served by the unusual inspection regime, are considered a sufficient justification for the exceptional treatment. They are said to imply a form of consent by anyone who chooses to enter into that line of work to permit the extraordinary degree of official snooping.

Not many industries have been deemed pervasively regulated. Fire-arms sellers, mines, and food preparation services are a few of the niches of the general economy that have been singled out for the special oversight. The chemical industry, in general, has not been considered pervasively regulated; perhaps the segment of it concerned with toxins and potential weapons could be. The case of the nuclear power industry has not been tested in court, but it seems likely that it would be considered pervasively regulated.

Additional industries could qualify for this category, and it is possible that future regulation schemes could enlarge the sectors of special interest to arms control on-site inspections and that are then deemed pervasively regulated. At one time, the courts seemed to be especially impressed with the long duration of the pattern of close regulatory oversight as a factor in establishing inclusion in the industry; this would have made the articulation of additional categories problematic. More recent cases, however, have been driven less by the extent of the history of the regulation and more by its comprehensiveness. That is, courts will not consider an industry to be per-vasively regulated merely because it is subject to the ordinary network of environmental, health, safety, and wage regulations that applies to virtually all American enterprises. There must be something especially demanding in the oversight plan applicable to this particular industry. When the scope, regularity, and frequency of the government's inspection rise to these unu-sual heights, then the industry may be considered pervasively regulated and thereby subject to even closer warrantless scrutiny than the Fourth Amend-ment would ordinarily tolerate.

Administrative Searches

Another category of Fourth Amendment cases concerns administrative searches. These include a raft of governmental inquiries, usually by state or local agencies, into industry or residential compliance with zoning codes, health ordinances, fire safety codes, and the like. Although these investiga-tions are relatively short in duration and small in consequences, they are enormous in frequency. Thousands of investigations of this sort are con-ducted annually in every part of the country. And while the usual purpose of the administrative searches is not criminal prosecution (it is, instead, to prompt conformity to the local ordinances), they usually do carry some modest criminal sanctions for repeated noncompliance.

Administrative searches are of special interest in the context of arms control on-site inspections because they have become the subject of a unique regime for providing a flexible, manageable form of oversight of government searches in a way that might provide a useful precedent. That is, the Supreme Court had initially determined that these administrative searches were sufficiently unimportant, and sufficiently unthreatening to the target, that they were entirely outside the reach of the Fourth Amendment and could be conducted without any necessity for the target's consent or a judicial warrant. Subsequently, however, the Court reversed itself, concluding that however benign the purpose and conduct of an administrative search, it was nevertheless a governmental search and constitutional protections would have to apply.

What the Supreme Court did next was especially interesting. It fashioned a special inspection protocol applicable only to these administrative searches in which the usual requirements of the Fourth Amendment were relaxed in important ways in recognition of the unique circumstances. The Court required that nonconsensual administrative searches would require a search warrant, but for this special purpose, the warrant could be issued under relaxed circumstances. The inspector need not show "probable cause" and a "particular" expectation that evidence of wrongdoing would be found in a specified premises. Instead, the warrant would issue whenever the inspector shows (1) that the inspecting agency has a regularized, routinized plan for inspecting all the buildings or facilities within its jurisdiction, with appropriate priorities for inspecting the oldest, or the most hazardous, or the most frequent violators first, and (2) that this particular inspection of this specific building fits into that orderly plan. When that showing has been made, the issuing official (who need not be a federal or local judge but could be a hearing officer affiliated with the agency, as long as sufficient detachment and independence were retained) could sign the administrative search warrant.

Administrative searches, therefore, may provide a fruitful source of analogy for arms control on-site inspections. Insofar as the arms control inspections are relatively routine, common, quick, and episodic and insofar as they are motivated by a desire other than collecting evidence for a threatened criminal prosecution, many of the same policy considerations apply. Perhaps a similar compromise can be fashioned here, where the inspectors have recourse to an expedited warrant procedure that protects the targets against undue harassment but does not intolerably delay the completion of legitimate searches. At the very least, this area of law suggests that courts will try to approach the arms control on-site inspections with sensitivity and finesse and will attempt to marshal their creativity to reconcile the competing public objectives.

Fourth Amendment Searches

The three foregoing categories (nonsearches, pervasively regulated industries, and administrative searches), while numerically accounting for a large percentage of government search activities, are conceptually merely the exceptions. For most purposes, the starting point for analysis will instead be the cases demonstrating the full reach of the Fourth Amendment, as in ordinary criminal prosecutions, with all the procedural protections intact.

The Fourth Amendment permits two kinds of searches and seizures: those undertaken pursuant to a warrant and those warrantless actions that are nonetheless "not unreasonable." The warrantless searches that are most nearly opposite to arms control on-site inspections have already been addressed; this section now considers the regime that would be applicable if arms control inspectors were required to follow the procedures common to the enforcement of the basic criminal law.

Issuance of a search warrant requires three factors: probable cause, particularity, and a detached magistrate. Probable cause mandates that the investigators have some articulable reason for focusing their attention on their target; it helps ensure that police are not proceeding on an arbitrary or discriminatory basis and are not disrupting the solitude of the citizenry based on a mere hunch or an unreliable tip.

The requirement of particularity means that the police must be able to focus their attention in a relatively narrow way; they must be able to specify the particular premises where a particular type of evidence is likely to be found. This antipathy to the English colonial practice of issuing general warrants underlies much of the spirit of the Fourth Amendment, and it reinforces the standard of probable cause by ensuring that police do the necessary legwork and preliminary investigation and assemble a substantial set of concrete reasons before they will be authorized to enter a premises without consent.

The third requirement is that a warrant shall be issued only by an independent magistrate, who can provide a distinct safeguard upon police discretion. The magistrate's task is to interpose an autonomous buffer between the concerns of law enforcement and the privacy of the citizens and to double-check the police conclusion that a search is appropriate. The magistrate must therefore be divorced from investigatory or prosecutorial functions and must be positioned to supervise the process.

The activities of arms control on-site inspectors would be constrained and restricted in many of the same ways in which the activities of local police already are. Opinions obviously differ on whether the constitutional restraints upon police investigatory powers are currently too high or too low and on whether the courts have significantly interfered with law enforcement tactics. In the context of arms control, however, it seems obvious that the full application of the Fourth Amendment would carry a substantial price.

The ordinary warrant procedure, for example, would probably prohibit arms control inspectors from making random entries. The inspections would have to proceed along some orderly schedule, with probable cause for entering any premises that did not voluntarily consent. Inspectors could not simply walk down a street or look at a map and decide capriciously which buildings they wanted to enter.

Moreover, inspectors would have to present their evidence before an independent tribunal, where it will be examined more or less skeptically, before a warrant will be issued. Foreign on-site inspectors will be naturally distrustful of the court procedure, fearful that delays will provide opportunities for the target of the investigation to be tipped off and for violations to be concealed. Even if the magistrate who issues the warrant need not be a judge and even if a warrant-issuing authority is always available on short notice, due process requires that the magistrate be institutionally separated from the inspectorate and sufficiently independent so as not to become a mere rubber stamp.

Principles Affecting the Legality of an On-Site Inspection

Although it is mostly simply informed guesswork to try to estimate how future courts will deal with future inspections to be undertaken pursuant to a future arms control treaty, it may nonetheless be possible to make some useful observations about the guiding principles that are likely to underlie that judicial reasoning. This section parses seven factors that will probably be important to the judges and that ought to be important to the treaty negotiators.

Scope of the Right to Inspect

Anytime, anyplace inspections are hard to square with the U.S. Constitution. Fundamental to any scheme of orderly inspection—whether under the rubric of the conventional criminal law or under the lowered standards of administrative searches—must be a sense of order, that the inspectors are not behaving capriciously, and that they have utilized a reasoned process in order to organize their investigations.

In fact, arms control inspectors may not need to operate in a truly anytime, anyplace fashion. They may be able to confine their operations, or at least the most intrusive and nonconsensual searches, in various ways: by specifying in advance the types and sizes of facilities of greatest interest, by indicating the sorts of external features or activities that might trigger special concerns, or by stating the categories of evidence (such as that gathered by remote national technical means) that could justify a closer look. Of course, there are costs associated with that kind of inspection regime, too, and there may be intelligence losses from having to display the original data in order to win the right to conduct an on-site inspection.

In general, the more narrowly focused the on-site inspection right is, the more likely it is to pass constitutional muster. If the arms control inspectors' access is concentrated on particular types of buildings or activities, if it is triggered by articulable reasons, and if it is a part of an overall, routinized pattern of inspection, then an on-site inspection is more likely to be upheld.

Importance of the Government's Interest

Courts inevitably balance competing interests, and whether or not there is an acknowledged national security exception, there is every likelihood that the importance of the government's operation will be a key factor in weighing the lawfulness of an on-site inspection measure.

In this context, it will not be sufficient to stop at a general level and proclaim simply that the inspection effort is connected in some vague way to national security and that weapons of mass destruction are implicated. Instead advocates will have to demonstrate that the particular inspection in question is a necessary part of the treaty's overall verification scheme, that the verification arrangements are an indispensable aspect of the accord, and that the treaty is essential to U.S. security. The government will have to demonstrate (if it is, in fact, true) that the frustration of this particular on-site inspection will jeopardize the reliability of the entire inspection apparatus, and that if the verification system is imperiled, the treaty's delicate balance of security risks will fall.

It may not be possible to make this showing for all types of on-site inspection that arms control inspectors would consider nice to have. If remote monitoring would work almost as well as on-site inspection, if there is no necessity for instantaneous access (because nothing effective could be done within a short period of time to remove or conceal a violation), or if an episodic rather than continuous presence would do the job, then the courts would likely decide that the government's interest in conducting the inspection is insufficient to outweigh the competing concerns of civil liberties.

Availability of Less Invasive Alternatives

Associated with the prior factor is the possibility that the government could attain its objectives and satisfy the interests of the arms control inspectors with a system that is less invasive than a full-scale on-site inspection. Courts frequently scrutinize a governmental search or seizure for precisely this purpose and are appreciably more sympathetic where the government has attempted to achieve its ends by lower-level intrusions prior to escalating the level of intervention.

Thus, courts are wary about authorizing a wiretap in a situation where more conventional approaches might suffice. Similarly, courts are less sympathetic to a warrantless entry when the police could have waited for a warrant without appreciable danger that the evidence they seek would be destroyed. And courts will not approve a permanent inspection presence in cases where even an occasional visit would succeed in deterring or detecting improper activities.

Intrusiveness

In general, the less intrusive the government inspection is, the more likely it is to be sustained; remote sensing, for example, is usually less problematic than an on-site inspection. Intrusiveness, however, is a particularly difficult concept to define. Some might consider an unmanned videotape camera to be less intrusive than the physical presence of human observers; to others, however, the technology raises the specter of an invisible big brother who is constantly watching every detail. Similarly, regularized inspections, which occur with great frequency and predictability, might become a major factor in the life of a business, but perhaps the very fact of their becoming routine, and therefore familiar to the management and employees, will make them seem less threatening and hostile than are the more episodic and spontaneous variety.

The element of surprise is sometimes a key criterion in the assessment of intrusiveness. If the hosts or targets of the inspection know that visitors are coming, they will be able to prepare (psychologically, as well as physically) in a manner that may make the on-site inspection feel less intrusive. On the other hand, the advance warning may also degrade the value of the inspection as a verification device if violations can be quickly and effectively concealed.

Additionally, the more powerful are the sensors used in the on-site inspections, the more critical will be the judicial review. If the inspector use highest-technology systems, providing access to information that the public does not generally realize is at risk, the courts will be more concerned, especially where the apparatus collects information going well beyond the authorized scope of inspectors' need to know. The selectivity of a system— its ability to collect only treaty-related information, filtering out other matters—may therefore be as important as its technical sensitivity.

Probability of Success

Courts are more generous with inspection rights when the probability is greater that the search will result in the acquisition of important evidence. The requirement of probable cause is designed for exactly this purpose: to ensure that fishing expeditions are disallowed. Therefore, where on-site inspectors have a genuine reason, based on information from other sources, to believe that a particular facility is worth inspecting, the warrant system should be supportive. Courts do not, of course, require a priori absolute certainty that the search will be successful, but they are more attentive when there is a demonstrably greater probability of obtaining the specified payoff.

Character of the Place to Be Searched

An important slogan of the criminal law is the notion that "the Fourth Amendment protects persons, not places." Associated with this, however, is the idea that degree of protection to be accorded to a person and his or her effects will vary substantially according to the character of the place and the way that the person habitually uses it. That is, the courts are more prone to authorize an entry into a business than into a home and more likely to permit the government to examine a vehicle than a briefcase. The more personal a place is considered, the more likely the courts are to conclude that the individual has developed and retained a subjective expectation of privacy regarding it.

For arms control inspection, the most frequent nongovernmental targets will surely be businesses, and heavily regulated businesses at that. The expectation of privacy will be at its minimum here, and the searches can accordingly proceed at their fullest. If inspectors have reason to want to visit a dwelling, however, they will have to conduct themselves in a more gingerly fashion. Any activities that the home owner conducts in the outer fringe of private property (the "open fields") are generally deemed less private than those carried on closer to the residence (in the area referred to as the "curtilage"); activities conducted inside the house are protected even more zealously. The greatest expectation of privacy inheres in the security of one's own body, and diagnostic examinations or other medical procedures (such as might be appropriate in the search for chemical or biological evidence) can be ordered only for the most compelling reasons.

Purpose of the Search

One additional factor informing the court's balancing tests will ordinarily operate to the advantage of arms control inspectors. In most instances courts are motivated at least partly by an assessment of the purposes of the government's inquiries and the nature of the corresponding threat to the individual target. Where (as with administrative searches) the sanction for a violation is relatively insignificant, the protections demanded by the Fourth Amendment will be mitigated. On the other hand, where the government has a less benign motivation (as with criminal prosecutions), the courts will erect a more substantial barrier.

Arms control on-site inspections will, in this sense, be among the least threatening types of government inspections. The primary motivation will be detection of violations, not criminal prosecution. Associated with this function, inspectors (and their hosts) will have an interest in compiling a great deal of information about violations or ambiguous behavior, and they will attempt to discover the identities of any malfeasors, the sources and methods of their activities, and the like; and the inspectors will be interested in observing and confirming any activities that are undertaken to rectify inconsistencies and to prevent reoccurrences. But criminal prosecution will ordinarily be of only incidental interest to the inspectors, who will not usually share the primary police interest in depriving criminals of their liberty.

Conclusion

This survey of the legal aspects of arms control inspections prompts three partially conflicting conclusions. First, most of the activities of treaty verification on-site inspections can be accomplished consistently with the commands of the U.S. Constitution. The vast majority of inspections will be outside the reach of the Fourth Amendment because the government is the target, because the private party has ceded a measure of consent, because the activities are conducted in plain view, or because of other legal theories. It will, fortunately, be the exception, rather than the rule, where the legal regime drives the on-site inspection system.

Second, however, there are clearly many hypothetical inspection regimes, including some that have been taken seriously by the superpowers as negotiating positions, that would not pass constitutional muster. Anytime, anyplace inspections, done without the protections of a search warrant or its equivalent, would be hard to sustain, especially where the inspectors wanted to intrude into ordinary (that is, not pervasively regulated) industries or private dwellings.

Third, and most important, the analysis suggests that careful attention to the details of the inspection scheme, as well as to the precedents of Fourth Amendment litigation, can ameliorate the difficulties in the category of close, intermediate cases. Treaty negotiators who are sensitive to the seven principles sketched and who attempt to confine the inspection scheme to the least burdensome arrangements compatible with sustaining the important purposes of national security will have to find accommodations between the demands of effective verification and the law of constitutional limitations. And with their new-found friends among the legions of lawyers that will soon rally to their aid (as to the small town noted at the outset), they should be able to chart such a course.

Bibliography

Books and Articles

Aronowitz, Dennis S. *Legal Aspects of Arms Control Verification in the United States.* Dobbs Ferry, New York: Oceana Pub. Inc. (1965).

Connolly, Thomas A. "Warrantless On-Site Inspections for Arms Control Verification: Are They Constitutional." *Stanford Journal of International Law* 24 (1987): 179.

———. "Does the Constitution Limit On-Site Inspection?" *Arms Control Today* (June 1988): 8.

Henkin, Louis. *Foreign Affairs and the Constitution.* Mineola, New York: Foundation Press (1972).

———. *Arms Control and Inspection in American Law.* 1958.

Koplow, David A. "Arms Control Inspection: Constitutional Restrictions on Treaty Verification in the United States." *New York University Law Review* 63 (1988): 229.

Tanzman, Edward A. "Constitutionality of Warrantless On-Site Arms Control Inspections in the United States." *Yale Journal of International Law* 13 (1988): 21.

———. "Legal Aspects of Implementing A Global Chemical Weapons Convention under Domestic Laws." Paper delivered at 1989 Annual Meeting of the American Association for Advancement of Science.

Cases

Reid v. Covert, 354 U.S. 1 (1957) (supremacy clause hierarchy of Constitution, treaties, statutes).

Sei Fujii v. State, 38 Cal. 2d 718 (1952) (self-executing treaties).

United States v. United States District Court, 407 U.S. 297 (1972) (national security exception to warrant requirement).

Zweibon v. Mitchell, 516 F.2d 594 (D.C. Cir. 1975) (national security exception to warrant requirement).

Katz v. United States, 389 U.S. 347 (1967) (expectation of privacy).

Dow Chemical Co. v. United States, 476 U.S. 277 (1986) (aerial observation of activities in plain view).

California v. Ciraolo, 476 U.S. 207 (1986) (aerial observation of activities in plain view).

Donovan v. Dewev, 452 U.S. 594 (1981) (pervasively regulated industry).

New York v. Berger, 107 S. Ct. 2636 (1987) (pervasively regulated industry).

Camara v. Municipal Court, 387 U.S. 523 (1967) (administrative searches).

See v. Seattle, 387 U.S. 541 (1967) (administrative searches).

Michigan v. Clifford, 464 U.S. 287 (1984) (purpose of search affects legal procedures).

O'Connor v. Ortega, 107 S. Ct. 1492 (1987) (scope of employer's consent to search employee's areas).

IV
On-Site Inspection Strategy

12
Striking a Balance: Toward an On-Site Inspection Strategy

Lewis A. Dunn
with *Amy E. Gordon*

R ecent arms control agreements and negotiations have thrust on-site inspection to center stage of treaty verification.[1] The 1986 Stockholm Accord of the Conference on Disarmament in Europe provided for the first time for Western inspections of military exercises in the Warsaw Pact and the Soviet Union. The 1987 U.S.-Soviet Treaty on the Elimination of Intermediate-Range and Shorter-Range Nuclear Forces (INF) contains extensive provisions for such inspection.

Practical experience with on-site inspection has developed quickly. Twenty inspections of exercises in the East and West were carried out in the first two and a half years of the Stockholm Accord, not because of concerns about compliance but to assert the right to inspect. Since inspections began under the INF treaty in July 1988, the United States and the Soviet Union have undertaken more than three hundred routine and short-notice inspections of missile bases and related support facilities in the Soviet Union and the Warsaw Pact. U.S. inspectors also are monitoring on a continuous basis a Soviet missile production facility at Votkinsk. Soviet inspectors have undertaken comparable activities at North Atlantic Treaty Organization (NATO) and U.S. facilities and sites. To implement these precedent-setting inspections, new organizations and procedures had to be established.

Several types of on-site inspection are essential parts of U.S. verification proposals for strategic forces reductions in a treaty resulting from the Strategic Arms Reductions Talks (START), a complete chemical weapons ban, conventional forces reductions in Europe, and nuclear weapons tests. In particular, the United States has proposed mandatory challenge inspections of sites suspected of harboring illegal activities for verification of a chemical weapons convention and is discussing this concept with the Soviet Union for verification of strategic arms reductions. This reflects over four decades of U.S. demands for on-site inspection to verify arms control and disarmament treaties.[2]

The On-Site Inspection Debate

Since the INF treaty, there has been a growing debate within Washington about on-site inspection. Focused on its benefits, costs, and risks, the main elements of that debate have been interwoven throughout the preceding chapters of this book.

Some U.S. defense experts, legislators, and officials have begun to have second thoughts about the benefits of such inspection, particularly for deterring possible illegal activities. With the experience of the initial INF inspections now behind us—and of preparations for them—concerns have also grown about the economic burdens of even more extensive on-site inspection in other arms control agreements. The prospect of short-notice suspect-site inspections with no right to refuse has raised fears of losses of U.S. national security information, intelligence information, nuclear weapons–related information, and commercial proprietary information. The constitutionality of warrantless searches of suspect sites in an effort to detect cheating also has been questioned. New-found skepticism threatens to replace long-standing U.S. enthusiasm for on-site inspection.[3]

Neither the enthusiasts nor the skeptics are correct in their appraisals; a more balanced approach or strategy for on-site inspection is needed. Such a strategy would accept the limits of what on-site inspection can realistically be expected to accomplish, take advantage of its benefits, and acknowledge its potential risks and costs, while taking steps to contain them.[4]

Types of On-Site Inspection

Several broad categories of on-site inspection need to be distinguished as a first step toward a balanced appraisal. These are routine inspections, including continuous monitoring, short-notice inspections, and suspect-site inspection. In certain situations, tagging of legally permitted items could be an important adjunct.

Routine inspections in which the timing and location of inspection are predetermined by the text of an arms control agreement are by far the largest category of potential on-site inspections. Under the INF treaty, for example, routine baseline inspections have been carried out by both the United States and the Soviet Union to establish an agreed data base of INF missiles for monitoring and elimination. Elimination inspections have been undertaken to verify the destruction of INF missiles, equipment, and facilities. And there have been closeout inspections designed to monitor that facilities have ceased production or storage of INF missiles and equipment.

Another type of routine on-site inspection, continuous monitoring over time, has taken place under the INF treaty. Perimeter portal monitoring monitors the perimeter and main points of access to the Votkinsk missile plant in the Soviet Union and the Hercules Plant in Magna, Utah, both of which had produced parts of banned INF missiles. In other arms control areas, continuous monitoring could entail stationing of observers at key troop transit points, systematic surveillance of civilian chemical facilities with instruments, and reliance on seals and other technological measures to monitor storage and track shipments of treaty-limited items.

Short-notice inspection of a previously agreed list of declared activities or sites is a third category of on-site inspection. In the INF treaty, for example, closed-out INF missile operating bases, former INF missile production facilities, and facilities producing comparable but not treaty-limited missiles are among the listed agreed sites subject to short-notice inspections. For short-notice inspections, timely access is measured in hours, or at most one or two days, and the inspecting party specifies at the time of inspection which specific agreed site is to be inspected. Short-notice inspections already have occurred under the INF treaty (for example, of a General Dynamic plant producing nonprohibited cruise missiles) and under the Stockholm Accord in Europe to monitor the limits on military exercises.

Suspect-site inspection, intended to detect illegal activities, is the third broad category. Its most stringent version would call for quick-response inspections with no right to refuse requests, at any location, any time. Though yet to be implemented in a U.S.-Soviet arms control agreement, suspect-site inspection without a right of refusal is under consideration in both chemical and strategic nuclear arms control negotiations. It was included in the Treaty of Tlatelolco (creating a Latin American nuclear-free zone) and has been used since 1960 to monitor compliance with the Antarctic Treaty.

Closely related, tagging of legally permitted systems furnishes technical assistance in tracking items subject to routine or other types of on-site inspection. One approach to tagging would use a nonreproducible, nontransferable reflective particle paint; another approach would rely on identification of unique characteristics ("fingerprints") of specific items. Any systems discovered without such a tag would be in violation of the agreement (for example, untagged mobile missiles in excess of the number agreed in a strategic arms reductions agreement or untagged tanks in a conventional forces agreement).

In discussions of the benefits—and limits—of these types of on-site inspection, attention generally focuses on suspect-site inspection without a right of refusal as the ultimate form of on-site inspection. Public debates center on whether suspect-site inspections will uncover illegal activity. This approach is too narrow, since even unqualified suspect-site inspection is unlikely to be permitted to detect evidence of illegal activities—barring a mistake by the evader. But routine and short-notice on-site inspections can serve many important purposes, in some instances better than national technical means and other treaty-monitoring measures.

Suspect-Site Inspection and the Detection of Illegal Activities

Even without a right to refuse suspect-site inspections, the inspected party would have many ways to prevent detection of the proverbial smoking gun. Whether in a bilateral strategic arms reductions treaty or in a multilateral chemical weapons ban, excuses could be found, from transportation problems to the weather, to delay access and permit disposition of incriminating evidence. In extremis, an "accident" could befall the inspecting party or the facility. In any case, care would be taken in advance to reduce the likelihood that any illegal activity would be detected and to have a good cover story available in case it was. With a right to refuse suspect-site inspections, the issue would not arise, though the act of refusal (or of delay) without credible explanation would reinforce suspicions.

Nonetheless, under some conditions, suspect-site inspection without a right of refusal (or short-notice inspections of declared sites associated with treaty-limited activities) might detect evidence of a violation. Detection could occur due to a mistake on the part of the evader. For instance, mixed signals might be given as to when an inspection team would arrive (for example, at a declared but no longer operating strategic missile base) so that all evidence would not have been cleaned up. Or cleanup could be too slow, or an extremely small amount of residue (for example, in illegal chemical weapons production at a civilian plant) might be overlooked.

The likelihood of mistakes also may be greater in the context of a multilateral chemical weapons convention with many Third World countries than in a bilateral U.S.-Soviet context. This is because most Third World countries have fewer trained technicians, poorer communications, and less developed industrial and technological bases.

In addition, the procedures for implementing suspect-site inspections could add to the likelihood that an evader might make a mistake. If the allotted time between the notification of an impending inspection and the arrival of inspectors were kept short, an evader could be forced to rush a cleanup, making missteps more likely. Similarly, if inspection procedures provide for broad and relatively unfettered access to a site at which illegal activities are suspected (such as to all parts of a civilian chemical plant), chances again would increase that some unintended sign of that illegal activity might be uncovered.

Particularly in the area of chemical weapons arms control, advances in monitoring technologies could improve the likelihood of detection. Assuming access in twelve to twenty-four hours, the development of robust, portable, highly sensitive instruments, designed to analyze wastewater samples at a particular site, would make it more feasible to detect extremely small trace residues. The right to remove samples for extensive off-site analysis would also add to the probability of detection. Again, however, this assumes timely access, permitted by the evader in the mistaken belief that all evidence of illegal activity had been eliminated (perhaps by flushing the pipes and tanks with other chemicals and mixing in other chemicals to mask residues).

Detection also might occur through coordination of national technical means and on-site inspection. In particular, the prospect of a request for a suspect-site on-site inspection would make elaborate cover-ups more and more necessary for successful noncompliance. This would add to the risk of detection by either intelligence assets or national technical means. Then a request for a suspect-site inspection could be used to prod a country to clean up a violation discovered by other monitoring means or to focus global attention on a problem, especially if a refusal was anticipated.

Nonetheless, the deterrent impact of this risk of unintended discovery by suspect-site inspection—or by other monitoring means due to a request for suspect-site inspection—appears at best uncertain. A potential evader could not completely discount the risk of detection, especially if on-site inspection requirements are strict and different monitoring means are mutually reinforcing. Besides, mistakes do happen. Consequently, if strong incentives to take illegal action were absent in the first place, this risk of detection would help to deter cheating. By contrast, an evader who thought that the benefits of illegal activities were substantial would likely not be greatly influenced by the fear that something might go wrong.

Given these limits of suspect-site inspection, the main benefits of on-site inspection clearly must be sought elsewhere. They center partly on the impact of routine and short-notice inspections in increasing the difficulty, expense, and risk of detection by other monitoring means of illegal activities. Both routine and short-notice inspections also have other less adversarial, more political purposes, including increased public assurance of treaty implementation, confidence building and warning, and greater transparency and openness.

Increasing the Difficulty, Expense, and Risk of Detection by Other Means of Illegal Activities

Exchanges of data on treaty-limited items, routine inspections (as well as continuous monitoring and tagging), and short-notice inspections of agreed declared sites can increase in various ways the difficulty and expense of carrying out illegal activities. These types of inspections would made it harder to use the most cost-effective, appropriately equipped and configured sites and facilities to conduct illegal activities. Further, although national technical and other monitoring means will continue to play a large role in arms control verification, by forcing a potential evader to use other new or reconfigured facilities, to make special preparations, and to take steps out of the ordinary, on-site inspections would heighten the chance of detection by these other monitoring means.

In the case of a START treaty, for example, continuous inspection of missile production facilities, including tagging of newly produced missiles, would force the Soviets to construct new covert production facilities to produce extra illegal missiles. If illegal missiles were produced, it would also be harder to service and repair them without access to legal repair facilities. Or, short-notice inspection of missile operating bases would likely force covert deployments to occur at new bases or storage facilities elsewhere.

To take a different example, continuous monitoring of former chemical weapons production plants, as called for by the Chemical Weapons Convention, would require construction of replacement covert facilities or attempted covert misuse of civilian chemical plants to accomplish illegal production. Systematic inspections of civilian chemical facilities, in turn, make necessary elaborate planning and preparations to misuse those plants to produce chemical weapons agents. Or, again, production of illegal chemical weapons would require construction of new, hidden facilities.

More generally, the extent of increased difficulty, expense, and risk of detection of noncompliance by other monitoring means would vary according to several factors. These include the ease with which other sites could be reconfigured to produce, service, or house treaty-limited items or activities; how readily illegal facilities or activities could be disguised; how much effort would be needed to avoid detection (for example, by cleanup) if an attempt were made to misuse an inspected facility or site; and the extent to which dual-use items, with both prohibited and permitted applications, were limited.

Granting that routine and short-notice inspections are likely to increase the difficulties, expense, and risk of detection of illegal activities by other means, what impact would that have on the thinking of a political leader contemplating cheating? There is no easy answer to this question. The deterrent impact would depend on the calculations that might lead a country's leaders to violate an agreement, on the evader's decision-making process, and on the perception that strong responses would ensue in the event of detected noncompliance.

Experience suggests that some countries, including possibly the Soviet Union, might undertake illegal activities for small gains, or to hedge against the risk of cheating by a rival, or simply because the difficulties and risks of actions not in strict compliance with an agreement seemed low. Ambiguities about what is and is not permitted would heighten that possibility. In this case, increasing the difficulties and expense of illegal activities (and the risk of their detection by other means) would help raise the threshold at which they would appear to be justified. That is, the perceived payoff would need to be higher to justify the greater difficulty and expense.

In some cases, moreover, limited cheating for small gains could stem less from a purposive decision by the highest authorities than from the actions of officials or bureaucrats, possibly driven by an unwillingness to cut back their own programs or to accept new constraints. The increased difficulty and expense could make such officials less likely to act on their own, without explicit authorization from the top.

Finally, a potential evader's perceptions of whether other countries would react strongly to illegal activities and whether noncompliance would be penalized would affect its behavior. But here, recent experience—not least the global failure to punish Iraqi use of chemical weapons—is discouraging. It demonstrates that the prospects for strong and effective future responses to alleged treaty noncompliance are low. This lessens considerably the potential deterrent impact of using routine and short-notice inspections to increase the difficulties, expense, and detectability by other means of illegal activities.

Increased Assurance of Treaty Implementation

Turning to other, less adversarial purposes, routine inspections of several sorts as well as short-notice inspections of declared sites, backed by prior data exchanges, offer a valuable means by which countries can visibly and publicly demonstrate that they are faithfully implementing treaty provisions. In some instances, on-site inspections would be able to offer a higher level of confidence in treaty implementation than would reliance on national technical or other monitoring means alone. This comparative advantage results from the ability of on-site inspection to look inside buildings and objects, to track small, mobile items, and to take a closer or continuous look at activities.

Routine baseline inspections (for example, with U.S. and Soviet inspections under the INF treaty of missile bases and support facilities) can help provide an agreed foundation for carrying out a treaty's terms and for monitoring its implementation. By providing such a data base, moreover, baseline inspections would make any future anomalies or suspicious developments more readily visible. They also might isolate irregularities in the data (for instance, missiles stationed in the wrong place or excess stocks of certain precursor chemicals that could be used to make weapons), which national technical means could not. The very prospect of inspections provides an incentive for a complete and accurate exchange of data on treaty activities.

The extent to which baseline inspections are able to count and confirm declared data will depend partly on the numbers and types of treaty-limited items. For the type of conventional arms control restrictions on tanks, artillery, and other systems now being discussed at the Vienna negotiations, for example, baseline inspections would provide a better estimate than is possible with national technical means because the types of treaty-limited items are so numerous, mobile, small, and/or dispersed. Unfortunately, those same characteristics would make it hard to count and confirm the declared baseline of conventional forces. More important, questions would persist about whether all such conventional arms had been declared, much less counted. Similarly, in both future chemical weapons and START treaties, a critical question will be whether all treaty-limited items—from stocks of chemical weapons to mobile missiles—have been declared.

Assurance that an arms control agreement is being implemented comes as well from routine elimination inspections. Under the INF treaty, these inspections are used to monitor destruction of ground-launched intermediate and shorter-range missiles, launchers, and support equipment. They provide unquestionable assurance that real (not dummy) missiles are being eliminated, while publicly demonstrating compliance. Similarly, the draft Chemical Weapons Convention requires elimination inspections to monitor destruction of declared chemical weapons stockpiles and production facilities. This type of on-site inspection is likely to be part of a future conventional arms agreement that eliminated specified military equipment. Moreover, in these specific future instances, routine elimination on-site inspections would offer better assurances of treaty implementation than would national technical means. Such inspections would furnish samples of chemical agents to be destroyed and would provide a count of the large number of items to be eliminated under a conventional arms accord, despite their small size.

Still another type of routine inspection—systematic or continuous monitoring, most often with instruments—can offer a level of assurance in treaty implementation of certain arms control limits that is unattainable with national technical means alone. This would be so, for example, in a future chemical weapons convention for monitoring declared chemical weapons production facilities and stockpiles (with cameras, remote monitors, seals, and sampling devices) to ensure that no chemical weapons were produced or diverted in the interim period before their destruction. Continuous on-site monitoring of storage parks for conventional military equipment removed from Central Europe or of mobile missile production plants could be key elements in monitoring compliance with future conventional or strategic arms reductions pacts. Similarly, direct on-site measurement of the yields of nuclear tests can provide better assurance of Soviet compliance with the 150 kiloton Threshold Test Ban Treaty and with any future lower yield nuclear testing limits.

Confidence Building and Early Warning

On-site inspection and the on-site presence that accompanies it can be important political confidence-building steps between governments. In part, this results from the public, visible, and readily usable assurance provided by certain types of routine inspections that treaty requirements are being met. For example, both the United States and the Soviet Union are publicly destroying their declared INF missiles. Continuous monitoring of peaceful nuclear facilities by the International Atomic Energy Agency (IAEA) has also added to political confidence in many cases. On-site inspection to monitor elimination of declared chemical weapons stockpiles and facilities would likely have a comparable effect.

In other instances, the very purpose of an agreement would be to establish a legitimate on-site presence, unattainable with national technical means or intelligence assets, to strengthen political confidence and to facilitate improved political relations. This has been one result of the inspections and observations of Eastern bloc military exercises conducted by the West under the terms of the 1986 Stockholm Accord. Moreover, an on-site presence and related confidence-building measures could increase each side's familiarity with the operational details and procedures on the other side under future conventional arms control agreements. The result would be to build confidence and contribute to more predictable East-West relations.[5]

Because cooperation is required, implementation of all types of on-site inspection serves as a political barometer, which can signal deterioration or breakdown of the political consensus or basis for an arms control agreement. A decrease in Soviet cooperation in implementing the INF or Stockholm provisions, or a decrease in another country's readiness to cooperate with inspections under a chemical weapons convention, would be examples. Strict implementation, by contrast, signals continued commitment to the status quo. For example, Egyptian and Israeli readiness to honor the inspection provisions for monitoring the Sinai Accords (including challenge inspections) demonstrated that neither desired a wider war in the midst of the Israeli invasion of Lebanon in 1982.[6]

Under some conditions, an on-site presence or on-site observers could provide warning of a conventional surprise attack. Inspectors at equipment storage parks, observers at key military mobilization points, and observers in selected zones could serve that purpose. Under future conventional arms control agreements, for example, their reports could signal major shifts of the status quo, as would their failure to report or their denial of access to given areas. The increment of warning over that provided by national technical means might be low, but on-site observation could reduce the political ambiguity and increase the political usability of information gained. This would be especially so if warning were provided by a clear-cut violation of inspectors' access rights to particular sites or zones.

On-site inspections also can provide limited warning of preparations to break out from an agreement and rapidly resume activities prohibited by an arms control treaty. Repeated refusal to permit inspection of suspect sites identified by national technical or other means is one source of warning, especially for nuclear or chemical arms control activities. Under a future chemical weapons convention, if on-site continuous monitoring equipment—or the process of data monitoring and accounting—detected a jump in anomalies at a civilian chemical facility, warning would also be triggered.

Transparency and Openness

Extensive routine and short-notice inspections can provide another important political benefit not associated with national technical or other monitoring means by reinforcing trends already under way toward reducing Soviet secrecy. This has long been one purpose of on-site inspection. In particular, such inspections are likely to provide more information to both outsiders and the Soviet public about Soviet military activities. Acceptance of on-site inspection also runs counter to—and can help to weaken—the presumption of secrecy in Soviet politics and society.

The INF inspection process, for instance, already has provided previously unavailable information on Soviet INF programs to the Soviet public by press coverage of inspections. The Stockholm inspections have served to open up Soviet military exercises to outside scrutiny. Further, Soviet proponents of greater openness have argued that a reimposition of secrecy would be at odds with this broader process of agreements and inspections.

On-site inspection under conventional arms control could reinforce basic political and cultural trends already at work toward greater openness in many Eastern bloc countries as well. Inspections under a Chemical Weapons Convention might have a similar effect in some Third World countries.

Assessing the Risks of On-Site Inspection

The loss of sensitive national security or proprietary information stands out as a major potential risk of on-site inspection. Although potential loss is difficult to measure or evaluate in advance, analysis and contingency planning over the past several years indicates that some loss must be assumed likely.[7]

More specifically, under some scenarios, on-site inspection, particularly unqualified suspect-site inspections, could result in losses of information about

U.S. defense programs, nuclear weapons programs, intelligence programs and assets, military procedures and practices, and proprietary commercial processes and technology. Potentially hostile countries might be able to obtain a better understanding of U.S. forces and systems and be better able to design countermeasures to them. Long-term U.S. research and development paths also could become evident. Specific information might be obtained about manufacturing processes, trade secrets, and technologies. Access by inspectors would make it easier to identify plant workers and personnel for later targeting by intelligence agencies.

The actual scope of information losses and their impact, however, will be likely to vary considerably in practice. The risk of information loss would be most substantial for suspect-site inspections with no right to refuse requests for inspection, as currently envisaged in the draft START treaty and the draft Chemical Weapons Convention. Inspectors from other countries could request access to U.S. nuclear weapons laboratories, defense sites with black programs, and intelligence facilities. By contrast, addition of a right to refuse access to such sensitive sites would drop the risks considerably. The risk would be much less, though still present, with routine and even short-notice inspections of agreed declared sites. In those cases, considerable information would already be known, and preparations to protect sensitive activities would be easier to make with more advance warning.

Depending on the specific arms control agreement, the extent of risk also will vary. For example, either routine or short-notice inspection of declared military bases and defense contractor facilities under a nuclear arms reductions agreement (assuming, as in INF, no destruction of warheads) would likely pose little risk to U.S. nuclear weapons information since nuclear weapons laboratories would be excluded. By contrast, the risk would be somewhat greater under chemical weapons arms control, depending on whether some of the national laboratories were subject to agreed inspections. On-site inspection for verification of limits on nuclear testing, with extensive access to the U.S. nuclear weapons test site, might well pose greater risks to information about the testing program. At the least, information would become available about specific U.S. test practices. Conventional arms control, almost by definition, would pose less of a risk of exposing national security information located in the United States, but it would expose military information at bases abroad. An extensive on-site presence would disrupt military activities and reveal information about NATO plans and procedures. In all of these areas, if agreed sites also included areas where compartmented sensitive research and development is performed, on-site inspection could risk intelligence losses in areas unrelated to treaty-limited activities.

Which country's nationals had access to the information from these inspections could also make a difference. This would vary between bilateral and multilateral agreements. For instance, losses of basic nuclear weapons information to the Soviet Union, while undesirable, would likely have a less damaging impact (since the Soviets already possess nuclear weapons) than loss of the same information to certain potential nuclear weapons states (for example, Pakistan or India). Conversely, access to information about U.S. defense programs would be of more use to the Soviets than to a Third World country. In the case of loss of industrial information, there could well be some concern about access by other industrialized countries.

The direct impact on U.S. national security of any such losses of information is hard to assess. Fairly detailed knowledge of some military assets (such as new aircraft and missiles) must eventually become known in any case. For other areas, such as intelligence assets, knowledge of even their existence could be damaging. But distinguishing potentially serious losses from those with little direct security effect in advance of actual incidents is likely to prove very difficult.

Besides, even without on-site inspection, there will be some loss of sensitive information. If so, will the United States or the Soviet Union gain most from added information from on-site inspections? Opinions differ, and the answer is uncertain. For example, with a greater baseline knowledge of U.S. activities, the Soviet Union might be most able to make use of new information to fill in old puzzles. In contrast, because it starts with less information, the marginal value to the United States of new information could be much greater. The answer also could change according to the arms control area and over time, assuming that the Soviet trend toward openness continues. In any case, in thinking about the risks of on-site inspection, it is important to remember that loss of national security information is not a one-way street.

A somewhat different risk that warrants brief mention is the danger that on-site inspection procedures could result in a false sense of confidence.[8] An inspected party could undertake covert illegal activities at locations not subject to inspection while carefully honoring its obligations at facilities subject to inspection. On-site inspection can only confirm that illegal activities are not under way at a given site at the time of inspection. In turn, while deteriorating cooperation with on-site inspection would signal a breakdown of an arms control regime, ongoing cooperation with inspections, taken alone, would not necessarily provide conclusive evidence that the Soviet Union or some other country were continuing to comply fully.

In assessing the magnitude of this risk of false confidence, however, it is important to keep in mind that national technical means and other means of monitoring provide a backdrop for on-site inspection. Thus, the risk of incurring false confidence is likely to be greatest to the extent that on-site inspection bears the bulk of the verification burden. Indeed, as the variety of monitoring tools expands to include on-site inspection and to create more redundancy, overall confidence is likely to increase.

Financial Burdens of On-Site Inspection

Until recently, direct U.S. experience with on-site inspection was limited to inspections of a small number of U.S. nuclear power plants by the IAEA and occasional exercise of the rights of inspection under the Antarctic Treaty. With the INF inspections, it has become increasingly clear that implementation of on-site inspection in the many arms control areas for which it is proposed would be a significant management and financial undertaking. In that regard, two types of financial burdens stand out: the costs of the inspections themselves and the costs of preparations for them. Here, too, however, care is needed in estimating (and then evaluating) how much will be spent (and for what). In addition, costs—such as risks—should be thought of in terms of the incremental expense over and above what may already be spent (for example, to protect classified information in the defense field or prepare for national safety inspections in the chemicals area).

Carrying out the provisions for on-site inspection in the INF treaty already has proved a demanding management and organizational task.[9] A new agency, the On-Site Inspection Agency (OSIA), had to be created and staffed rapidly, inspectors recruited and trained, and the many logistics details resolved. Although total figures are difficult to obtain, some estimates of the financial costs of on-site inspections are possible. The fiscal year 1988 budget of the OSIA was $19 million, but this covered only part of the calendar year because inspections began in July 1988. For fiscal years 1989, 1990, and 1991, OSIA's budget request is approximately $50 million. In addition, there are other costs not covered by the budget, including personnel seconded to the agency as inspectors and escorts, costs for airlift of inspector teams, and costs of activities conducted by other U.S. government agencies and by the military services.

Proposed new on-site inspection measures in other arms control areas would place new management and organizational demands on the United States. They also would drive the financial costs higher, quite probably resulting in total expenses for all arms control areas in the low billions of dollars. Under a START agreement, more numerous inspections, with more continuous monitoring and technical support, could add several hundreds of millions of dollars annually. Monitoring of a chemical weapons convention, with widespread systematic inspections, as well as of a conventional arms reductions agreement, could be of comparable magnitude.[10] It is said to have cost tens of millions of dollars to carry out direct measurement of a single Soviet nuclear test in the summer of 1988.

These costs of carrying out on-site inspections are but one side of the coin. Perhaps of greater importance would be the significant financial burdens on facilities subject to inspection under currently proposed provisions—

whether defense contractors, Department of Energy nuclear weapons laboratories and plants, or the civilian chemical industry.

Experience with preparations for the INF inspections indicates that one type of cost would be the direct financial costs preparations for inspections, which run from salaries of personnel (to plan for, prepare for, and host inspections) through purchase of protective safety garments for inspectors. Potential operational costs are equally important though often overlooked. Workers might be sent home and plants shut down for an inspection, resulting in lost production, lessened efficiency, and salary expenses. (During one defense facility INF inspection, for example, workers were sent home.) Disruption and delay of planned work schedules can incur other financial costs, which could vary considerably depending on specific operating schedules and activities. Still another expense might result from changing security plans and relocating sensitive activities to accommodate the possibility of on-site inspection.

The magnitude of these preparation costs clearly would depend on the specific provisions of the on-site inspection regime. It would be the highest with provision for short-notice suspect-site inspection without a right of refusal. This type of suspect-site inspection in START or a chemical weapons convention, for example, would require that a wide range of U.S. defense contractor, nuclear-weapons-related, intelligence, and other national security facilities assume that they could be inspected on only hours notice. All of these various facilities would need to pay for necessary preparations. If the number of facilities and sites on agreed lists for short-notice inspections of declared sites were large, that too would incur high costs. The amount of preparation time before commencement of a short-notice inspection, as well as the duration of an inspection, would influence the cost of preparations.

By contrast, in industries that already are heavily regulated, the incremental costs of preparing for yet another set of inspections might be considerably less. This might well be the case in the civilian chemical industry under a chemical weapons convention.

As for dollar estimates of the total costs of preparing for on-site inspection, representatives of the Martin Marietta Corporation have stated that it spent $5 million in preparation for an INF inspection at its Baltimore facility.[11] This covered steps from shrouding sensitive equipment, through sending workers home and removing nameplates, to rekeying over 2,500 door locks to permit rapid entry with a master key. Even assuming this is heavily loaded with initial start-up costs, it still suggests that the preparation costs of unqualified suspect-site inspection for START or a Chemical Weapons Convention—with upwards of a hundred or more defense and other sites at risk—could run into several hundred million dollars, if not higher. The final cost figures would depend as well on the number of facilities, whether delay is permitted, and the nature of any modifications to suspect-site inspection.

For the INF inspections, it proved necessary to adopt procedures for the U.S. government to defray such costs, as well as to ensure defense contractors that they would not be placed at a competitive disadvantage due to their susceptibility to on-site inspection. These costs will ultimately be borne by the U.S. economy.

Are these costs too high? That ultimately will be a policy judgment, based partly on public and congressional appraisal of the benefits of on-site inspection. It also is likely to reflect comparisons to other defense spending, as well as nondefense activities. Finally, discussion will focus on what must be given up at the margin to fund such inspections (for example, from new intelligence satellites to more military procurement). Taking these elements together, however, costs are unlikely to be the main driver of future U.S. positions on on-site inspection.

Legal Issues Raised by On-Site Inspections

In striking a balance among the benefits, risks, and costs of different types of on-site inspection, it is becoming evident that several important legal issues cannot be overlooked. Though a complete discussion exceeds the scope of this chapter, the implications of some issues warrant brief mention.[12]

Under the Fifth Amendment to the U.S. Constitution, the U.S. government is prohibited from taking private property without due process, including just compensation. Owners of private facilities subject to inspection could claim compensation from the U.S. government for the costs of preparing for inspections and for losses attributable to their disruptive effect. It is unlikely that a court would block an inspection on the basis of a claim of threatened damage. But it also will be increasingly important to the smooth operation of future on-site inspection regimes to put in place needed mechanisms to handle any claims and resolve disputes. This issue also could result in congressional revision of on-site inspection due to constituent pressures.

A somewhat different legal issue arises because inspections could accidentally result in the unauthorized disclosure of classified or other controlled information inconsistent with U.S. legislation requiring its protection. The Atomic Energy Act of 1954, for example, has strict requirements for the protection of restricted data concerning nuclear weapons and includes penalties for its disclosure. Other legislation directed against espionage also could come into play. It is unlikely that a court would uphold prosecution of individuals for not protecting such information in this instance, since U.S. law treaties supersede existing statutes. Here, too, however, steps to reassure employees may prove necessary.

By contrast, on-site inspections, whether in START or a chemical weapons convention, also raise issues pertaining to the Fourth Amendment to the U.S. Constitution, which states that

> the right of the people to be secure in their persons, houses, papers, and effects, against unreasonable searches and seizure, shall not be violated, and no Warrants shall issue, but upon probable cause, supported by Oath or affirmation, and particularly describing the place to be searched, and the persons or things to be seized.

The question of the legality of warrantless suspect-site inspections, whether in START or a Chemical Weapons Convention, would not arise in the case of U.S. government facilities, such as military bases, because the federal government has no Fourth Amendment rights. Moreover, inspections of private facilities are exempt from the amendment if the owners have explicitly or implicitly given their consent. (The U.S. government, for instance, successfully solicited the consent of the relatively small number of firms affected by the on-site inspection provisions of the INF treaty.) But if some on-site inspections called for by an arms control agreement were not covered by the explicit or implied consent of the private parties concerned, as seems likely, the courts would have to decide whether those inspections could legally be carried out without warrants.

In assessing the constitutionality of on-site inspections, the courts could be expected to give considerable, but not necessarily overriding, weight to the importance of the inspections in fulfilling the government's commitment to arms control and national security. The intrusiveness of the inspections, the availability of alternative means to monitor compliance, the invasion of privacy suffered by the parties inspected, and the threat to those parties' interests posed by the inspections also would be considered. Overall, prospects for court approval of routine inspections and short-notice inspections of declared facilities, without warrants or consent of the inspected parties, appear relatively good. But reconciling warrantless short-notice suspect-site inspections with the Fourth Amendment is likely to prove difficult.

Elements of an On-Site Inspection Strategy

For more than four decades, U.S. officials and academics have taken the lead in demanding on-site inspection to monitor compliance with arms control and reduction agreements. More recently, there are signs of a backlash against this verification measure. What is needed is a long-term on-site inspection strategy that stresses what this type of inspection does best and makes use of the advantages it offers in comparison to national technical and other monitoring means. Such an approach would balance the benefits, costs, and risks of this verification measure.

Specifically, routine inspections (including continuous monitoring) and short-notice inspections of agreed declared sites—whether in START, chemical weapons, or conventional forces arms control—can increase the difficulties, expense, and risk of detection by other monitoring means of illegal activities. Both types of inspection also offer greater assurance that certain treaty provisions are being implemented. In addition, routine and short-notice inspections, as well as an on-site presence, can serve broader political purposes, from confidence building to increasing transparency.

By contrast, the potential benefits of unqualified short-notice suspect-site inspections are much more limited, both viewed in their own terms and in comparison to national technical means for monitoring treaty compliance. The likelihood is very low that an evader would permit detection of illegal activities, barring a mistake on its part. In turn, the deterrent impact of the possibility of unintended or accidental detection is at best uncertain. Moreover, the risks and costs of short-notice suspect-site inspection without a right of refusal, though hard to specify precisely in advance, could be considerable.

Consequently, as part of a strategy for on-site inspection, the United States should revise its support for unqualified suspect-site inspection, whether in START or in a Chemical Weapons Convention. The core of its strategy needs to be the realistic recognition that routine and short-notice inspections can serve useful purposes rather than the hope that suspect-site inspection will detect and deter noncompliance.

Several approaches might be taken to modify the current position of unqualified suspect-site inspections. Efforts could be made in each arms control area to reach agreement on criteria, (for example, physically observable unique characteristics of a missile production facility or a chemical weapons plant) as a basis for initiating a suspect-site inspection. Development of and agreement on such criteria, however, is likely to prove quite difficult. Or the parties to agreements could exchange lists of sites and facilities, off-limits for suspect-site inspection. This, however, would have the disadvantage of identifying some facilities that for national security and intelligence reasons, it would be essential to keep secret.

The simplest way to revise the U.S. position is likely to be to add a right of refusal to requests for inspections, subject to certain conditions. A right of refusal would permit protection of sensitive facilities and activities on a case-by-case basis. Following a proposal made by the United Kingdom in the chemical weapons negotiations, exercise of that right of refusal could be conditioned on a requirement that the country rejecting a request for inspection explain its action and the activities of concern, as well as offer alternative means to demonstrate compliance. In addition, agreed lists for short-notice inspections could be expanded to include facilities and sites with a less direct link to treaty limits but of potential concern for illegal activities. Procedures might be established to update such agreed lists periodically, with an understanding that all new plants or sites with comparable technical characteristics would become subject to inspection. Further, in some areas (for instance, chemical weapons arms control), emphasis could be placed on development of less intrusive monitoring technologies that could provide information from a near site rather than an on-site location.

A U.S. decision to step back from support for unqualified suspect-site inspection would likely be welcomed by the Soviet Union in START and by most other countries in the chemical weapons negotiations. Possible congressional reaction to backing away from suspect-site inspection is more difficult to judge. The on-site inspection provisions of the INF Treaty (which did not include suspect-site inspection) helped to win congressional support for that treaty. Since the consequences of Soviet noncompliance would be greater in a START agreement, a shift of position could be viewed mistakenly as relinquishing an important monitoring measure. However, consultations with Congress about the relatively low likelihood that an evader would permit a violation to be detected would temper this reaction. Besides, there is growing congressional sensitivity to U.S. industry concerns about the potential burdens of unqualified suspect-site inspections.

Revision of support for unqualified suspect-site inspection would go far to limit the overall risks of on-site inspection. At the same time, more direct steps continue to be warranted to prevent and minimize losses of national security and proprietary information. "Red-teaming" and mock inspections have already proved their value as means to identify information at risk. Preparations can be taken to protect sensitive information during inspections by shrouding equipment, removing identifying tags, and ensuring sufficient numbers of escorts for inspections. Some sensitive activities could be moved to other sites. In the negotiations on routine and short-notice inspections, the United States also needs to be cognizant of sensitive activities and should seek to shield them.

The costs of preparing for on-site inspections would be reduced by eliminating unqualified suspect-site inspection. In particular, sites and facilities not on agreed lists for inspection would no longer need to take special precautions. There is another step that could be taken to reduce further the preparation costs of inspections. Consideration might be given in some arms control areas to permit a delay before interior access to a site takes place, with provision for a temporary portal monitoring system at access and egress points. In the case of strategic systems, for instance, this would preclude removal of evidence of cheating but still add time to prepare for inspection, thereby reducing costs. By contrast, such an approach would not be acceptable for a chemical weapons convention in which elimination of evidence of illegal activities would take place inside the site.

Design and implementation of on-site inspection provisions for future arms control agreements will be a learning process. From the INF and Stockholm inspections, as well as the more extended IAEA experience, there are lessons to be learned about what to do and not do in areas such as personnel, logistics, equipment, legal drafting, and day-to-day interaction with inspected countries.[13] Efforts already under way to distill the lessons of the INF inspections should be followed by examination of other experiences. The resulting conclusions should be reflected in future agreements and operations.

Finally, even with sophisticated national technical means, cooperative measures, and extensive on-site inspection, high-confidence verification of some provisions of potential arms control agreements may not be attainable. Nevertheless, in some instances and despite such verification uncertainties, an agreement, backed with suitable safeguards, might still serve overall U.S. national security interests. Conversely, even with highly effective verification, some arms control agreements might not be consistent with U.S. interests. Both possibilities need to be kept in mind in making use of on-site inspection to support U.S. arms control and national security goals.

Notes

1. Arms control verification is taken here to mean the process whereby monitoring data on the treaty-related activities of parties to a particular arms control agreement is compared to the limits set by that agreement to make a judgment about the extent of their compliance (or noncompliance) with that agreement.
2. See chapter 5.
3. Some of these concerns are reflected in Sidney Graybeal and Michael Krepon, "The Limitations of On-Site Inspection," *Bulletin of the Atomic Scientists* (December 1987).
4. In setting out an overall on-site inspection strategy, this chapter draws on the discussions of the Workshop on On-Site Inspection for Arms Control Verification held by the Center for National Security Negotiations (CNSN) in 1988–1989. Many of the ideas presented here appeared in somewhat different form in the report of that workshop, Lewis A. Dunn, with Amy E. Gordon, *On-Site Inspection for Arms Control Verification: Pitfalls and Promise* (May 1989).
5. On this idea of on-site presence and on-site observation, see chapter 7.
6. Itshak Lederman pointed out this example during the CNSN Workshop on Conventional Arms Control Verification.
7. The following is based on the CNSN discussions, which included individuals with responsibilities to assess potential risks to information and to design approaches to minimize such losses.

8. This point was stressed to the authors by Howard Stoertz.
9. On the INF experience, in addition to chapter 1, also see "On-Site Inspection Agency," Report to the Committee on Foreign Affairs, U.S. House of Representatives, March 1989.
10. The IAEA's annual budget is about $52 million, covering the monitoring of several hundred nuclear facilities. However, the task of monitoring a chemical weapons ban would be technically more demanding.
11. Briefing to the CNSN workshop.
12. For a more complete assessment, see chapter 11. The following discussion draws on Koplow and on Edward A. Tanzman, "Constitutionality of Warrantless On-Site Arms Control Inspection in the United States," *Yale Journal of International Law* 13, no. 1 (1988).
13. See chapters 1, 2, and 3.

Index

About the Contributors

John Barrett is with the Arms Control and Disarmament Division of the Canadian Department of External Affairs. He is the former deputy director of the Canadian Centre for Arms Control and Disarmament, a private, non-profit research organization.

James R. Blackwell is a partner and director of the International Security Division at the Meridian Corporation. As deputy director of political-military affairs in the Department of State, he was actively involved in drafting verification requirements for the INF Treaty.

David A. Koplow is a professor of law at the Georgetown University Law Center and director of the Center for Applied Legal Studies.

Edward J. Lacey is the principal deputy director of the U.S. On-Site Inspection Agency.

Christopher J. Makins is vice-president for policy programs, the Aspen Institute.

Janne E. Nolan is a visiting fellow at the Brookings Institution and served as senior adviser for national security and foreign policy to Senator Gary Hart.

William C. Potter is executive director of the Center for International and Strategic Affairs, University of California, Los Angeles, and program coordinator for the Rand/UCLA Center for the Study of Soviet International Behavior.

Timothy J. Pounds is a defense analyst at the Center for National Security Negotiations, Science Applications International Corporation.

Carl F. Romney is the director of the Center for Seismic Studies at the Science Applications International Corporation and has served as deputy director for science and technology at the Defense Advanced Research Projects Agency.

Don O. Stovall, a retired U.S. Army colonel, is a senior staff member with the BDM Corporation. He led the first on-site inspection (under the Stockholm Accord) of a Soviet ground force exercise in Belorussia and led subsequent inspections in Hungary, Poland, and the German Democratic Republic.

Archelaus R. Turrentine is a consultant on defense, international security policy, nuclear energy, and space issues and has served as acting assistant director for multilateral affairs at the U.S. Arms Control and Disarmament Agency.

About the Editors

Lewis A. Dunn is assistant vice-president (Negotiations and Planning Division), Science Applications International, Corp., and deputy director of the Center for National Security Negotiations. He is a former assistant director of the U.S. Arms Control and Disarmament Agency and served as ambassador to the 1985 Nuclear Non-Proliferation Treaty Review Conference and to the 1987 United Nations Peaceful Uses of Nuclear Energy Conference. In addition to numerous articles on arms control and national security issues, he is the author of *Controlling the Bomb*, an assessment of policies to contain nuclear proliferation and manage its consequences. Dr. Dunn is managing projects on a broad range of arms control issues. He holds a Ph.D. in political science from the University of Chicago.

Amy E. Gordon is a national security policy analyst in the Negotiations and Planning Division of Science Applications International, Corp. Her current work concerns nuclear and chemical weapons arms control issues as well as on-site inspection and treaty verification. Ms. Gordon has an M.A. in international affairs from the School of International Affairs at Columbia University and is a certificate candidate at the W. Averell Harriman Institute for Advanced Study of the Soviet Union at Columbia University.